Monsters in the Classroom

Monsters in the Classroom

Essays on Teaching What Scares Us

Edited by Adam Golub *and* Heather Richardson Hayton

Foreword by W. Scott Poole
Afterword by Jeffrey Jerome Cohen

McFarland & Company, Inc., Publishers
Jefferson, North Carolina

ISBN (print) 978-1-4766-6327-2
ISBN (ebook) 978-1-4766-2760-1

Library of Congress cataloguing data are available

British Library cataloguing data are available

Printed in the United States of America

McFarland & Company, Inc., Publishers
Box 611, Jefferson, North Carolina 28640
www.mcfarlandpub.com

Acknowledgments

We would both like to thank our students for welcoming monsters into our classrooms and for inspiring us to explore monstrous pedagogies. We are grateful for the opportunity to work with such excellent scholars and teachers on this project—to continue learning from them and their monsters. We would also like to thank our graduate research assistants, Jasmin Gomez and Anna Rider, for their editorial assistance, as well as the two anonymous readers of this manuscript for their time and suggestions.

Adam Golub would like to thank his colleagues in the American Studies department at California State University, Fullerton, for supporting his mid-career turn to monster theory and pedagogy. He is also grateful to family, friends, and the many random strangers who have talked to him about their favorite monsters over the years.

Heather Richardson Hayton would like to thank her colleagues at Guilford College who enthusiastically welcome her monstrous experiments, even when they spill out into the halls of Archdale and onto the lawns of campus. She has benefited enormously from conversations about monsters over meals, drinks, and long plane rides with friends and family.

Table of Contents

Foreword

W. Scott Poole

"I'm looking forward to the class. I just don't understand how we can do a whole U.S. history course about monsters."

In varying forms, students have said these words to me before the beginning of almost all my American Monsters courses. I'm a historian who studies and teaches American cultural history, but it is very likely that anthropologists, sociologists, communications scholars, and English professors have heard various versions of this idea from undergraduates eager to take "a monsters class," but uncertain what they are signing on for.

It is not that they aren't excited to take a course on monsters. In fact, sometimes it is fair to say their enthusiasm for the topic itself supersedes their spirit of scholarly inquiry. Many of them are undoubtedly hoping to get to watch a lot of horror movies. Some of them may enter our classes assuming that nothing could be easier than thinking and talking about zombies, vampires, and Frankenstein's monsters. More than a few *Game of Thrones* fans fill the seats hoping that a dragon will glide by. No such luck in American history; another way that some of my colleagues studying medieval and East-Asian monsters have it over us. We do, however, have an embarrassment of riches when it comes to sea serpents swimming around in the 19th century, making these creatures of legend to the 1820s through the 1850s what the zombie has become to the early 21st century.

So, our students come sometimes giddy with excitement but uncertain of what we will actually do. Unfortunately, sometimes colleagues are equally dubious. "I hear that's a popular class," they sniff, which translated means "I'm doing serious historical work in my class and so that's why it's less popular." Perhaps this unfortunate attitude only plagues professors who examine American culture and modernity more generally? Medievalists, early modernists, and classicists are often less surprised by the topic as they have worked on monster narratives for decades, through the explication of everything from saga and epic (*Gilgamesh* can lay claim to both the earliest known human story and the first monster narrative), to the legal records of European witch trials and early-modern folktales of monstrous births and demonic rites.

Now, over the last few years, condescension toward the idea of a monsters class has slowly begun to erode in my particular corner of academia. I certainly have colleagues in the wider historical profession who have realized how much monster narratives play a role in American history and are building courses around the idea. One of the editors of this volume teaches one such course at California State University, Fullerton.

Although historians are playing catch-up in this area, scholars of film studies and communications theory have long taught the reading of the horror film, and how cinematic texts frame the monstrous and depend on certain audience assumptions about what constitutes a monster (while of course sometimes subverting those notions). The work of Robin Wood, Andrew Tudor, and Carol Clover has been key here, as was an extraordinary and very classroom-friendly essay collection that appeared almost 20 years ago, edited by Barry Keith Grant and entitled *The Dread of Difference: Gender and the Horror Film* (1996). Though often depending too much on Freudian and Neo-Freudian readings of horror for my tastes, the collection surveyed an astonishing array of material and placed gender and sexuality at the center of our understanding of horror, as I think it needs to be if students are to fully grasp their relevance.

Why have other academic disciplines only made their way slowly to the darkest part of the forest? Skepticism about the pedagogy and the study of monsters comes, knowingly or unknowingly, from scholars influenced very much by the Frankfurt School's grumpy evaluation of pop culture as mind-numbing, apolitical mass culture. Some may have some version of Marshall McLuhan's conception of "cool" media bouncing about in their heads: pop culture as mellow disengagement. The most *trendinista* of our postmodern colleagues may see us lost in Baudrillard's "desert of the real" in our study of monsters, certain we are mistaking media illusion without substance for meaningful narrative. Of course, my fellow monster scholars who study the ancient Near East would quickly explain that it's in just such haunted wastes that monsters make their lair, from Pazuzu of *Exorcist* fame to the jinn who remain part of Islamic thought both in the Quran and in numerous hadith.

Noting the ancient pedigree of studying the monstrous highlights the obvious fact that they have long been essential to various kinds of histories. Pliny the Elder collected monster tales in the first century from across the rather restricted limits of his known world. Long before anyone spoke of a hermeneutic of suspicion, Pliny showed some healthy skepticism toward the stories of werewolves at Lycos. In the Middle Ages, monastic encyclopedist

Isidore of Seville catalogued the existence of "monstrous races" who lived beyond the borders of Latin Christian Europe. Sadly, when European explorers, settlers and conquerors made their way to West Africa, Asia, and the Americas, they took such conceptions of monstrous races with them.

In the modern era, two strands of scholarship emerged to examine the monster and its many heads, bloody claws, or blood-curdling screams. Psychoanalysis viewed the monster as many-tentacled or furry or fanged ids that come out to play in our dreams and sometimes our walking nightmares. In many respects, Freud's interpretation of the *unheimlich*, the uncanny, laid the basis for this reading with his 1919 essay of the same name.

Julia Kristeva's *Powers of Horror: An Essay on Abjection* (1980) fundamentally reframed Freud's reading while building on certain aspects of it. Her concept of the abject helped explain why we are both attracted and repelled by the "Terrible Thing" or the "Terrible Place." Or, just the *terrible stuff* of the body. What disgusts and terrifies us, she insisted, comes grossly intermixed with what we want and desire, a complex psychological fact that lies at the root of our fascinations, obsessions, and phobias.

Freud's interest in folk and fairy tales as cutting a path into the wilderness of the unconscious finds a parallel in the study of folklore as unveiling the secrets of culture. In fact, I would nominate Jacob and Wilhelm Grimm as the first modern monster scholars. "The Brothers Grimm," as they became known, transcribed over two hundred folktales in the late 18th and early 19th centuries, stories of monsters and magic that had previously only circulated in oral form. Oddly known today as collectors of allegedly harmless children's tales that are anything but, they shaped a methodology highly influential in the professionalization of anthropology and literary scholarship.

These brothers with grim stories unpacked their tales of dark wonder to discover a rural *volk* at the heart of German culture. Meanwhile, Anglo-Saxon scholars like Edward Tylor and Andrew Lang focused their efforts on using folklore to trace the genealogy of tales that had, they believed, terrified human beings since prehistoric times. The seminal *Golden Bough* (1890) of James George Frazer represents the apogee of these efforts.

Understanding these first scholarly forays into terror tales requires an understanding of the political and historical context in which folklorists sought to define the national characteristics of their own folk cultures. They worked at a time that incubated modern notions of nationalism. Their scholarship reflected this new way of thinking about identity and the collection of folktales supposedly aided in finding an irreducible national spirit. In the case of the Grimms, they sought a "Germanic" volkish spirit in the decades before Germany existed as a single nation-state. Folklore became, unwittingly, part of the rising tide of European nationalism that had such utterly horrific effects by the 20th century.

British anthropologists took their folkloric studies, and their ethnocentrism, abroad to their colonial possessions, often wreaking havoc in our understanding of the cultures of South Asia. British anthropological studies of Hinduism, for instance, discovered "monsters" everywhere in the mythic narratives and ritual practices of India. To repurpose the famous line in James Whale's *Bride of Frankenstein* (1935), it became a new world in which gods *became* monsters (a concept that even made an unfortunate cameo in the Indiana Jones franchise of the 1980s). Even more damaging, this British imperial gaze turned like the all-seeing Eye of Mordor on South Asian religious practices to create the very notion of "Hinduism" as a monolithic religion rather than a loose collection of highly localized practices that must be studied in their specificity and particularity.

The folklorist and the psychoanalyst long dominated the idea of "monster studies" but such scholarly interest also found a home, or a lair, in literary criticism. They especially cast their eldritch shadows over medievalists who built on, or directly challenged, J. R. R. Tolkien's famous essay "Beowulf: The Monsters and the Critics" (1936), in which he argued against previous readings that understated, or simply ignored, the role of the monstrous in the saga in favor of emphasizing its style. Take away the monsters, Tolkien noted, and you take away the hero and his struggle with time and fate. Suddenly, he insisted, you have an epic with no conflict. This leaves you with a story as eviscerated as Hrothgar's doomed warriors after one of Grendel's nighttime visits.

Tolkien's view that monsters cannot be discarded has won the field in a variety of disciplines. Over the last decade, the study of the monster in folktale, popular culture, media narrative, public memory, historical archives, urban legends, and moral panics has exploded. The cynical will say this has to do with our current fascination with monsters, as evidenced by the continuing zombie obsession embodied in small screen hits like *The Walking Dead* (2010–) and *Game of Thrones* (2011–). But the truth is that these pop culture phenomena simply reflect a deep and enduring obsession with what hides in the darkest part of the forest or the empty caves of the desert, an experience as old as primordial Sumer and Çatal Hüyük.

Recent approaches to the teaching of monsters break with older models, often adopting a wonderfully rich interdisciplinary approach. The essays in this volume point to the proliferation of methodologies brought to bear on these strange, dangerous, wondrous, sad, and terrifying creatures.

Several significant current interpretations of the monster have fought shy of the Freudian approach and deeply affected how most of us teach the meaning of monsters. Jeffery Jerome Cohen's 1996 *Monster Theory* collected a number of important essays that perhaps helped stage our contemporary monster mash in a variety of disciplines. His own contribution, "Monster

Culture (Seven Theses)," remains a landmark discussion of the monster as cultural signifier. Unfailingly useful in starting a discussion of the meaning of monsters in that first, essential week of class, it clears away some of the more simplistic psychological assumptions about the monstrous still current in the 1990s and even today. He reminds us that cultures, contemporary and ancient, have found in the monster a liminal space, a conduit of desire, and a savage other. We cannot reduce them to a single set of meanings. Employing J. Jack Halberstam's perfect phrasing in his brilliant book *Skin Shows: Gothic Horror and the Technology of Monsters* (1995), "monsters are meaning machines," able to represent all manner of identities, desires, and even nationalist projects, in their complex and often horrific bodies.

Timothy Beal's *Religion and Its Monsters* (2001), as the title suggests, begins with the insight of theologian Rudolph Otto, who saw what he called a "mysterium tremendum" in his 1917 *The Idea of the Holy*. A masterful survey taking us from biblical concepts of order and the cosmos to the sadomasochistic power politics of the *Hellraiser* series, Beal identifies monsters with religion's tendencies to bridge, or to widen, the gap between ourselves and others.

More recently, Stephen T. Asma's reflective and compelling *On Monsters* (2009) sees the terrors of the night as part evolutionary imperative and part cultural development and change that forces on us confrontations with the problem of evil and our desperate need to tell stories about it. Asma's book has moved scholarship fully beyond the truism that individuals and societies use the monster simply to legitimize their desire to destroy "the other" (that much overused term). Monsters do provide a language, if limited, for talking about the problem of evil. He also, despite certain characteristics he calls the "historically provincial," finds continuities across time in our ideas about the monster, discovering themes he considers universal in the stories we tell ourselves in the night.

My own reading of monster narratives has been wary of any psychological reading of the monstrous or any pedagogical approach that establishes a clear definition of the monster. Monsters, I've argued, are creatures of historical context and cultures get the monsters they deserve, the vengeful ghosts they have raised. The rituals that evoke these daimonic forces are the very stuff of historical forces and events. Nineteenth-century Americans feared the sea serpent because their frontiers seemed full of lake monsters and their whaling ships allegedly encountered terrors on the entrepreneurial frontiers of the high seas. This mirrored the violence settlers and maritime entrepreneurs perpetrated in the working out of their mythical manifest destiny.

In a new context, the 1930s and '40s, the mad scientist emerged out of the shadow of two world wars and Oppenheimer's weapon of apocalyptic peril. By the 1970s, American imperial adventures in Southeast Asia had made "body bags" part of the vocabulary. Following a war that brought the realities of combat into living rooms and a plastic surgery and dieting/exercise revolution in the 80s, the body became the haunt of the undead, the zombie and the vampire, creatures that in different ways reflect historical ideas about the ruined body and its fate.

Monster scholarship continues to proliferate as monster culture continues to grow. Currently, our students are consuming horror narratives that raise new and interesting questions, reflect the historical moment and even recall, in a revisionist manner, earlier interpretations of the monster that are in themselves now historical artifacts.

In fact, Jennifer Kent's *Babadook* (2014) makes us feel that Freud deserved a writing credit. Kent, both in her short film *Monster* (2005) and the major feature that followed, resurrected a fairy tale monster and hybridized it with the possession narrative popular since 1973 when Regan spewed pea soup and did bad things with a crucifix. In making these connections, Kent created a truly terrifying scenario that alludes to the patriarchal father recrudent and the id unleashed.

What most interested me about this film, even beyond its exquisite pacing, cinematography, and ability to scare jaded old horror nerds like myself, relates to its deep roots in what Freud saw as some of the most basic elements of terror: the stories from which we weave both civilization and religion. There is good evidence that ceremonial burial may have functioned as the first religious act of human beings. Rites of internment came from the need to make sure that the dead, some of whom may have taken a well-placed mammoth bone to the back of the head, stayed where they had gone, did not return to regain their place in the tribe, take back their many wives and avenge themselves on their killers. Kent's film fed off such primordial fears in an especially effective way while also creating an ending that echoes a somewhat modern conception of what we do with the monsters that stalk us.

But monsters are not all in our heads and the popularity and critical acclaim of *Babadook* doesn't force us back into the hands of the Freudians and folklorists. Ana Lily Amirpour's *A Girl Walks Home Alone at Night* (2014) reminds us that monsters are creatures of politics and particular historical contexts. Perhaps the most important horror film since Danny Boyle's *28 Days Later* (2002), it explains post-revolutionary Iran both in terms of its complex relationship to modernity and the struggle of women caught in the rip-tides of Shi'a traditionalism and an indigenous middle eastern feminism that wants to mutilate patriarchal systems, old and new. It is also a revival of the vampire film, somnolent and stumbling since the *Twilight* phenomenon, but clearly alive (or undead) with possibilities. Amirpour's monster comes at us as a sympathetic, deeply political, and also utterly vicious killer—murderous and primal.

We don't need to convince our students that monsters matter. They can turn on the TV, queue up Netflix, or spend a few minutes online and learn this, if they somehow have missed the horrific menagerie that lives in our current popular culture. But, beginning on that first day of class when they sit curious, uncertain, and maybe a little spooked, we do need to convince them how much and how deeply monsters matter in making sense of human strivings and failings, how they are primary sources of personal and collective horrors, and how they live at the intersection of politics, history, desire, and meaning. We have to teach about monsters.

W. Scott Poole, *a professor of history at the College of Charleston, has written widely on American history, horror and popular culture, including his award-winning* Monsters in America *(2011) and his study of Cold War America, horror films and celebrity culture,* Vampira: Dark Goddess of Horror *(2014) and a new biography of H.P. Lovecraft,* In the Mountains of Madness *(2016).*

Introduction

Monstrous Pedagogies

ADAM GOLUB *and*
HEATHER RICHARDSON HAYTON

The 2013 animated film *Monsters University* is set at a college in the imaginary city of Monstropolis where young monsters take classes to learn how to scare humans. At Monsters University (MU), monsters are the students, the teachers, and the subject matter. In classes like "Scaring 101," monstrous professors teach the mechanics of fear. Monstrous students—only a few of whom will pass the final exam and graduate from the School of Scaring—study the proper role of monsters in society. Monstrosity is at the heart of the curriculum and the campus culture at MU. "Scariness is the true measure of a monster," says Dean Abigail Hardscrabble, herself a dragon-like creature with millipede legs and bat wings. "If you're not scary, what kind of monster are you?" *Monsters University*—a pop culture phenomenon that appealed to audiences of all ages and was one of the highest grossing animated films in history—notably locates monsters directly in the classroom. At MU, teaching and learning converge on monsters and the lessons of fear.

This book engages with the notion that we are living in an age of *Monsters University* writ large.

Monsters, of course, have always been educational. Since ancient times, societies around the world have invented monsters in art, literature, folklore, and religion as a way to *teach* something to members of a group. Monsters sometimes perform supernatural and mythical functions in a community, serving as portents, as object lessons, or as central figures in a society's construction of culture heroes. Monsters have also performed sociological functions, embodying a society's deepest fears, signifying difference and defining the Other, and reinforcing cultural boundaries. Monsters "produce wonder and demand explication," writes Lisa Verner.[1] They both frighten and instruct.

While we have always learned from monsters in one way or another, we seem to be living in a peak moment of monster pedagogy. There is a distinct cultural conversation taking place today surrounding the educational possibilities inherent in monsters. In the 21st century, monsters have become both a subject of formal study and a means of teaching people useful knowledge. On and off campuses, in books, television, and film, in training workshops and online communities, we are seeking out opportunities to teach with and learn from monsters. More than ever, like the pupils of Monsters University, we are being schooled in the monstrous.

For example, the same year that *Monsters University* appeared in theaters, the University of California, Irvine, offered a massive open online course (MOOC) called "Society, Science, Survival: Lessons from AMC's *The Walking Dead.*" The class taught students the physics, chemistry, and biology of the zombie apocalypse. Sixty-five thousand people worldwide enrolled.[2]

That's right. Sixty-five thousand people took a class on zombies.[3]

Meanwhile, in-person courses on monsters have grown exponentially on college campuses in recent years.[4] Students are studying monsters in a variety of academic departments, in classes with titles like "Monsters and Monstrosity," "Monsters and the Monstrous," "Making Monsters," "What Is a Monster?," "Monsters, from Folklore to Reality," "Monsters in Literature, Film, and Culture," "Ghosts, Monsters, Demons, and Aliens," "Witches, Vampires, and Other Monsters," "Monsters in America," and "American Monsters." At George Mason University, students interested in "Monster Studies" can take a cluster of recommended courses offered by different departments in the College of Humanities and Social Sciences.[5] In 2012, the University of Virginia offered a year-long interdisciplinary course called "The Art of the Moving Creature" that taught students how to design and build their own monsters.[6]

Monster pedagogy is also being practiced outside the classroom.

Since 2011, millions of fans of *The Walking Dead* (2010–) have been tuning into *Talking Dead*, a show that airs immediately after each episode of the popular television series. *Talking Dead* has been described as an "hour-long monster mash" that "invites you to make your couch another forum for discussion" and explore "what it all means."[7] The show is essentially a televised seminar that encourages guests—and viewers at home—to practice analysis of character, plot, theme, and symbolism in *The Walking Dead*. In 2016, one episode even featured a teacher as a panelist; the winner of the "Ultimate Fan" contest, he discussed how he used *The Walking Dead* to teach his high school students close reading skills.

Recently, a number of documentary television series about monsters have also appeared on educational TV channels. From 2007 to 2010, History aired *MonsterQuest*, a show that purported to use science to investigate eyewitness accounts of monster sightings. The National Geographic Channel similarly applied archeological methods to examining vampire lore in *Vampire Forensics* (2010). On the Discovery Channel, viewers can catch episodes of *Monsters and Mysteries in America* (2013–).

For people who want to get off of their couch to learn about monsters, the outdoor equipment retailer REI has been offering "zombie preparedness" courses at store locations across the United States. The classes teach participants survival skills that would be helpful in the event of an undead invasion, but would also come in handy in the aftermath of an earthquake or major storm.[8] In May 2011, the Centers for Disease Control released an emergency preparedness guide for "the zombie apocalypse." Aimed at an American population fixated on zombies, it was a tongue-in-cheek attempt to teach important community safety issues. The CDC website crashed in the first 48 hours under the weight of its popularity and viral marketing.[9]

Books have also been using monsters to teach us things of value. The novel *Zombies and Calculus* tells the story of a math professor who uses calculus to help his students survive an undead apocalypse (be sure you know about tangent vectors and gravitational acceleration). *Economics of the Undead* applies economic theory to such monstrous phenomena as vampire investment strategies, the implications of taxing zombie labor, and the odds of finding undead love (not good). Monsters are also vehicles for teaching philosophy in books like *True Blood and Philosophy*, *The Philosophy of The X-Files*, and *Planet of the Apes and Philosophy*.[10]

"The mind needs monsters," writes anthropologist David Gilmore. "Since earliest times, people have invented fantasy creatures on which their fears could safely settle."[11] We are still inventing monsters—and still being scared by them—but at this moment in time, we seem to want to discover new and different ways to learn from monsters. Today, the mind does not just need monsters—it also needs monster pedagogy.

In *The Joy of Teaching*, Peter Filene writes, "Teaching is only as successful as the learning it produces. Indeed, the teaching/learning relationship is not simply dialogic, between professor and student, but polylogic.... Together, students and professor interact with the other member of this process: namely, the subject matter."[12] *Monsters in the Classroom* asks what happens when *the monster* is the other member of the learning process. How do we interact with it? What learning does it produce? The essays gathered here examine how and when we bid the monstrous into our classrooms—and why we might invite such fearful creatures into a space commonly devoted to creating safe learning communities. These essays detail the potential dangers of welcoming monsters into the classroom, as well as highlighting how the monstrous, as an epistemological category and site of abject desire, holds transformative power for one's pedagogy. How does teaching monsters reshape the dynamics of the classroom, the socio-politics of the curriculum, and the mission of the university? How can monster pedagogy transform the classroom into a safe enough space to discuss topics that incite fear and dread, and to focus students' attention on the uncanny, the unseen, and the underexamined? Each essay in this edition explores the intersection of monstrosity and pedagogy, describing what transformative learning looks like while drawing on diverse theoretical frameworks as well as the authors' own experiences with interdisciplinary teaching at a variety of institutions across the United States and the world.

Twenty years ago, Jeffrey Jerome Cohen's *Monster Theory* gathered together essays that explored "what happens when monstrousness is taken seriously, as a mode of cultural discourse."[13] In a similar vein, this book examines what happens when monstrousness is taken seriously as classroom pedagogy. Over the years, monster studies has provided teachers with a wealth of theoretical tools for investigating the monstrous. Monster scholars have taught us how to read the monster as repressed Other, as disrupter of categories and binaries, and as embodiment of sexual, racial, and foreign threats to the community.[14] We have learned to read the monster as a figure of repulsion as well as a figure of desire and fantasy.[15] Monster scholars have taught us to contextualize monsters in order to understand how they resonate with issues, fears, and anxieties—and with real-life acts of monstrosity—in the larger culture (monsters are the things "hiding in history's dark places," as W. Scott Poole puts it).[16] From monster studies we have learned about the circuit of consumption and (re)production whereby we consume imaginary monsters and then regulate our own behavior while also surveilling other people for signs of monstrosity (the monster "polices the borders of the possible," writes Cohen).[17] For over two decades, scholars have been conceptualizing the monstrous in important and exciting ways, but surprisingly little work has been done to translate this research into practical pedagogical strategies.[18] *Monsters in the Classroom* explores ways to apply monster theory to diverse learning situations and to operationalize the monstrous as a teaching practice.

In his 2013 essay, "Towards a Monster Pedagogy: Reclaiming the Classroom for the Other," John Edgar Browning argues that monstrosity can be taught as a "means of inquiry" into how particular societies construct normalcy. Monsters, he writes, represent "the endeavors of organized societies to classify what they deem 'normal.'" When students engage with monsters, they must necessarily confront the cultural logics of difference and belonging, which in turn opens up a whole other avenue of inquiry into the workings of ideology, social structure, and hegemony. Monster pedagogy, therefore, "can provide educators with a critical tool with which to facilitate the reexamination of cultural and historical prejudices."[19] Browning's point—that the study of monsters is never just about monsters—is one we explore in this volume. The contributors to *Monsters in the Classroom* do not choose to teach monsters simply as a way to bolster enrollment or cater to students' pop culture tastes. Nor are they simply teaching rote surveys of monsters that treat them only as imaginary beasts. Rather, the educators in this collection have found that monsters are a highly effective vehicle for teaching cultural analysis, fostering a critical imagination, making interdisciplinary connections, and encouraging students to "build new mental models of reality."[20]

The book is organized into three parts that playfully and generatively replicate the monster's trajectory. First the monster appears, shaking us out of our complacency and making us immediately aware of difference. Then the monster roams, wreaking havoc on landscapes and rendering familiar places unsafe. Finally, the monster attacks, upending systems and transforming how we live our everyday lives. A number of the essays feature appendices that include sample syllabi, assignments, and class materials, offered with the hope that the monster will return, resurrected in other classrooms, the inspiration for new monstrous pedagogies.

Part I, "Teaching Difference: The Monster Appears," features four essays that demonstrate how bringing monsters into the classroom can focus student learning around questions of identity formation and the construction of "the normal." Monsters are frightening in part because they smash distinctions and "conflate or collapse cognitive boundaries recognized as the foundations of order."[21] As the contributors here show, monsters expose and destabilize classification systems such as race, class, gender, and sexual identity, allowing students to interrogate the categories (and biases) by which we organize our society and our everyday lives. Asa Simon Mittman explains how he uses monsters in art history to teach the "wonders of difference" and prompt students to explore their own prejudices and preconceptions about the "abnormal." In Pamela Bedore's English capstone course, students examine how monster literature engages with issues of power, liminality, gendered epistemologies, and vulnerability, while at the same time reflecting on how these issues circumscribe their own experiences as students and aspiring writers and teachers. Nancy Hightower challenges students in her composition course to produce their own visual rhetoric projects, creatively integrating research, writing, and photography in an attempt to understand the "monstrous grotesque" as both an aesthetics of difference and a rhetorical mode of argument. Jessica Elbert Decker's essay invites monsters into the philosophy classroom, showing how texts like *Jurassic Park* (1993), *Alien* (1979), and Margaret Atwood's *Oryx and Crake* (2003) can teach students to grapple with the conditions of oppression and the ways in which we codify difference in our cultural narratives and social relations.

Part II, "Transforming Space: The Monster Roams," explores how geography can shape our sense of the monstrous. The essays in this section suggest that monsters can provide students with a vehicle for studying spatial culture and learning how to read—and meaningfully interact with—the landscapes and places around them. Adam Golub offers an interdisciplinary American studies framework for teaching monstrous geographies, explaining how he uses monsters like King Kong, Godzilla, and the vampire to help students think about the meanings we attach to nature, the built environment, and imagined political communities. Bernice M. Murphy introduces cinematic and literary representations of Gothic landscapes and the specter of the Wendigo to her university students in Ireland in order to help them interrogate the doctrine of Manifest Destiny as a kind of monstrous devouring of space, people, and resources. Kyle William Bishop describes how he uses place-based teaching practices and "fear experience learning" in his London study abroad program to bring literature students into contact with monstrous spaces that incite physiological responses. Phil Smith explains how he teaches "zombie walking" to theatre students in the United Kingdom to push them to reflect on the relationship between their bodies and the spaces they move through during performance, while also learning the importance of acting in—and in response to—a larger group.

Part III, "Disrupting Systems: The Monster Attacks," considers what happens when teachers introduce monstrous pedagogies into deep-rooted systems. How can we use monsters to shake up established disciplinary practices, modes of inquiry, and institutional values? These essays advocate for the infusion—the *unleashing*—of monsters into the curriculum in order to engage students, to discomfort them, and to teach them required content in fresh ways. Each essay also hints at the possibility that monsters can helpfully disrupt what schools think students should know and what students themselves think they already know. Joshua Paddison, a scholar of religious history, uses monsters to challenge students' understanding of faith and belief systems that are typically associated with religion but that also pervade the ways in which people "believe" in monsters. In her undergraduate Japanese courses, Charlotte Eubanks injects the monstrous into foreign language instruction in order to provide an important cultural diagnostic that helps students find their own voice and linguistic agency. Shifting our attention to secondary education, Brian Sweeney suggests that high school teachers can use monsters to disrupt an institutional emphasis on outdated methodologies and overly-simplistic assessments, and better prepare students for the analytical writing and critical thinking they will need to do in college. Finally, Heather Richardson Hayton describes how she staged a simulated zombie attack on her students and discovered that their reactions severely tested the core values of community, collaboration, and transformational learning at her Quaker liberal arts college.

Monsters in the Classroom is a timely collection of 12 essays written by experienced educators that explores the pedagogical value of monsters. Each contributor reflects on how monsters can augment the curriculum, inspire new instructional strategies, and transform student learning. Taken as a whole, this book is designed to serve as both a primer on monster theory and a casebook of teaching practices. The following essays address our broader cultural fascination with monsters—and our need to process the *meaning* of monsters—by showcasing innovative approaches to teaching the monstrous across disciplines, in high school, college, and university classrooms.

Notes

1. Lisa Verner, *Epistemology of the Monstrous* (New York: Routledge, 2005), 43.
2. "Infrastructure, UC Irvine Reveal Results of 'The Walking Dead' MOOC," http://ps.uci.edu/news/8289 (last accessed July 2015).
3. In the fall of 2015, UC Irvine offered another online class about monsters, "The Science Behind *The Strain*," based on the television series about a vampire pandemic. Class topics included parasites, cyber attacks, and disease dynamics—all themes in the show. Casey Fabris, "A MOOC Hopes to Sink Its Teeth into a New Audience: TV Fans," *The Chronicle of Higher Education*, May 13, 2015, http://chronicle.com/blogs/wiredcampus/a-mooc-hopes-to-sink-its-teeth-into-a-new-audience-tv-fans/56577 (last accessed August 2015).
4. Erica E. Phillips, "Zombie Studies Gain Ground on College Campuses," *The Wall Street Journal*, March 3, 2014, www.wsj.com/articles/SB10001424052702304851104579361451951384512 (last accessed July 2015).
5. "College Courses Study Monsters?" http://chssundergrad.gmu.edu/articles/6193 (last accessed July 2015).
6. Erin O'Hare, "Monster Mash: Modern-Day Dr. Frankensteins Bring Creatures to Life," *Virginia: The UVA Magazine*, October 16, 2012, uvamagazine.org/articles/monster_mash/ (last accessed August 2015).
7. Greg Braxton, "Chris Hardwick's 'Talking Dead' Walks Off with Zombie Fans," *Los Angeles Times*, March 20, 2013, http://articles.latimes.com/2013/mar/30/entertainment/la-et-st-talking-dead-walking-dead-amc-20130330; Jake Mann, "How Chris Hardwick's Talking Dead Is Changing TV," *The Motley Fool*, December 3, 2013, www.fool.com/investing/general/2013/12/03/how-chris-hardwicks-talking-dead-is-changing-tv.aspx; Sonia Saraiya, review of *Talking Dead*, *The A.V. Club*, April 1, 2013, www.avclub.com/tvclub/emtalking-dead-em-95849 (last accessed July 2015).
8. Cascene Gibson, "REI Hosing 'Zombie Preparedness' Classes," http://q13fox.com/2013/11/15/rei-prepares-you-for-zombie-apocalypse/. The REI website even features an infographic of "essential gear" for a zombie outbreak that includes everything from matches and moleskin to a cast iron skillet (for cooking *and* for whacking zombies in the head). http://blog.rei.com/social/infographic-13-essential-tools-for-surviving-a-zombie-outbreak (last accessed August 2015).
9. "Zombie Preparedness," http://www.cdc.gov/phpr/zombies.htm (last accessed September 2015). For representative reactions to the release of the survival guide, see http://www.zdnet.com/article/cdc-launches-zombie-apocalypse-survival-guide-supplementary-tech-tips/ and http://content.usatoday.com/communities/sciencefair/post/2011/05/cdc-helps-americans-prepare-for-a-zombie-apocalypse/1#.VfwENmRViko (last accessed September 2015).

10. Colin Adams, *Zombies and Calculus* (Princeton: Princeton University Press, 2014); Glen Whitman and James Dow, eds., *Economics of the Undead: Zombies, Vampires, and the Dismal Science* (Lanham, MD: Rowman & Littlefield, 2014); George A. Dunn and Rebecca Housel, eds., *True Blood and Philosophy: We Wanna Think Bad Things with You* (New York: Wiley, 2010); Dean Kowalski, ed., *The Philosophy of The X-Files* (Lexington: University Press of Kentucky, 2009); John Huss, ed., *Planet of the Apes and Philosophy: Great Apes Think Alike* (Chicago: Open Court, 2013). See also Wayne Yuen, *The Walking Dead and Philosophy: Zombie Apocalypse Now* (Chicago: Open Court, 2012) and Galen A. Foresman, ed., *Supernatural and Philosophy: Metaphysics and Monsters … for Idjits* (Oxford: Wiley-Blackwell, 2013).

11. David D. Gilmore, *Monsters: Evil Beings, Mythical Beasts, and All Manner of Imaginary Terrors* (Philadelphia: University of Pennsylvania Press, 2003), 1.

12. Peter Filene, *The Joy of Teaching: A Practical Guide for New College Instructors* (Chapel Hill: University of North Carolina Press, 2005), 2–3.

13. Jeffrey Jerome Cohen, "Preface: In a Time of Monsters," *Monster Theory: Reading Culture*, ed. Cohen (Minneapolis: University of Minnesota Press, 1996), viii.

14. On the monster as Other, see Robin Wood, *Hollywood from Vietnam to Reagan* (New York: Columbia University Press, 1986), especially Chapter 5, "The American Nightmare: Horror in the 70s." On monsters and category crisis, see Jeffrey Jerome Cohen, "Monster Culture (Seven Theses)," in *Monster Theory: Reading Culture*, 3–25. On monstrous bodies and the nation, see J. Jack Halberstam, *Skin Shows: Gothic Horror and the Technology of Monsters* (Durham: Duke University Press, 1995). See also the essays collected in Barry Keith Grant, ed., *The Dread of Difference: Gender and the Horror Film* (Austin: University of Texas Press, 1996).

15. For example, see Harry M. Benshoff, *Monsters in the Closet: Homosexuality and the Horror Film* (New York: Manchester University Press, 1997); Carol J. Clover, *Men, Women, and Chain Saws: Gender in the Modern Horror Film* (Princeton: Princeton University Press, 1992); and James B. Twitchell, *Dreadful Pleasures: An Anatomy of Modern Horror* (New York: Oxford University Press, 1985).

16. W. Scott Poole, *Monsters in America: Our Historical Obsession with the Hideous and the Haunting* (Waco: Baylor University Press, 2011), xv. In addition to Poole, there is a large body of work that deeply contextualizes and historicizes monsters. See, for example, Kendall R. Phillips, *Projected Fears: Horror Films and American Culture* (Westport, CT: Praeger, 2005); Heather Urbanski, *Plagues, Apocalypses, and Bug-Eyed Monsters: How Speculative Fiction Shows Us Our Nightmares* (Jefferson, NC: McFarland, 2007); Brian Regal, *Searching for Sasquatch: Crackpots, Eggheads, and Cryptozoology* (New York: Palgrave Macmillan, 2011); Cynthia Erb, *Tracking King Kong: A Hollywood Icon in World Culture* (Detroit: Wayne State University Press, 2009); Kyle William Bishop, *American Zombie Gothic: The Rise and Fall (and Rise) of the Walking Dead in Popular Culture* (Jefferson, NC: McFarland, 2010); Sarah Juliet Lauro, *The Transatlantic Zombie: Slavery, Rebellion, and Living Death* (New Brunswick: Rutgers University Press, 2015); and Stephen T. Asma, *On Monsters: An Unnatural History of Our Worst Fears* (Oxford: Oxford University Press, 2011).

17. Cohen, "Monster Culture (Seven Theses)," 12. Cohen and Halberstam both talk about this circuit of consumption and re(production). Poole similarly observes that monsters "not only symbolize, but also help to configure, worldviews and play a role in those worldviews" (24). See also Elizabeth Young, *Black Frankenstein: The Making of an American Metaphor* (New York: New York University Press, 2008).

18. A small but growing body of work has started to explore the pedagogical dimensions of monsters and horror. See, for example, Aalya Ahmad and Sean Moreland,

eds., *Fear and Learning: Essays on the Pedagogy of Horror* (Jefferson, NC: McFarland, 2013) and Lisa A. Nevarez, ed., *The Vampire Goes to College: Essays on Teaching with the Undead* (Jefferson, NC: McFarland, 2014).

19. John Edgar Browning, "Towards a Monster Pedagogy: Reclaiming the Classroom for the Other," in Ahmad and Moreland, 40–41.

20. Ken Bain, *What the Best College Teachers Do* (Cambridge: Harvard University Press, 2004), 27.

21. Gilmore, 18.

Part I

Teaching Difference
The Monster Appears

Teaching Monsters from Medieval to Modern

Embracing the Abnormal

Asa Simon Mittman

Monsters are, at their base nature, by their essential ontology, pedagogic tools. The theorizing of their instructional function can be traced at least as far back as the Patristic period. Though Augustine of Hippo and Isidore of Seville differed on the precise messages and mechanisms of discovery, they both maintained that monsters existed to teach the careful viewer essential truths.[1] As they saw the world designed in all its myriad detail by an omniscient god, everything bore meaning, but the monstrous was thought to be especially pedagogic, because the monster is the exception, the distortion, the deviation from the general rules that were seen as governing the natural world. This exceptionality required explanation, and both of these influential theologians, as well as many others, concluded that a monster's function was to teach humanity something important.

What *was* God trying to teach us by placing the head of a dog on the body of a human? This was the central question. Augustine concluded that God's point was that he would be able to resurrect the dead, even if their bodies were no longer extant by the Day of Judgment, "with no difficulty to impede him, with no laws of nature dictating to him."[2] Isidore, by contrast, saw them as general warnings against sin. I would take a very different message from the monsters I study and teach, and hope my students do, as well: a message that is not about judgment, fear, and restraint, but instead about the wonder of difference, and the possibility of unburdening ourselves of the judgments placed upon us, and which we place on others.

At its heart, Monster Studies exists to uncover, examine and, when necessary, fight the fundamental binarisms and taxonomic assumptions upon which our cultures are based. This is also the basic goal of my course "Monsters and the Monstrous," which I offer as an upper division seminar at a mid-sized state university. The course is located in, but by no means limited to, the content or methods of my home department, Art History.[3] As I explain to students in the syllabus:

> Monsters haunt culture. They gnaw at the edges of societies. They capture our fears and give bodies to our anxieties. This course will look at the role of monsters and the monstrous in cultures from throughout the world. We will study monsters from Europe, Asia, Africa, and the Americas, from the oldest surviving records of monsters to contemporary incarnations—literary, artistic and cryptozoological. This course will not be a traditional art history course, but rather, will be a cultural studies course, with foci on art, literature, scientific discourse, religion and on.
>
> The course will have two main units, monster theory and monster culture. In the first, we will read texts that lay out some of the key concerns of "monster studies," and some of the central approaches of "monster theory." In the second, we will focus on particular examples of monsters from throughout global culture. We will look at images, read short stories and a novel, and watch a film. Students will choose their own subjects for research and will pursue them with help from me.[4]

The monsters we study in art and literature are, by definition, challenges to systematizations of the messy world and its content; this is what makes them monsters. Consequently, they draw attention to the systems they defy. In narratives, they are often then vanquished by the forces of order and authority (though more recently, monstrous heroes have become popular). In the classroom, they provide an opportunity to explore the biases and preconceptions that students bring with them, and with which they judge themselves and others. The slight remove that attends the examination of monstrous beings allows for us to explore openly the constructs underpinning our culture, leading students to discuss issues they might not ordinarily feel comfortable talking about in class; monsters also occasionally draw out prejudices students might not realize that they bear.

Queering Medieval Monsters and Modern Monstrosity

Monsters are, in a sense, traps. Like sirens on their rocks, they draw us into dangerous waters without our realizing it. Elsewhere, I have described a disturbing episode in a medieval art course in which a student expressed with ferocity and at length her anti–Semitism, to the collective horror of the rest of the class.[5] We would not have found ourselves in this unnerving, and deeply powerful classroom moment were it not for the monsters on the screen, in this case the Winchester Psalter's wild, contorted, fanged horrors, with crude weapons in their hands and their eyes rolling back in their oversized heads (Figure 1). These are figures that were intended to represent "Jews," though I place this in scare quotes since the figures are artificial constructs, not exaggerated caricatures rooted in material realities. I had not engendered the discussion in order to draw out latent bigotry—far from it!—but once I calmed down, I had to admit that it should not have been as surprising as it was. The medieval lives on in the present, and I often think that every bad idea anyone ever had is still alive and kicking.[6]

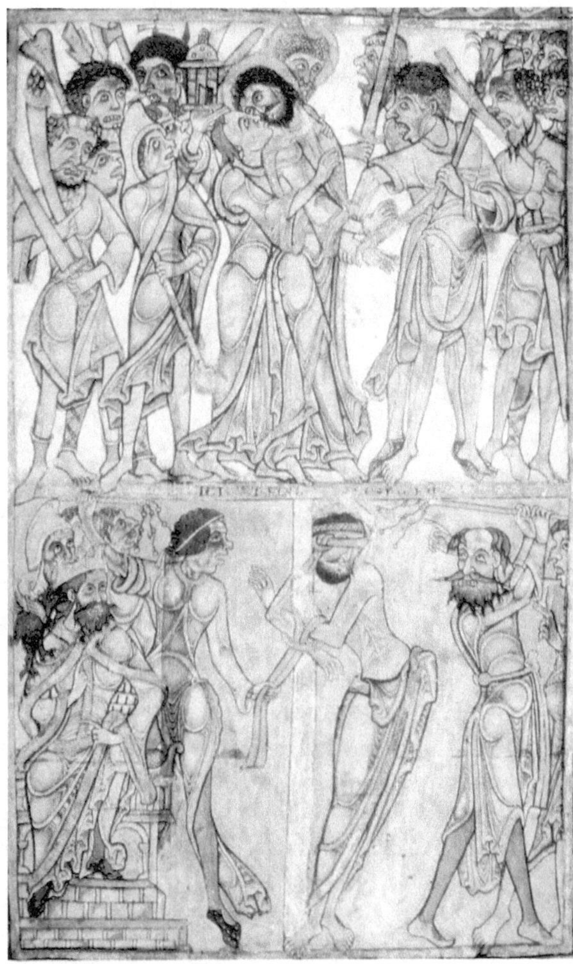

Figure 1: *Betrayal and Flagellation of Christ*, Winchester Psalter, ca. 1150, London, British Library, Cotton Nero C.iv, f. 21r, ©The British Library Board, all rights reserved. Photograph: The British Library Board, reproduced under Creative Commons.

The medieval is, in essence, non-normative in the modern world, which is overwhelmingly presentist in orientation. It thereby functions like the monstrous, in that it disrupts expectations and thereby reveals them. I would stress this value of teaching medieval material in favor of one rooted in the facile equation of medieval and modern, or predicated on the con of "relevance," mistakenly used to justify our existence to administrators and politicians, and wrongly limited to moments when we can draw (justly or not) straight(ish) lines between "then" and "now." The study of medieval culture, like the study of monsters, is not important because (or just because) we can see ourselves reflected in it, but instead, because we often cannot. Rather, I wish to queer the modern via the medieval. There has been wonderful work in medieval studies to queer the medieval, as nicely encapsulated by Karl Whittington, who argues that such work stands "as a kind of position against normative or dominant modes of thought."[7] He is here not talking about so-called non-normative sexualities, but rather, about a mode of viewing and encountering the world. Whittington is relying, among others, on David Halpern, who sees the "queer" as "whatever is at odds with the normal, the legitimate, the dominant.... It demarcates not a positivity but a positionality vis-à-vis the normative."[8] In this sense, there is a very strong kinship between this academic usage of "queer" and the "monstrous." The central point of relevance is that neither category exists in the abstract, but only in relation to artificially defined and ever-shifting norms that, despite their nature as cultural products, are often treated as if existential and unchanging facts. Individuals and communities can only be queer in relation to a purported (and often legally and violently enforced) norm; so too, the monstrous only exists as a moment of interaction. It has no essential features, and is only defined by its difference from whatever artifice of normality a given monster has been summoned to define and defend.[9]

Whenever we study the monstrous, it is really these norms that we are interrogating, sometimes in sympathy with our objects of study and sometimes against their intents. Monsters both establish *and* challenge the normative categories they menace, and in both cases, draw our attention to these norms. All of this is to say that in the classroom, the medieval and the monstrous and, most especially, the medieval-monstrous, provide excellent moments of estrangement from the norms of our modern present, and thereby allow me to queer my students' understanding of their own time and place and, on occasion, even their sense of identity.

What Is "Normal"?

Whenever I teach the monstrous, one of the issues that inevitably arises is its necessary doppelgänger, its uncanny twin, the "normal." We cannot discuss the "monster" without reference to the "norm" from which it deviates, nor the "monstrous" without the "normal" that defines it, nor "monstrosity" without an examination of the "normativity" that grants it meaning. Points of difference may be obvious surface elements attendant to (nearly) universal human norms—dog-headed people, headless people, and so on—but the most interesting examples are those that hew closer to the bone by being closer to home. For example, in the Middle Ages, we might look at the wondrous "Woman-Givers," who are included in the *Wonders of the East* along with fire-breathing, dog-headed giants and people with no heads (Figure 2).[10] They are "wondrous" because, the text tells us, "this kind of person lives for

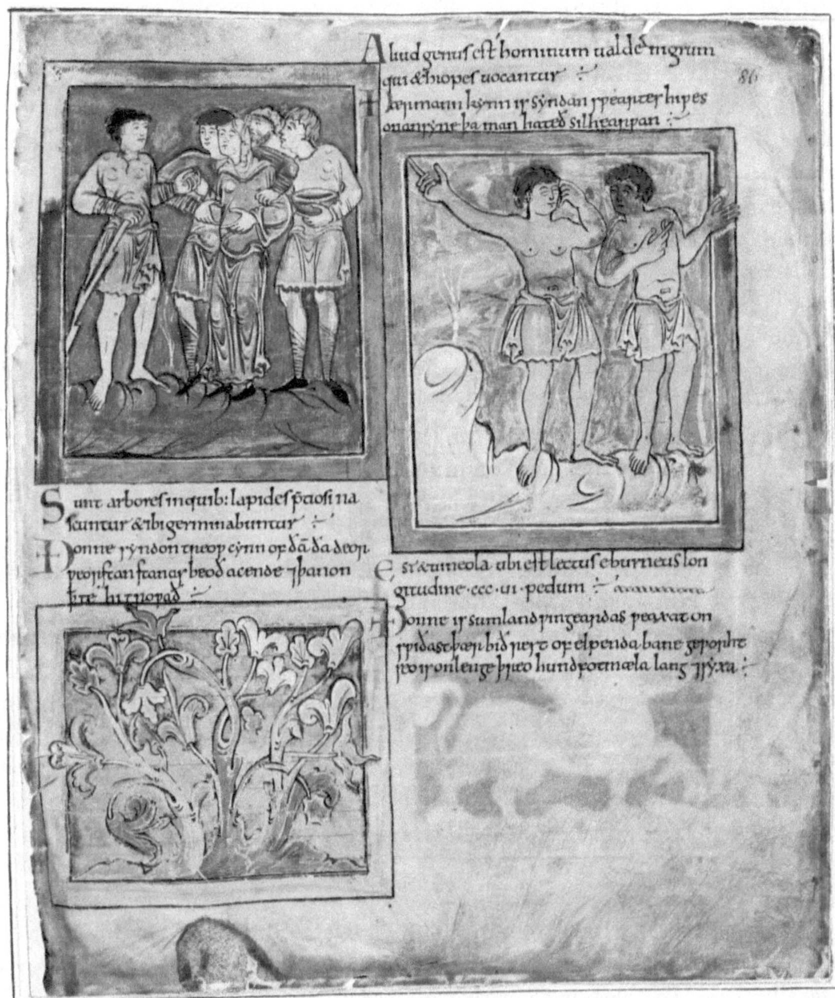

Figure 2: Woman-Givers (left) and Ethiopians (right), *The Wonders of the East*, ca. 1025–50, London, British Library, Cotton Tiberius B.v, f. 86r, ©The British Library Board, all rights reserved. Photograph: The British Library Board, reproduced under Creative Commons.

many years, and they are generous people. And if anyone comes to them then they give him a woman before they let him go away. The Macedonian Alexander, when he came to them, was wondering at their humanness, nor did he wish to kill them nor do them any harm."[11]

What *is* the point of difference, here? Why are these people included in the *Wonders*, which is a catalogue of monstrosity? From our perch in the

21st-century West, it is of course the giving away of women to passing travelers that stands out as anomalous and troubling. Looking at this strange passage draws our attention to our own practices and mores. But for the original Anglo-Saxons, this would have been a barely discernable point of difference, since the giving of women in a variety of contexts was a normal part of their society. For the original audience, then, Susan Kim and I have posited that the risk of sameness would perhaps overwhelm difference, giving the presumably male readers of this volume more points of identification than separation.[12]

This effect would be enhanced by the image, which presents the "exotic" wonder as essentially indistinguishable from the presumably English traveler they converse with, and from the English reader-viewer for whom he is clearly a stand-in. How different, though, is this scene from the lived experience of our students? In the illumination, they see one man giving a woman to another man, who clasps her hand while others from her community bear witness. Again, we start out with a stance of difference, but find that it erodes quickly beneath our gaze.

I have taken a fairly easy example, a "wonder" that, while presented along with giant carnivorous ants and hens that light on fire anyone who touches them,[13] is apparently human. The destabilizing moment of identification, though, is a process that plays out again and again as we confront the monster with a seriousness of purpose, when we look and read closely and think carefully about where and how it stands in relation to ourselves. The valuably destabilizing role of monsters, the queering work that they can do for cultures, is to a degree predicated on their difference not being *quite* absolute. I suspect that blob monsters are not especially popular because, while they threaten bodily integrity, they do not threaten societal norms in as potent ways as more humanoid horrors would. The original poster and trailer for the 1958 film version of *The Blob*, starting Steve McQueen in his debut role, tells us that the blob is "INDESCRIBABLE."[14] This is not, of course, literally true—the blob is a carnivorous, animate, shape-shifting, glistening, semi-transparent red gelatinous mass. I *can* describe it, but I cannot much relate to it.[15]

But both sorts of monsters—the more accessible humanoids and the largely inaccessible others—ultimately cast their glare on us. In my experience, my college students have thought about a great many subjects, but few have spent significant energies examining the most basic categories and qualities out of which their own senses of identity are constructed. Many come from largely homogenous, mid-sized, predominately white, middle-class northern Californian communities (though recent outreach and recruitment efforts have yielded some increasing ethnic diversity).[16] In these communities, issues of identity can, with care, be avoided. It might seem to many readers for it to be impossible in our current political moment, with news cycles dominated by same-sex marriage and race-based police brutality,[17] for any Americans to fail to consider their understanding of sexuality or race, and yet many seem to have taken their normative, "unmarked" status for granted. Many of the students who sign up for "Monsters and the Monstrous" would not have taken an art history course called "The History of Sexualities" or "Representations of Race." They come for vampires and werewolves, but they get rather a lot more than this in the course of 16 weeks, and much of this is directly intended to inspire them to think through their race, gender, sexuality, nationality, religion, ethnicity, class, subcultures, and individuality.

In the first weeks of the course, we not only cover some of the new classics of Monster Studies (including Jeffrey Jerome Cohen's deservedly-popular "Monster Culture: Seven Theses" and Rosemarie Garland-Thomson's "Introduction: From Wonder to Error—A Genealogy of Freak Discourse in Modernity"[18]). We also spend significant time with the classics of postcolonialism (Edward Said, Homi Bhabha, and Partha Mitter[19]). We cover some of the basics of the history of sexuality (Michel Foucault[20]). We cover abjection (Julia Kristeva[21]) and horror (Noël Carrol[22]) and disgust (William Ian Miller[23]). This is a lot of very heavy material to hit my students with, week after week, and I have been surprised that it does not scare more of them off. Surely, some of them are dying to ask, "*Where are the vampires?*" But all of this hard work is accumulative, with each angle on otherness deepening our collective understanding of how the process works, how othering is systemic and culturally endemic, rather than individualized and incidental to the "normal" course of life. We are, of course, building toward the big one, the category that is often seen in the world of identity politics as the trump, the goal, the marker of success within a given rights movement: humanity.

If we can get to a sense of *shared humanity*, surely we can congratulate ourselves, call it a day, and put down the Kristeva, right? Thanks to the posthumanists, no. We still have to interrogate the basis of that top-level category, to break down the notion that there is solid, enduring coherence within the very notion of their (and my and your and our) *humanity*. Other "Others" might well suffice for explorations of many aspects of identity, but monsters are central to our defining and understanding and asserting of our most basic taxonomy: we are human. Through serious and sustained confrontation with the theoretical constructs offered by the readings, and by our close looks at several primary sources, we can slowly start to gain a picture of the category of humanity, itself. From Said and Bhabha, we learn about the deployment of inherently unequal binaries to describe the unmentioned viewing subject; from Cohen, we learn about the cultural construction and force of monsters; from Carrol, we learn about the centrality of emotions to the definition of horror and the monsters at its core; and so on. Of course, these are reductive one-line encapsulations, not careful expositions of the theses and importance of these readings, each of which casts a different shadow on the complex and shifting notion of the monstrous, ultimately building up a penumbra by which we can recognize, use and defy its claims on us.

The (Ab)normal

In my "Monsters and the Monstrous" course, I build slowly toward one of the most challenging readings, Patricia MacCormack's "Posthuman Teratology."[24] The essay, which we read six weeks in, on the last day of the "Monster Theory" unit, is dense and complex, in part because it resolutely (and purposively) avoids exemplification. When I was editing the collection in which MacCormack's essay appears, I pressed her for a few examples to clarify her points, and she explained persuasively why doing so would contradict (by reduction and constraint) the very points she was aiming to prove; she was right, and I relented. And students struggle a bit—in a way that is good for them.

I have come to use this essay as a sort of recap of all that we've covered to this point. Once, as we began our discussion of MacCormack's essay, I asked students to list the themes it engages, and those from the course, to date. I scrawled these on an increasingly overfilled whiteboard (Figure 3). "Other(ness)" came first, unsurprisingly, and then "Abject(ion)," "Hybrid(ity)," "Disgust(ing)," and "Alterity." Adjectives and nouns jostled for primacy. We mapped a dozen binaries, such as "(Dis)ability," "(in)organic," "(Un)known," "(Un)containable," and, of course, "(Ab)normal," and I relied on that 80s lit-crit use of parentheses to fuse many of these terms with their theoretical opposites, since each is meaningless without its other.

At first, we thought we were mapping the key terms for one essay. Then, we decided we were mapping the key terms for our course. In the end, it was clear that we'd charted our civilization, which is predicated on these very mechanisms. In her well-known "Cyborg Manifesto," Donna Haraway enumerates what she finds to be the most essential dichotomies "persistent in Western traditions," those that are "chief among these troubling dualisms": "self/other, mind/body, culture/nature, male/female, civilized/primitive, reality/appearance, whole/part, agent/resource, maker/made, active/passive, right/wrong, truth/illusion, total/partial, God/man."[25]

Many of these pairings are represented in our chaotic list, because the dualisms of our "Western traditions" are the primary ingredients used to construct monsters. In essence, they might all be subsumed under the über-rubric "(Ab)normal." It is no surprise that the normal and abnormal are made a point of dramatic comparison at the outset of James Whale's thoughtful

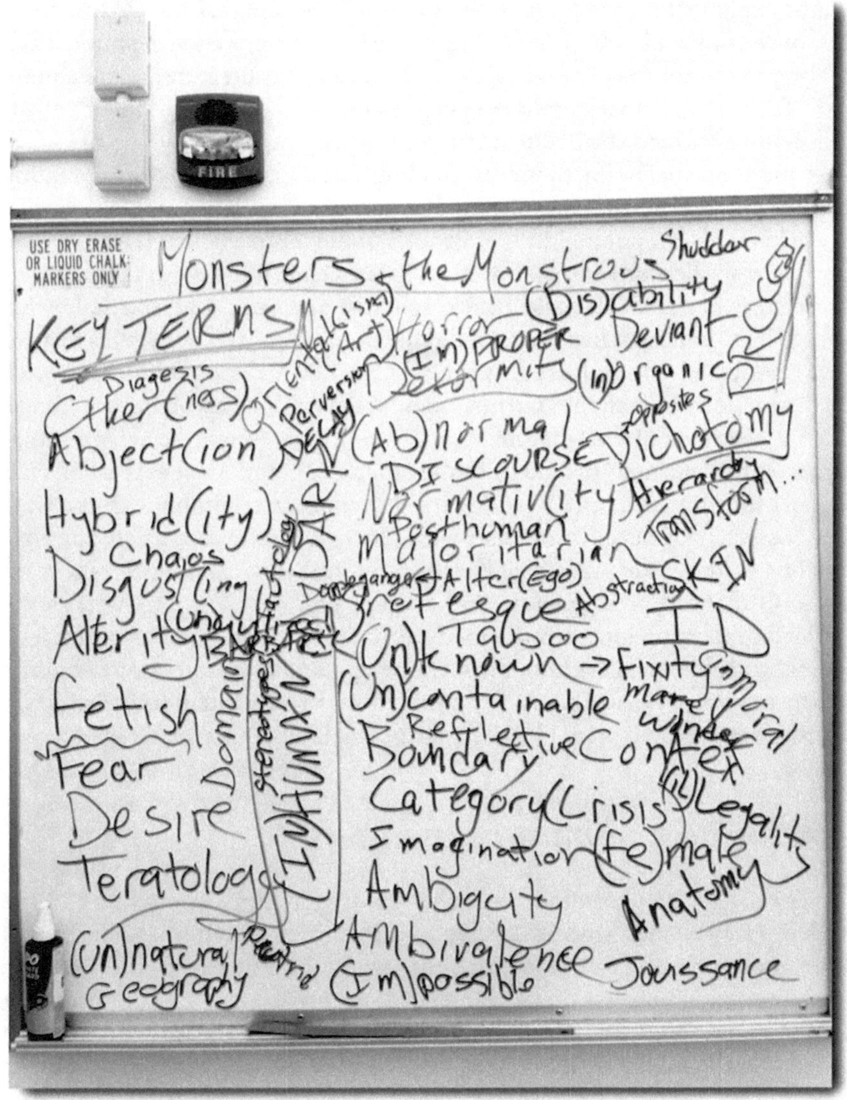

Figure 3: Key Terms Whiteboard, "ARTH400: Monsters and the Monstrous," California State University, Chico, October 2, 2014.

Frankenstein.[26] Only seven minutes in, Doctor Waldman (Edward Van Sloan) explains the difference between two brains, one in a jar labeled "normal brain," containing "one of the most perfect specimens of the human brain," and the other in a jar labeled "abnormal brain," characterized by its "degenerate features." The camera pans back and forth between the jars as the good doctor explains that the folds of the brain tell the story of the personalities they once animated. At the end of this scene in the film, we see the hunchback stealing the brain that Frankenstein will place in his creature.[27] The abnormally formed hunchback grabs the jar containing the normal brain, but drops and shatters it when startled by the ominous ringing of a gong. He therefore takes the *ab*normal brain, thereby providing a new rationale to the impending disaster not present in Mary Shelley's novel.

This is all lampooned in Mel Brook's *Young Frankenstein* (1974), where Igor (Marty Feldman) sneaks into the "Brain Depositary," with the intent of stealing the brain of "Hans Delbruck, scientist and saint" but, startled by his own ghastly, hunchbacked, bug-eyed reflection, drops it.[28] Igor settles instead for a jar labeled "Do not use this brain! ABNORMAL." Comic or disastrous, the distinction between the "normal" and "abnormal" makes all the difference. Doctor Waldman offers what many of us want: clear, scientific evidence that separates the "normal" people from the "abnormal" and "degenerate." His pat explanation—offered in 1931—of course has more in common with the Nazi pseudoscience of degeneracy than with Shelley's subtle construct, but both versions of the Frankenstein narrative offer students chances to reflect on the ways that cultures generate and actively enforce norms, as well as the modern preoccupation with the medical pathologization of difference. The normal and abnormal are human creations, granted meaning by one another, and through such discussions, my students and I generate new, hybridized, interdependent categories like the "(ab)normal," in which we all live.

"We are all and must be monsters"

Monsters are ubiquitous in global culture, as close as anything to the student essay cliché, "since the dawn of humanity…." I tell my students that there is nothing that can follow this that would be true except for "…so far, everyone dies." But even this is not really true. I will put it down in print, for the first time since I was a freshman (and I hope I did not use the trope, even then): *Since the dawn of humanity, people have produced monsters.* They *do* appear in art, from the caves to the present, West and East, North and South.[29] Of course, they do not always serve the same functions, and are not always objects of rejection and loathing, though this is their most common role. It does not, though, have to remain so.

While varying throughout the United States (and the rest of the world), there has certainly been an erosion of reflexive trust in the signs and symbols of authority. All of the badges and lab-coats on the heroes of old monster movies, all of the noblemen and men of science of Victorian novels, all the knights and kings and bishops of medieval accounts are, for most of my students, already and immediately suspect. Monster aficionados enjoy feeling superior as we push our glasses up our collective nose and point out that Frankenstein is the doctor, *not* the monster, but we are wrong when we do so; Victor Frankenstein is *both* the doctor *and* the monster in the narrative, and my students achieve this flash of insight before the lighting strike even arrives to grant the beautiful, murderous *creature* animation.[30] They are suspicious of the powerful and the confident from the start, since they have lived through too many false heroes and corrupt leaders. In reading *Frankenstein*, many do not pity or have sympathy for the lost, lonely creature, lacking a reliable father and a stable family, lacking a community, lacking even a sense of clear and unified identity; they empathize with him. And they *loathe* the craven Victor.

We live in a time when a great many of our students feel alienated, when, at last, the cool kids are no longer cool (only 60 years after *Rebel Without a Cause* tried to convince us),[31] when postmodern decentralization and its attendant digital narrowcasting has fragmented us into increasingly small interest groups. Netflix has me pegged correctly as someone who likes "critically-acclaimed, violent suspenseful movies" and "sci-fi & fantasy featuring a strong female lead."[32] These were not genres in the past. Without a center to hold us in, we are each that much closer to spiraling outward to the edge, to becoming a *mearcstapa*, a monstrous walker of the margins.[33] The question, then, is not whether we have any sympathy with the devil—of course we do, and have, in varying degrees, at least since the Junius 11 manuscript was produced in the era of the *first*-millennium millennials.[34] The question is: what do we do with this sympathy? What are the pedagogical and ethical implications of teaching monsters in a post team-Edward/team-Jacob world, wherein at least some of our students are as ready to join the monsters as to fight them?

I would argue that it is here, in my students' willingness to identify with the monstrous, that I can find the greatest advantage to teaching this material. They often arrive in my class—an elective not required for any students—with an interest in monsters. They say they "like" or "love" monsters, but generally do not seem to have thought through what they mean by this. Some are thrilled by the power and majesty of famous screen titans, and by the heroics resulting in their inevitable defeat, casting themselves in the role of vicarious dragon slayer. Others, though, are suspicious of the beautiful, powerful, noble heroes, and are compelled by the horrible antagonists and mutant antiheros.

Since I teach in Northern California, I do not confront a great deal of traditionally defined social conservatism, at least as it is presented by media outlets. However, most of my students initially accept at face value a fairly standard set of American social assumptions (the scientific legitimacy of racial and gender divisions, the fixed nature of sexuality, and so on). Once we can really get under the skin of the monstrous, though, we can fundamentally queer these assumptions so that they not only crumble but also, at times, give way to something *better*. What I want my students to take away from the experience of a sustained confrontation with monsters and the monstrous is a realization carefully articulated by MacCormack:

> We are all, and *must* be, monsters because none are template humans. The human is an ideal that exists only as a referent to define what deviates from it. Just as the monster is predicated on a judgment based upon what defines a normal human, so too, the human is a conceptualized idea which can be figured as a referent defined only through that which deviates from it. Through teratology we discover in the posthuman what can be thought as ethical, material, experimental, creative, and yet which escapes definition—the inhuman, the a-human, the non-human. In the most reduced sense then, through concepts of adaptability and evolution itself, all organisms are unlike—we are all, and must be monsters because nothing is ever like another thing, nor like itself from one moment to the next.[35]

That is, we all—you, me, our students, our political opponents and our allies, those who might attack us, and those who would defend us, all of us—are monsters, since the monster is the embodiment of difference, and we are all different. Not one of us matches the idealizing templates labeled "human" in biology books, not even the most avowedly normative members of society. Not all students are longing for difference, or to be accepted despite their differences, and perhaps those who sign up for a course called "Monsters and the Monstrous" are a more eager audience for this line of reasoning than others. Perhaps. This discussion about what it means to be monstrous, though, is the only one I have held in a dozen years of teaching, in lectures and discussions conducted with well over seven thousand students, that resulted in their tears.

These tears bore both personal and ethical significance. First, I believe, they stemmed from the sense of the possibility of total acceptance of difference represented by our embrace of the complete monstrosity of humanity; if we are all monsters, then none of us need be cast out into the wilderness for our individual varieties of difference. Second, these tears represented an opening of empathy, an extension of it beyond the confines of the known and the familiar and the *like*. Their realization, at its heart, is that we need to do better than to "tolerate" difference, to bear up under the burden of being surrounded by entities—human, a-human, non-human—that make us uncomfortable, those whom cultures train us to reject as monstrous.[36] If we are ourselves not examples of a legitimate "norm," we cannot unthinkingly and reflexively reject others for failing to be like us. This expansion of empathy, surely imperfectly realized and perhaps fleeting, is, I would argue, even more important than the acceptance of our individual, internal difference. That students might feel more at ease in their own skin is a very good thing, and some of my students are profoundly in need of this, having been raised to reject fundamental aspects of their identity. Better still, though, is that they accept the different skins of others who, in this moment, have ceased to be their Others.

Notes

1. Augustine, *The City of God Against the Pagans*, trans. G. E. McCracken, et al. (London: William Heinemann, 1965), 56–58: "And to us the monsters, signs, portents, prodigies, as they are named, ought to demonstrate, ought to signify and portend and prophesy that God is going to do with the bodies of men what he foretold he was able to do, with no difficulty to impede him, with no laws of nature dictating to him." *The Etymologies of Isidore of Seville*, trans. Stephen A. Barney, et al. (Cambridge: Cambridge University Press, 2006), 241: "A portent is therefore not created contrary to nature, but contrary to what is known in nature. Portents are also called signs, omens, and prodigies, because they are seen to portend and display, indicate and predict future events." For extended discussion, see Asa Simon Mittman and Susan M. Kim, *Inconceivable Beasts: The Wonders of the East in the Beowulf Manuscript* (Tempe: ACMRS, 2013), 75–76.

2. Augustine, *The City of God*, 56–58.

3. This course has no prerequisites, and has majors, minors and others. I offer it every few years, and have had generally strong student outcomes.

4. My "Monsters and the Monstrous" syllabus is online with several others at "Pedagogy," *MEARCSTAPA Website* (updated May 2015), http://www.mearcstapa.org/#!pedagogy/ch9r (accessed May 2015). This is the website of MEARCSTAPA, an organization "committed to the scholarly examination of monstrosity as an area of social and cultural interest to past and present societies. Our inter/trans/post/pre-disciplinary approach allows us to explore the significance of monstrosity across cultural, temporal, and geographic boundaries. We are interested in a multivalent approach using materials on monsters and monstrosity from literary, artistic, philosophical, and historical sources." See "Mission Statement," *MEARCSTAPA Website*, http://www.mearcstapa.org/#!mission-statement/cnec (accessed May 2015).

5. Asa Simon Mittman, "Introduction: The Impact of Monsters and Monster Studies," in *Research Companion to Monsters and the Monstrous*, ed. Mittman, with Peter Dendle (London: Ashgate, 2012) 1–14; 11–14.

6. For more on this, see Asa Simon Mittman, "The Greatest Zombie Lie Ever Told," on The Conversation (November 11, 2014), https://theconversation.com/the-greatest-zombie-lie-ever-told-33915 (accessed May 2015).

7. Karl Whittington, "Queer," *Studies in Iconography* 33 (2012): 157–68; 157. See also the seminal Glenn Burger and Steven F. Kruger, eds., *Queering the Middle Ages* (Minneapolis: University of Minnesota Press, 2001).

8. David Halpern, *Saint Foucault: Towards a Gay Hagiography* (New York: Oxford University Press, 1995), 62; also cited in Whittington, 158.

9. For more on this, see Mittman, "The Impact of Monsters and Monster Studies."

10. This text survives in three medieval manuscripts, all heavily illustrated, all English. London, British Library, Cotton Vitellius A.xv, the *Beowulf* Manuscript, is the oldest, probably produced around 1000 CE. See Andy Orchard, *Pride and Prodigies: Studies in the Monsters of the Beowulf-Manuscript* (Cambridge: D. S. Brewer,

1995), 2; David Dumville, "Beowulf Come Lately: Some Notes on the Palaeography of the Nowell Codex," *Archiv* 225 (1988): 49–63, 63. London, British Library, Cotton Tiberius B.v, the second version of this text and that under present discussion, has been dated by Temple, *Anglo-Saxon Manuscripts*, 104, no. 87, to the second quarter of the 11th century. The third *Wonders* text is Oxford, Bodleian Library, MS Bodley 614. Alun Ford, "The 'Wonders of the East' in its Contexts: A Critical Examination of London, British Library, Cotton Mss Vitellius A.xv and Tiberius B.v, and Oxford, Bodleian Library, Ms Bodley 614" (Ph.D. diss., University of Manchester, 2009), chap. 3, locates it at the Abbey of St. Martin, Battle, where it could have been copied from the Tiberius manuscript, which was sent there in the 1150s.

11. My translation. "Ðis mannkynn lifað fela geara 7? hi syndon fremfulfe men 7? gyfhwylc mann to him cymeð þonne gyfað hi him wif ær hi hine onweg lætan. Se macedonisca Alexander þa ða he him to com þa wæs he wundriende hyra menniscnysse ne wolde he hi cwellan ne him nawiht laðes don." London, British Library, Cotton Tiberius B. v, f. 85v. For a discussion of this subject, see Asa Simon Mittman, "Are the Monstrous 'Races' Races?" *postmedieval* 6.1 (2015): "Making Race Matter in the Middle Ages," ed. Cord Whitaker, 36–51, 42–43; and Mittman and Kim, *Inconceivable Beasts*, Chapter 2, "Unworthy Bodies: Editing the Female Wonders of the East."

12. Mittman and Kim, *Inconceivable Beasts*, Chapter 2, "Unworthy Bodies: Editing the Female Wonders of the East."

13. See Mittman and Kim, *Inconceivable Beasts*, 61 and 58, for these wonders, and 57–72 for a translation of the full text of the Vitellius *Wonders*. Orchard, *Pride and Prodigies*, 175–203, provides the slightly longer texts and translations of the Tiberius *Wonders*.

14. "The Blob," *The Criterion Collection* (no date), http://www.criterion.com/films/630-the-blob (accessed April 2015).

15. Even blob monsters, though, *can* bring about moments of identification, as John Block Friedman describes in his foreword to the *Research Companion to Monsters and the Monstrous*, xxv–xxxix. *The Heap*, a Hillman Comics series from the 1940s, featured a sort of blob monster that had once been a German fighter pilot, transformed into "a gigantic hairy heap like a walking bale of peat moss." While this seems to provide little for an American boy of the era to identify with, as Friedman explains, "the monster was of good family, brave and valiant, skilled as a pilot, and politically right thinking, even if exiled to the margins for his ugliness and uncertain humanity. The Heap also had a youthful human sidekick, Ricky, whom I envied immensely at the time" (xxvii).

16. "95% of the total student population comes from California: 31.1% from CSU, Chico's service area; 20.4% from the rest of Northern California." CSU, Chico Public Affairs & Publications, "Chico Facts," www.csuchico.edu/pa/chico-facts.shtml (accessed June 2015).

17. As of the editing of this essay, the Supreme Court has just, following heated public debate, announced its historic ruling on *Obergefell v. Hodges*, creating a nationwide right to marriage for all couples. See, for example, Linda Greenhouse, "The Morning After the Same-Sex Marriage Decision," *New York Times* (May 14, 2015), www.nytimes.com/2015/05/14/opinion/OpinionTodayEmail/the-morning-after-the-same-sex-marriage-decision.html?ref=topics (accessed May 2015), followed by The Editorial Board, "A Profound Ruling Delivers Justice on Gay Marriage," *New York Times* (June 26, 2015), www.nytimes.com/2015/06/27/opinion/a-profound-ruling-delivers-justice-on-gay-marriage.html?_r=0 (accessed June 2015). This has also been a grim political season dominated by Ferguson, Eric Garner, "#blacklivesmatter," the

white supremacist murders at Emanuel African Methodist Episcopal Church in Charleston, South Carolina, and the renewed debate over displays of the Confederate battle flag. For an excellent and nuanced discussion of race and racial thought in the United States present and past, see Alison Kinney, *Hood* (New York: Bloomsbury Academic, 2016).

18. Jeffrey Jerome Cohen, "Monster Culture (Seven Theses)," in *Monster Theory: Reading Culture,* ed. Cohen (Minneapolis: University of Minnesota Press, 1996), 6–31. Rosemarie Garland Thomson, "Introduction: From Wonder to Error—A Genealogy of Freak Discourse in Modernity," in *Freakery: Cultural Spectacles of the Extraordinary Body*, ed. Rosemarie Garland Thomson (New York: New York University Press, 1996), 1–19.

19. Selections from Edward Said, *Orientalism* (New York: Pantheon, 1978); Homi K. Bhabha, *The Location of Culture* (New York: Routledge, 1994); Partha Mitter with Asa Simon Mittman and Peter Dendle, "Postcolonial Monsters: A Conversation with Partha Mitter," in *Research Companion to Monsters and the Monstrous*, ed. Mittman, with Peter Dendle (London: Ashgate, 2012), 329–342.

20. Michel Foucault, *Abnormal: Lectures at the Collège de France 1974–1975,* ed. Valerio Marchetti, Antonella Salomoni, trans. Graham Burchell (London: Verso, 2004).

21. Julia Kristeva, *Approaching Abjection: Powers of Horror* (New York: Columbia University Press, 1982).

22. Noël Carroll, *The Philosophy of Horror or Paradoxes of the Heart* (New York: Routledge, 1990).

23. William Ian Miller, *The Anatomy of Disgust* (Cambridge: Harvard University Press, 1997).

24. Patricia MacCormack, "Posthuman Teratology," in *Research Companion to Monsters and the Monstrous*, ed. Mittman, with Peter Dendle (London: Ashgate, 2012), 291–208.

25. Donna Haraway, "A Cyborg Manifesto: Science, Technology, and Socialist-Feminism in the Late Twentieth Century," in Susan Stryker and Stephen Whittle, eds., *The Transgender Studies Reader* (London: Routledge, 2006) 103–18; 113.

26. James Whale, *Frankenstein* (Universal, 1931).

27. This character, played by Dwight Frye, is named Fritz. The more famous Ygor does not appear until the subsequent *Son of Frankenstein* (Universal, 1939) and *The Ghost of Frankenstein* (Universal, 1942) films.

28. Mel Brooks, *Young Frankenstein* (20th Century Fox, 1974).

29. See, for example, David Wengrow, "Gods and Monsters: Image and Cognition in Neolithic Societies," *Paléorient* 37.1, *Néolithisations: nouvelles données, nouvelles interpretations à propos du modèle théorique de Jacques Cauvin* (2011): 153–63.

30. Mary Shelley, *Frankenstein*, rev. ed. (London: Henry Colburn and Richard Bentley, 1831), x: "perhaps the component parts of *a creature* might be manufactured, brought together, and endured with vital warmth" (emphasis added). Available online as *Frankenstein or The Modern Prometheus, Rev., corr., and illustrated with a new introd.*, Open Library (originally posted April 2008, last update August 2012), https://openlibrary.org/books/OL20443134M/Frankenstein_or_The_Modern_Prometheus (accessed May 2015).

31. Buzz Gunderson (Corey Allen): "Oh, he's real abstract. He's, um, he's different." Jim Stark (James Dean): "That's right. That's right. I'm cute too." Nicholas Ray, *Rebel Without a Cause* (Warner Brothers, 1955) at 29 mins.

32. For a full (and astonishing) list of the *first 100,000* Netflix categories, see

Zack Lovatt, "NETFLIX GENRE LIST (BY AGID)," *ZackLocatt.com* (August 15, 2014), http://zacklovatt.com/netflix-genre-list-by-agid/ (accessed May 2015).

33. "mearcstapa," Anglo-Saxon masculine noun: *"One who wanders about the desolate mark* or *border-land," Bosworth-Toller Anglo-Saxon Dictionary* (digital edition) (2013), http://bosworth.ff.cuni.cz/022497 (accessed June 2015). See also R.D. Fulk, Robert E. Bjork, and John D. Niles, eds., *Klaeber's Beowulf,* 4th ed. (Toronto: University of Toronto Press, 2008), line 103.

34. Asa Simon Mittman and Susan M. Kim, "Locating the Devil '*Her*' in MS Junius 11," *Gesta* 54.1 (2015): 3–25.

35. MacCormack, 294.

36. For more on the problematic notion of "toleration," see Jeremy Cohen, *Living Letters of the Law: Ideas of the Jew in Medieval Christianity* (Berkeley: University of California Press, 1999), passim; Marcia Kupfer "'. . . lectres . . . plus vrayes': Hebrew Script and Jewish Witness in the *Mandeville* Manuscript of Charles V," *Speculum* 83.1 (January 2008): 58–111, 102; Sara Lipton, *Images of Intolerance: The Representation of Jews and Judaism in the Bible moralisée* (Berkeley: University of California Press, 1999), 56; and Asa Simon Mittman, "Mandeville's 'East,' Colonialism, Certainty, and Art History," *Postcolonising the Medieval Image*, ed. Eva Frojmovic and Catherine Karkov (London: Ashgate, 2015).

Gender, Sexuality and Rhetorical Vulnerabilities in Monster Literature and Pedagogy

PAMELA BEDORE

> Vampires. Werewolves. Zombies. Serial killers. Monsters appear in all sorts of literary and media contexts, raising questions from the sidelines of society, threatening the core values of civilization, illuminating the problems of really understanding what it means to be human. What is a monster? Why are monsters present in every human society? How has the figure of the monster evolved along with changes in literary and artistic representations of the human experience? As a form of popular literature, does monster literature construe power as the province of a small elite group, or does it offer its readers potentially transgressive narratives? Sometimes menacing, sometimes pitiable, the monster often tracks cultural anxieties—about social trends, political conflicts, and changing understandings of identity markers like race, gender, class, and sexuality. We'll look at literature and film in trying to figure out how the monster works as a popular trope and why its appeal is at a particular high point today.
>
> —Course Description, "The Monster in Literature and Culture" (see appendix)

This is the opening foray of the syllabus for my capstone course for English majors, a seminar-style class that usually enrolls ten to 15 students, all nearing the completion of their major. I teach at the University of Connecticut's Avery

Point campus, which has a population of approximately 800 students and combines the feeling of a small liberal arts campus with the structure of a large state university. Almost all the capstone students already know me, as their major advisor, or have taken classes with me in previous semesters, and/or been part of a club or activity I organized. The students are planning, in about equal numbers, to attend graduate school, to become teachers in the K–12 system, and to become professional writers; the main course objective for all English capstones is to provide an advanced research context in which all students can synthesize the elements of their undergraduate education and look forward. The capstone course with a monster theme is popular with students, perhaps because it echoes their own experience as they enter the liminal space between college and whatever is to follow. After all, the monster embodies the personal and cultural anxieties many of us face at this moment of our lives, it is a central character in numerous provocative texts, and it provides a genuine need for the theoretical approaches to literature that sometimes feel a bit forced to students.

My teaching style is Socratic and students are often responsible for leading off discussions and identifying the topics they want to cover. In the course, we begin by identifying the monsters that are most familiar to us, and we very quickly move into discussions of sex, gender, power, and knowledge construction as we think about how analysis of the monster in popular cultural artifacts (novels, TV series, films, advertisements, news stories, and video games) helps us to understand some of the key issues we face as a culture. Through these discussions, grounded in literary and critical readings, and through a great deal of writing both formal and informal, students are asked to come up with their own research projects, some of which they have presented at local and national conferences. They are also asked to think explicitly about the complex interactions of themes central to monster literature (power, liminality, and vulnerability, for example) with the issues they face in higher education, and especially in writing classrooms. At a time when many students are hesitant to identify as "feminists" even though they believe strongly in gender equity, the concept of the monster becomes a powerful pedagogical space for introducing the tools of literary theory—and especially gender theory—in helping students think through issues of contemporary identity politics.[1] This essay examines some of the ways we can use the monster to interrogate complex theoretical issues, including subversive sexualities, gendered epistemologies, and rhetorical vulnerabilities. Throughout the essay I provide questions designed to prompt discussion in any class dealing with monsters.

Subversive Sexualities

Is the monster a sexual sadist or a romantic hero? Or something else entirely? As with many questions about popular representations, the answer tends toward "all of the above, except when it is none of the above." As students have generally intuited from reading or watching *Twilight*, *Vampire Diaries*, and *True Blood*—or adamantly refusing to consume these texts as either "too fluffy" or "too misogynistic"—the monster is often figured in explicitly erotic terms, and the monster's sexuality is often one of the most central, but complex, aspects of his or her identity. If we see popular literature as charting cultural anxieties, we might think of the monster figure as particularly involved in exploring anxieties around sexuality.

Take *Twilight*, as I often do on the first day of class.[2] Here we have a coming-of-age story about Bella, a young girl who falls in love with Edward, the century-old vampire that inspired E. L. James' *Fifty Shades of Grey*, whose wild popularity rests on its exploration of the psychodynamics of a sadomasochistic relationship.[3] Employing the tried-and-true trope of triangular desire, *Twilight* also includes Jacob, the young Native American werewolf whose hot-blooded passion—and fantastic abs—makes him a perfect foil to Edward's cold sensuality. Bella is forced to choose between her two monstrous suitors, and the novel's surprise resolution ("Ew," say the students who did not know this part) introduces a pedophilic angle with a long history in vampire literature as Jacob imprints upon Bella and Edward's infant child, marking her as his future mate. I do not ask students to read or watch *Twilight*, since in general they have already done so, or rather vehemently don't wish to do so. But we use it as a touchstone in our discussions of sexuality throughout the course. Is this a misogynistic text? Is Bella the most powerful character in the novel, given that she has the ability to negate the supernatural power of other monsters? Or is she merely a pawn in a long-standing conflict between vampires and werewolves? Are the monsters intriguingly subversive or loathsomely perverse? Are they to be loved or feared? Or both? And how do we explain the astounding popularity of this monstrous text and its spinoff, *Fifty Shades*? Theoretically, we go to queer theory, where I give mini-lectures and reading suggestions on Judith Butler, Lee Edelman, J. Jack Halberstam, and Eve Kosofsky Sedgwick.[4] Historically, we go to the 19th century.

There are plenty of vampire novels from the 19th century, and each provides a window into constructions of normative sexuality and gender performance through detailed investigation of the monster. I highly recommend, and often require for my own course, two complementary texts: Sheridan LeFanu's *Carmilla* (1872), the first explicitly lesbian vampire novel, and Bram Stoker's *Dracula* (1897),[5] the prototype of vampire lit.

Written in a coy Victorian voice, *Carmilla* tells the story of Laura, an innocent eighteen-year-old girl living in relative isolation with her father when they take in Carmilla, a very pale and beautiful young woman left stranded near their home after a carriage accident. Laura feels like she recognizes Carmilla from a childhood dream in which a lovely woman bit her on the chest, and the two become close friends. Carmilla makes unsettling advances towards Laura, which Laura describes with conflicted emotions: "Now the truth is, I felt rather unaccountably towards the beautiful stranger. I did feel, as she said, 'drawn towards her,' but there was also something of repulsion. In this ambiguous feeling, however, the sense of attraction immensely prevailed."[6] And later Laura clarifies that "I experienced a strange tumultuous excitement that was pleasurable, ever and anon, mingled with a vague sense of fear and disgust. I had no distinct thoughts about her while such scenes lasted, but I was conscious of a love growing into adoration, and also of abhorrence."[7] Laura's confession of feeling both "abhorrence" and "tumultuous excitement" in the face of Carmilla's advances, of experiencing simultaneous "repulsion" and "attraction," speaks to the monster's potential to stand in for subversive sexual desire—in this case Laura's taboo desire for a lesbian relationship. This desire is decisively thwarted by novel's end, when Carmilla, actually the centuries-old Countess Mircalla Karnstein, is killed by General Spielsdorf, whose niece was, like Laura, seduced by the vampiress. This ending leaves students, understandably, a bit unsettled. If Carmilla stands in for non-normative desires, does her death—at the hand of male hunters—make the novel a cautionary tale against lesbianism? Or is the novel's engagement with questions of lesbian sexuality in itself a subversive act? Students often lean towards the latter reading, given that Laura is not shown to move on to a heterosexual marriage, but they also see the potential of twinned but contradictory readings.

Questions around subversive sexual desires and how they can be interpreted are also at the center of that most prototypical of vampire novels, *Dracula*. Most of my students have not read the novel before the class, although they are aware of its cultural power through movie versions or references in other popular culture artifacts. Upon reading, many are astonished that Dracula—whom they think of as a terrifying monster with a bad accent—is so explicitly sexualized: first in his dealings with Lucy Westenra, desired by most of the men she meets, then with Mina Harker, the faithful wife who uses her considerable intelligence to support her husband's career, and also with Jonathan Harker, the young man who provides our first glimpse of a human placed in the master vampire's thrall. Dracula is a deeply erotic being whose monstrosity, as Christopher Craft argues in his seminal essay, is constructed through the linking of sex and blood.[8] The vampire, as Craft notes, locates his or her many powers in the mouth, an ungendered organ that allows the vampire to give and take sexual pleasure, to act as a progenitor to a new vampire, and to pursue immortality. For Craft and others, the vampire stands in for subversive sexuality as a highly liminal creature whose desires and attractions reside outside genital constructions of gender identity. For instructors, the vampire is a highly recognizable but difficult-to-read figure that invites students to make theoretical forays into the nature of compulsory heterosexuality, queer desires, and monstrous bodies.[9]

Dracula's representations of gender identity and of libidinous desires are multifaceted and endlessly riveting. I like to ask students to create a schematic of the relationships between the main characters of the novel: Dracula, his three wives (or sisters, depending on the critic), Lucy, her three suitors (John Seward, Arthur Lord Godalming, and Quincey Morris), Van Helsing, Renfield, Jonathan Harker, and Mina. Students note immediately the many doublings: Lucy and Mina are both young nubile women who represent different attitudes towards courtship and work, and both are eventually objects of desire for the vampire; Dracula and Van Helsing are both elders, one constructed as evil and the other leading the so-called Crew of Light; Jonathan and Renfield are both in Dracula's thrall, with Renfield embodying Jonathan's potential fate should he remain a servant of the vampire; Van Helsing and John Seward are representatives of religion and science, respectively, although both are able to incorporate the other epistemological framework into their actions; and Dracula and Lucy both have three opposite-sex lovers/suitors. But each time we try to pursue a double, we end up in a kind of liminal space, with each of the doublings simultaneously revealing and concealing something about the characters and what they might represent.

Take Mina Harker, for example. In her early interactions with Lucy, she deliberately constructs herself in contrast to the New Woman, presenting herself as a proper young lady whose only goal is to support her fiancé, Jonathan. She is also shown in contrast to Lucy, who is sexualized in her initial presentation through her obvious pleasure at receiving three marriage proposals on the same day, as well as by her inappropriate midnight wanderings (in Dracula's vampiric thrall, we eventually learn) in nothing but her nightgown. As the novel progresses, though, Mina is equally eroticized when she is attacked by the vampire in her bedchamber while her enthralled husband sleeps beside her and the other men burst in just in time to see her sucking blood from Dracula's bare breast. Although she feels unclean from her interactions with Dracula, Mina avoids Lucy's fate of becoming both victim and predator, instead using her involuntary blood connection to enhance her role in the Crew of Light as not only the organizer of documents and schedules but also the tracker of Dracula's movements. As Van Helsing exclaims, "Ah, that wonderful Madam Mina! She has man's brain—a brain that a man should have were he much gifted—and a woman's heart. The good God fashioned her for a purpose, believe me, when He made that so good combination."[10] As a liminal character caught between the feminine and the masculine, between the human and the vampiric, between the rational and the libidinous, Mina becomes Dracula's fiercest and most effective opponent.

My class always has great discussions on why this is. Does Mina's power reside in her liminality? Is her power increased after she has consumed Dracula's blood? Does this connect her to the criminal profiler who must take on the perspective/power of the monstrous serial killer in more recent texts of crime fiction such as *Silence of the Lambs*, which we read later in the course?

Dracula and Carmilla, like other 19th-century vampires, represent non-normative desires unfettered by the sense of cultural repression that prevented many Victorians from acting upon such desires. The orality of the vampires' interactions leads to scenes that sexualize not only the vampires but also the humans with whom they interact. Laura recognizes that she is deeply attracted to another woman in the form of the female vampire and nonetheless acts upon that lesbian desire. Jonathan, while less articulate about his reactions to Dracula, narrates in his journal his overtly sexual encounter with three female vampires: "The girl went on her knees, and bent over me, simply gloating. There was a deliberate voluptuousness which was both thrilling and repulsive, and as she arched her neck she actually licked her lips like an animal, till I could see in the moonlight the moisture shining on the scarlet lips and on the red tongue as it lapped the white sharp teeth."[11] And if we see the mouth as a stand-in for genitals and the blood as a stand-in for more sexually charged bodily fluids, as Craft persuasively does, we find a complex queering of desire in the body of Lucy Westenra.

Let us follow the blood. When Dr. Van Helsing diagnoses Lucy with mysterious blood loss, her fiancé, Arthur, provides blood for a transfusion. Later, when she needs more blood, it is willingly given by her other suitors, Seward and Morris, and eventually even by Van Helsing himself. As Seward reports in his journal, even the characters code the blood as erotic: "Arthur was saying that he felt since then as if the two had been really married and that she was his wife in the sight of God. None of us said a word of the other operations, and none of us ever shall."[12] The blood of the four men, which marks the consummation of marriage "in the sight of God," then, literally mingles within Lucy's veins, only to be finally consumed by Dracula, who has already shown that his desire is not bound by gender. As Craft notes, "This repetitive contest (penetration, withdrawal; penetration, infusion), itself an image of *Dracula*'s ambivalent need to evoke and then to repudiate the fluid pleasures of vampiric appetite, continues to be waged upon Lucy's infinitely penetrable body until Van Helsing exhausts his store of 'brave men,' whose generous gifts of blood, however efficacious, fail finally to save Lucy from the mobilization of desire."[13]

In the end, of course, both Carmilla and Dracula are killed, their non-normative sexuality contained by intertwined but contradictory narratives: (1) in a fight between good and evil, the evil vampire is vanquished, and (2) following the permanent death of the vampire's body, the soul of the person involuntarily transformed into a vampire is released. These narratives provide a way of historicizing perspectives on alternate sexualities, presenting two ideas about people who act upon non-heteronormative desire: in the first, they are by nature evil, predators capable of despoiling pure and nubile girls and thus deserving of violent death, and in the second, they are victims who cannot control their desires despite their best efforts and whose souls need only be released from the prison of their treacherous bodies in order to return to God. Whether the vampire is male or female, is itself evil or is merely a victim and pawn of an evil force, the vampire's death in 19th-century novels is justified as a conquest of evil. The vampire also codes a simultaneous fear and loathing of non-normative desire that allows for the narration of violent actions: even in the homophobic 19th century, it would not be acceptable for a man to kill a lesbian because she has "converted" a young woman to Sapphic ways, but it *is* acceptable—and even grounds for celebration—to depict an authoritarian male character killing a paranormal monster who has done the same.

If the vampire has a history of standing in for queer desire, how do we explain the appeal of contemporary monsters—vampires, werewolves, hybrids, and so forth—in romance and young adult literature? At a basic level, the ability of such monsters to enact roles as romantic heroes can be seen as charting a sea change in attitudes towards non-normative sexuality. Look, for example, at HBO's *True Blood*, the enormously popular adaptation of Charlaine Harris' Sookie Stackhouse series.[14] Here we have a maelstrom of sexual activity in which the series, at one point or another, depicts almost every main character in a queer sex scene. And yet, the power dynamics of those scenes, and their emotional aftermaths when they are a result of vampire thrall or witchcraft, are complicated. Indeed, *True Blood*, like *Vampire Diaries* or *Twilight*, can be read as simultaneously celebrating and containing queer desires. The vampire, after all, is still a monster—misunderstood, usually concealed, at once terrifying and pitiable. And although some of the human characters may wish to become monsters, their transformation always comes with a high cost. Bella, for example, must give up her human family and friends to become Edward's vampire wife, suggesting, as many of these more celebratory monster narratives do, that the human and monster worlds—perhaps coded as worlds of heteronormative and non-heteronormative desire—do not easily coexist. Furthermore, the consumers of these texts continue to live in a world in which the reception given to the *True Blood* vampire coming out of the coffin is far too similar to that faced by LGBTQ teens coming out of the closet.[15]

The gender politics of vampire texts were ambitiously complex in 19th-century novels such as *Carmilla* and *Dracula*, and their complexity has only multiplied in recent years, especially if we read monster narratives through an intersectional lens that examines the imbrications of gender, race, and sexuality. A classic novel like Richard Matheson's *I Am Legend* (1954), which spawned highly distinct film versions including *The Last Man on Earth* (1964, directed by Ubaldo Ragona and Sidney Salkow, starring Vincent Price), *The Omega Man* (1971, directed by Boris Sagal and starring Charlton Heston) and *I Am Legend* (2007, directed by Francis Lawrence and starring Will Smith), leads to fascinating questions of individual identity politics (I teach only the most recent film, but I believe it would be worth assigning the others in a class spending more time on Matheson).

Robert Neville is, literally, the last human standing following an engineered plague that kills all of humanity. Fortified in his home with virtually endless supplies and a seemingly unbreakable spirit, Neville is surrounded by monsters he calls vampires but that share many of the traits we might associate with zombies, as they travel in hordes, are not seductive, and appear to have limited cognitive function. In the Matheson novel, written and set in the Civil Rights era, Neville, a middle-class white man, raises the specter of violent race relations in his musings about the monster: "Why, then, this unkind prejudice, this thoughtless bias? Why cannot the vampire live where he chooses? Why must he seek out hiding places where none can find him out? Why do you wish him destroyed? Ah, see, you have turned the poor guileless innocent into a haunted animal.... Robert Neville grunted a surly grunt. Sure, sure, he thought, but would you let your sister marry one?"[16] The answer to this rhetorical question in Matheson's novel is clearly "no." Jump forward in time to texts as diverse as Marta Acosta's deceptively light-hearted *Happy Hour at the Casa Dracula* (2006) or Glen Duncan's dark, angsty *The Last Werewolf* (2011) and we find the same thing: no, the characters would not let their sisters marry the monster. And in all three, perhaps those racist characters are wrong.

The adaptations of *I Am Legend* compound the complexities of representation. Given the breadth of my class, we spend only two weeks on Matheson and the adaptations, so I have students watch only the 2007 film version, which addresses questions of race head-on, as is ably demonstrated in Dorothea Schuller's insightful and accessible article.[17] We begin our discussions with the assumption that Matheson's narrative struck an important cultural chord when it was written, and that it continues to do so, perhaps because of its engagement with questions of intersectional identity.[18] As Schuller points out, the 1954 novel and the 2007 film reflect contemporary anxieties around race relations that are suited to their eras, in the lead-up to the Civil Rights movement and in the aftermath of 9/11. Matheson's novel includes a twist that students love: told entirely from the perspective of the lone able-bodied, middle-class white man who kills vampires by day and holes up in his fortified home by night, the novel turns in the last few chapters to Neville's dawning comprehension that the vampires have far more cognitive ability than he had imagined and that, in fact, some of them see themselves as the seeds of a new species, as the next step in human evolution. They see him, with his methodical clearing of the vampire population, as a perpetrator of genocide. To them, *he* is the monster whom they would not let their sister marry. After he has decided to commit suicide rather than undergo execution, Neville finally realizes what it all means: "Full circle, he thought while the final lethargy crept into his limbs. Full circle. A new terror born in death, a new superstition entering the unassailable fortress of forever. I am legend."[19]

Francis Lawrence's 2007 film substantially changes the narrative's inquiries about race relations through its representations of the main character, played by Will Smith, an African-American box office phenom, and the vampires, computer-generated albinos that, as Schuller points out, resemble voracious aliens more than humans-turned-vampire. The ending, too, opens up many questions, as Neville sacrifices himself for other humans in a suicide attack that also destroys the most powerful vampires. "This is his legend," intones one of the uninfected human characters, perhaps before she is to become a founding member in the restoration of the human race. What is gained and what is lost in the choices made by Lawrence in terms of his film's ending, which market-tested better than the alternate ending Schuller also discussed at length? Discussions of *I Am Legend* serve as an excellent place to push students to negotiate the scholarship, since here they can work between the insightful examinations of Craft on gender and Schullar on race. Robert Neville, after all, meets a woman he suspects of being a vampire (she is in the novel, she is not in the Lawrence film), and he desires that woman even as he fears her potentially monstrous nature. How can we interpret that desire and its consequences in the original and the adaptation?

We end our vampire unit by asking ourselves how questions of difference, race, gender, and erotic desire intersect at the site of the monster. What is gained or lost when we see the monster figure as coding non-normative desire? How do different adaptations of prototypical monster stories like *Dracula* and *I Am Legend* manipulate and recast these novels' investments in questions of gender, race, and sexuality? To what degree does the monster's sexuality reflect and/or push back at sociocultural anxieties about same-sex desire or race? Where does power ultimately reside in classic and contemporary monster literature? There are no easy answers to these questions, and vampire novels seem an ideal space to showcase how literature featuring monsters can pose these questions and how the tools provided by literary theory can be employed in helping students make sustained arguments on one or more of these topics. By the end of the vampire unit, I ask students to have strong research questions in place for their final paper, and we continue to workshop their formal and informal writing towards this paper throughout the semester.

Gendered Epistemologies

We cannot, of course, discuss gender and sexuality without addressing a term scholars often use more easily than students: feminism. I like to discuss the historical, social, and affective resonances of this term early in the semester. "How many of you are feminists?" I might ask on the second or third day of class, when students are still getting to know each other and me. They will already be used to my informal polls, though; I teach popular culture topics, so I regularly ask students which TV programs and novels they consume and enjoy as we prepare to apply cultural theory to our textual analyses. Results of the "are you a feminist?" question vary, of course, but they have something in common: students look around the class before putting up their hand or choosing not to.

"How many of you like *Housewives of New Jersey*?" "How many of you watch *World Wrestling Federation*?" Here, there is no hesitation. Some students put up their hands and others do not. Laughter and scoffing might break out. Students vote—accurately or not, I have no way of knowing—without checking in with their classmates. But "feminism" is different. Feminism is a loaded word, as many of us know, and as several scholarly monographs have recently explored, including Catherine Redfern and Kristin Aune's *Reclaiming the F Word: Feminisms Today*, which reports on surveys of women across age groups as well as detailed media analysis. Redfern and Aune note a rhetorical contradiction that will sound familiar to those of us who teach feminism: "Strangely, whilst being told they are as extinct as dinosaurs, feminists are simultaneously depicted as if they more or less rule the world."[20]

The term *feminism*, which many students readily admit is one they aren't quite comfortable using, serves as an excellent entry into cultural theory as well as into discussions of monster literature. What does it mean to be a feminist? Why do students committed to social justice and gender equity hesitate to identify as feminists? Who defines the term and how do competing definitions of feminism arise not only between feminists and non-feminists but also among different groups of feminists who focus on different issues and approaches to thinking about gender and equality? In thinking through these questions, we often end up at a postmodern conundrum familiar to students: to what degree do the major concepts of our existence—power, knowledge, and identity politics, for example—reside in biological essentialism or social construction? This question is equally important in thinking through how monsters get gendered. Are men and women different but fundamentally equal (Elaine Showalter, Catharine MacKinnon, and other second-wave American feminists), different and deserving a celebration of that difference (Hélène Cixous, Luce Irigaray, and other French feminists), or is sex itself a social construction just as gender is (Judith Butler, J. Jack Halberstam, and other queer theorists)? And what of monsters? Which differences get coded as monstrous? How do we construct *monster* epistemologically?

Octavia Butler's *Xenogenesis* trilogy (1987–89, packaged as *Lilith's Brood* in the 2000 omnibus)[21] provides an exceptionally rich representation of warring epistemological models that is equally illuminating for questions of gender, race, and monstrosity. *Xenogenesis* places us in a post-apocalyptic world in which the Oankali, a highly evolved alien species, has saved a relatively small number of humans during a human-caused extinction event. The Oankali, who are gene-traders, have allowed a few centuries to pass so that Earth can recover from human devastation and so they can study their salvaged human individuals, whom they see as exhibiting a never seen before and non-viable contradiction: intelligence and hierarchy. For the Oankali, all can be explained by biological essentialism: the destructive nature of the human species is coded into the human genome and can, therefore, be coded out. For the newly-awakened humans, many of whom become violently ill when they see and experience the grotesque physicality of the Oankali, whose tentacle-like sensory organs are widely dispersed over their humanoid bodies, human nature is much more than genetics. The Oankali give the humans two choices: they can live out their lives in sterility but with a longer lifespan and excellent health given Oankali gene therapy, or they can build a new society in which the Oankali reprogram their genetic code for reproduction in human-Oankali hybrid families in which all sexual contact goes through the ooloi, the Oankali third gender, who provides direct neurological pleasure during sexual encounters as well as disease-free offspring expected to live for centuries.

The *Xenogenesis* trilogy is a brilliantly executed exploration of the monstrous as it is embodied in these tri-gendered aliens, alternately seen as benign and malevolent, and in the post-apocalypse humans, who are trying to understand what it means to be human after the anthropogenic destruction of the planet Earth. The novels provide three perspectives: the first focuses on Lilith, a black human woman, the second on Akin, a human-Oankali hybrid boy as he grows to manhood, and the third on Jodahs, the first hybrid ooloi (third sex). Through these multiple perspectives, *Xenogenesis* examines the limits of how humans construct knowledge in general and at the site of personal identity, with particularly complex representations of gender, race, and sexuality. The issue of rape comes up repeatedly, since the Oankali claim—and believe fully, as we see when we get into their perspective—that they can read a human's biological desires, which they privilege over stated desires. The novel provides multiple examples of humans saying "no"—to sex with the Oankali or to pregnancy, for example—and the Oankali reading "yes" from their biochemistry. And from the Oankali perspective, humans are just as monstrous as the Oankali are to humans. Jodahs, the ooloi of the final novel, uses language similar to that of Laura looking at Carmilla when he thinks about the human female, Marina, "as incredibly complex as any Human, as full of the Human Conflict—dangerous and frightening and intriguing—as any Human. She was like the fire—desirable and dangerous, beautiful and lethal."[22]

Even as the Oankali believe that all knowledge can be reduced to biology, the novel shows that the monstrous is always a matter of perspective, and therefore a social construction. Octavia Butler is a master at logical contradiction, so this text and others (any of her novels would teach well in a monster class) repeatedly present an apparent truth moments before contradicting that truth by showing it from a different perspective. The scholarship on *Xenogenesis* abounds with highly accessible but theoretically complex articles that explicate Butler's ambitious project, and students become productively enmeshed in complex discussions of this trilogy.[23] Is *Xenogenesis* a feminist text? A queer text? Does it ultimately celebrate or punish the monster? In what ways do the Oankali-human relationships resonate with the history of slavery? Where do such comparisons break down? How do representations of monstrous sexuality here follow, and collide with, such representations in other novels studied in the course? Once again, the difficulty of pinning down answers to these and other theoretically complex questions about gender, sexuality, and epistemology make this novel especially suitable for a course on monster literature.

Rhetorical Vulnerabilities

As teachers, we may sometimes feel vulnerable. We are always performing to an extent, so we are vulnerable to bad reviews, snide comments about our course delivery, and even non-renewal of teaching contracts if we are contingent faculty, as an increasing portion of the humanities faculty seems to be. Students, of course, are even more vulnerable in the classroom, and the complex power dynamics of the university can be heightened in smaller writing classes, where students may feel like they are forced to reveal their weaknesses, real or perceived, through mandatory participation in processes such as in-class writing exercises, peer review, class discussion, and presentations. In monster courses, which naturally lead to discussions of liminality and power, it seems particularly appropriate to discuss explicitly *how* power works through rhetoric.

Because this is a capstone class for students about to complete their undergraduate degree, many of whom will go on to graduate study or careers in secondary education, we explicitly discuss a topic very much on their minds: higher education. We consider a number of provocative questions, including: Who has power in the university? How is that power deployed and deflected? Is there power in being an outsider, an "other"? In what ways is the university a liminal space for those who attend for four years, and for those whose working life is located there? How does the classroom echo the concerns central to any kind of outsider literature, including monster lit?

In setting the stage for explicitly discussing these questions, I use an assignment that could be adapted for any advanced writing class, but that contains an especially delightful resonance with understanding the monster. Many of us experience the writing process as we experience monsters—as messy but generative, alienating but pleasurable. Although I do not have a strong theoretical commitment to teaching students that there is some kind of "monstrous" element to writing, it is always a pleasure to me—and to them, I suspect—when the metaphors we have identified and discussed within monster texts can also be applied to the writing process. Writing, after all, can be considered a type of procreative process, as can many monstrous reproductions. And we might have the experience of being simultaneously attracted to and repelled by the act of writing, simultaneously shamed and empowered by the idea of sharing our writing with others.

In this class, I create a deliberately difficult—perhaps even monstrous—assignment. Since most students write most of their papers, even long research papers, in under two weeks (and, let's face it, sometimes under two days), I require them to gain experience in spending an entire semester working on a single argumentative piece. This means they must choose their topic early, usually by the third week of a 14-week semester. Topic in hand, they share drafts of their large research paper at least eight times in the ten weeks between topic selection and presentation. My suggestion is that they aim for 500–1000 new words per week, understanding that they will delete much of their early work, as professional writers tend to do. And each week, they must post their progress to the electronic class management system along with questions for peers who read their draft writing. This is a tough assignment, I readily admit, and it provides a process model for researching, thinking, and writing that many students may choose never to use again. But for some, it illuminates the power of spending an entire semester with a project, deepening their focus and spurring them to try new rhetorical strategies, since they have time and space to fail and still recover. It also provides them the space to really dig into the difficult theoretical apparatus that is often used in understanding the complexities of the monster at sites of gender, sexuality, race, and epistemology.

Since I am asking students to make themselves vulnerable by sharing early drafts, I make myself vulnerable as well, and I start a new project at the same time as they do, sharing drafts and working all the way through to a presentation. My early drafts are no more polished than theirs, and I reveal the false starts, the initial lack of editing, the anxious margin notes, and my own problems with procrastination in writing. For many students, the assignment initially increases the level of anxiety they feel when writing a large research paper with accompanying class presentation that is worth 50 percent of a course grade. It pushes students out of their comfort zones, asking them to begin writing before they've completed the research and thinking that will underlie the final products. In a strange way, the assignment does some of the same work that monster literature does: creates a space with the potential for vulnerability or power that is often simultaneously both. Of course I'm not suggesting that students are treated as monsters or act as monsters within this environment of continual drafting and peer review. But they *do* think about what it means to reveal oneself in an unfamiliar way as the research paper itself becomes a monstrous process, wherein we inhabit liminal space and conflicting desires, perhaps, whimsically, taking on the perspective of a Laura or Mina in the process.

Concluding Thoughts

Popular monster texts provide a particularly rich space for teaching literary and cultural theory. When students are able to read novels or watch films and TV series that they understand and enjoy at first consumption, they are often excited to read or view the text a second time more deeply with the class discussion and critical readings in mind. The concept of the "monster"—along with related concepts like the "grotesque," the "sublime," and the "liminal"—delivers numerous opportunities for students to explore theoretical work on such concepts as subject formation, subversive sexualities, epistemological frameworks, and the limits of language. Each of us surely has our favorite monster texts, and many of us probably use some of these in survey courses not devoted to the theme of the monster. But whether we are teaching a course in Victorian Literature or Contemporary Young Adult Film, talking with our students about how the "other" often gets conceptualized as monstrous will provide an opportunistic entry into insightful and engaging discussions about personal and cultural identity formation.

Appendix
Capstone Syllabus
ENGL 4600W: The Monster in Literature and Culture
Fall 2014
Dr. Pamela Bedore

Course Description

This is the capstone course required of all English majors, so if it isn't your most difficult course, I'm doing something wrong and you should let me know immediately. The capstone, whose theme revolves around the professor's current research interests, is designed to provide an opportunity for students to draw together the reading, writing, analytical and rhetorical skills they've been developing throughout their English courses. The course serves as the final step of information literacy instruction for the major and it gives students a sense of what they might expect should they pursue English studies at the graduate level. If you aren't an English major, you're absolutely welcome in the class, but be aware that you'll be working pretty hard here.

Vampires. Werewolves. Zombies. Serial killers. Monsters appear in all sorts of literary and media contexts, raising questions from the sidelines of society, threatening the core values of civilization, perhaps illuminating the problems of really understanding what it means to be human. What is a monster? Why are monsters present in every human society? How has the figure of the monster evolved along with changes in literary and artistic representations of the human experience? As a form of popular literature, does monster literature construe power as the province of a small elite group, or does it offer its readers potentially transgressive narratives?

Sometimes menacing, sometimes pitiable, the monster often tracks cultural anxieties—about social trends, political conflicts, and changing understandings of identity markers like race, gender, class, and sexuality. We'll look at literature and film in trying to figure out how the monster works as a popular trope and why its appeal is at a particular high point today. This course counts as a related course for the American Studies major.

Course Objectives

A student successfully completing this course should be able to:

- Intelligently discuss the major scholarly debates in popular culture
- Critically read both popular literature and literary theory
- Locate, evaluate, and enter into critical conversation with scholarly sources

- Write clearly and effectively
- Provide useful feedback to other writers

Course Policies

General Expectations about Reading: One of the challenges of this course will be keeping up with the reading. There will be three kinds of reading: 1) fairly long but not-too-difficult novels (get a sense of how many pages you read per hour and make sure you set aside enough time for these); 2) TV episodes and film (*read* these, don't just watch them. Keep a pencil—or its electronic equivalent—in hand to make notes as you're viewing); 3) theoretical readings (short but very tough—don't worry, we'll talk about these in class in depth, so just do your best). We'll refer to specific passages in the texts, so bring your book to class every day, ideally with important passages marked. We'll take some time to discuss reading strategies, but please let me know if you're having trouble with the reading.

Drafts/Redrafts: This is a "W" course, so it requires 15 or more pages of revised, edited academic writing. You'll be doing one long research paper for this class, and we'll work on it every week for the whole semester. You'll therefore get tons of feedback, from peers and from me, as we go. Because this is a "W" course, you must pass the writing component in order to pass the course.

Required Reading

Books

Mary Shelley. *Frankenstein*. 1818.
Sheridan LeFanu. *Carmilla*. 1872.
Bram Stoker. *Dracula*. 1897.
Richard Matheson. *I Am Legend*. 1954.
Thomas Harris. *Silence of the Lambs*. 1988.
Octavia Butler. *Lilith's Brood*. 1989.
Lindqvist, John Ajvide. *Let the Right One In*. 2004.
Max Brooks. *World War Z*. 2006.
Glen Duncan. *The Last Werewolf*. 2011.

Assignments/Grading Scheme

Response Papers (10%). 10 responses, 300 words each. You will write ten response papers throughout the semester. You may write about novels, films, or critical articles for the class. You can write a general response if you have one. You may also want to focus on one or two specific quotations for analysis.

Annotated Bibliography (20%). 5 entries, 400 words each. Choose a scholarly source from our class readings or that you've found on your own and write a summary (150 words) and evaluation (250 words). Students have told me that this is a boring assignment (yeah, yeah), but it's also a great tool for researchers. Should you end up doing graduate-level research in any discipline, you'll read so many interesting articles and books that your annotations on them will become extremely valuable to you. Ideally you'll be writing about the scholarly sources you're using in your research paper.

Research Paper (50%). 5000 words. That's right. Your research paper is worth half of your grade for this course. But don't be alarmed. We're going to pick topics for the research paper in Week 4 of the course and you'll get feedback all the way through. Indeed, you'll be posting a new version of your research paper every single week on HuskyCT and each week I'll give you a grade out of 10 for the progress you've made this week for a total of 10%. The final product will be worth 40%, and you should have a very good idea of what kind of grade you can expect by the time we get there.

Final Presentation (10%). You'll present your research during the last day of class and we'll open up those presentations to the public. I don't expect a huge crowd, but your projects will be fascinating, so I want to provide the opportunity for the campus to see what you guys have been up to throughout the semester. Each student will have 5–6 minutes to talk about the highlights of their research. This will be a summary of the key arguments you make in your research paper. If you would prefer not to do an oral presentation, you may choose instead to do a poster presentation of the kind one often sees at conferences. Guidelines will be forthcoming.

Peer Review (5%). You'll do at least five peer reviews throughout the course. We'll talk about logistics on the first day of class.

Final Assessment (5%). There will be no final exam in this course. We'll decide together on the best format for our final assessment as we move through the course.

Please note that there is no "Class Participation" grade in this class. This is the capstone, so regular attendance and participation are simply expected. Be aware that if you miss a lot of classes without letting me know what's going on or if you regularly come to class unprepared, I will be very sad. Let that be your punishment.

Course Schedule

8.26 Introduction: Who Cares About Monsters in Literature and Culture?

- Drawing the Monster
- Syllabus Review (with extensive discussion of the research paper and peer review process)
- The Big Folder

- PowerPoint: Course Readings
- Opening Day Questionnaire

8.28 *Monster Theory*

- Read: Marina Levina and Diem My T. Bui. "Towards a Comprehensive Monster Theory in the 21st Century" (2013)
- Read: Amit S. Rai. "Monstrosity and Ontology" (2013)
- Writing Workshop: Group Freewrite

9.2 *Zombies and Identity*

- Read: Max Brooks. *World War Z*, pp. 1–186
- Read: Aalya Ahmad. "Gray Is the New Black: Race, Class and Zombies" (2011)

9.4 *Zombies and Politics*

- Read: *World War Z*, pp. 187–end
- Read: Steven Pokornowski. "Insecure Lives: Zombies, Global Health, and the Totalitarianism of Generalization" (2013)
- Writing Workshop: Brainstorming

9.9 *Werewolves and Sexuality*

- Read: Glen Duncan. *The Last Werewolf*
- Writing Workshop: Finding Good Sources

9.11 *Werewolves and Postmodernism*

- Bring: 500 words of draft writing about a possible paper topic
- Writing Workshop: Annotations

9.16 *Vampires and Horror*

- Read: John Ajvide Lindqvist. *Let the Right One In*
- Writing Workshop: Peer Review Model (Annotated Bibliography)

9.18 *Vampires and Film*

- View: *Let the Right One In* (dir. Alfredson, 2008)
- Read: Jorgen Bruhn, Anne Gjelsvik, and Henriette Thune. "Parallel Worlds of Possible Meetings in *Let the Right One In*" (2011)
- Writing Workshop: Setting Up the Debate (writing your intro)

9.21 *Sunday 11:59 PM deadline*

- Post your research paper to HuskyCT (this and every Sunday for the rest of the semester)

9.23 *Reading TBA*

9.25 *Writing TBA*

9.28 *Sunday 11:59 PM deadline*

- Post your research paper to HuskyCT (this and every Sunday for the rest of the semester)

9.30 Old-School Monsters

- Read: Mary Shelley. *Frankenstein.*

10.2 The Monster and the Gothic

- Read: Ashley Craig Lancaster. "From Frankenstein's Monster to Lester Ballard: The Evolving Gothic Monster" (2008)
- Due: your first Annotated Bibliography entry
- Writing Workshop: Peer Review of Annotated Bibliography

10.7 A 19th-Century Lesbian Vampire?

- Read: Sheridan Le Fanu. *Carmilla.*
- Writing Workshop: Thesis Development

10.9 Vampire Evolution

- Read: Bram Stoker. *Dracula.* pp. 1–105 (first eight chapters)
- Read: Benson Saler and Charles A. Ziegler. "Dracula and Carmilla: Monsters and the Mind" (2005)
- Writing Workshop: Outlining Your Argument
- Midterm Evaluations (that's right, folks, this is the halfway point of our class!)

10.14 Vampires

- Read: Bram Stoker. *Dracula.* 106–End
- Writing Workshop: Free For All—What are you most concerned about as you work on your paper?

10.16 Vampires and Gender

- Read: Christopher Craft. "'Kiss Me with Those Red Lips': Gender and Inversion in Bram Stoker's *Dracula*" (1984)

10.21 Legends

- Read: Richard Matheson. *I Am Legend.*
- Writing Workshop: Entering into Critical Conversations

10.23 Legend and Genre

- Read: Simchi Cohen. "The Legend of Disorder: The Living Dead, Disorder and Autoimmunity in Richard Matheson's *I Am Legend*" (2014)
- Read Dorothea Schuller. "'Something Black and of the Night': Vampirism, Monstrosity, and Negotiations of Race in Richard Matheson's *I Am Legend*" (2009)
- Writing Workshop: Writing a Conference Abstract (discussion of PCA)

10.28 The Sci-Fi Monster

- Read: Octavia Butler. *Dawn* (Book 1 of *Lilith's Brood*)

10.30 Situating the Oankali

- Writing Workshop: Writing Process, A Self-Evaluation

11.4 Generational Monsters

- Read: Octavia Butler. *Adulthood Rites* (Book 2 of *Lilith's Brood*)

11.6 Monstrosity and Hybridity

- Writing Workshop: In-class peer review of research papers (bring two hard copies)

11.11 Monstrous Conclusion

- Read: Octavia Butler. *Imago* (Book 3 of *Lilith's Brood*)
- Theodora Goss and John Paul Riquelme. "From Superhuman to Posthuman: The Gothic Technological Imaginary in Mary Shelley's *Frankenstein* and Octavia Butler's *Xenogenesis*" (2007)
- Writing Workshop: Organizing a Long Paper

11.13 Class Cancelled—Individual Conferences

11.18 The Human Monster

- Read: Thomas Harris. *Silence of the Lambs.*
- Writing Workshop: Free For All—What are you most concerned about as you work on your paper?

11.20 Aesthetics of Murder

- Read Lisa Trahair. "A Taste for Murder: Aesthetics in *The Silence of the Lambs*" (2002)
- Writing Workshop: Turning a Paper into a Presentation

THANKSGIVING BREAK

12.2 Public Presentations

- We'll open up the class to the campus community for these final presentations

12.4 Wrap-Up

- Final PowerPoint
- Final discussions

12.7 Final Paper Due

12.9 Final Assessment Due

- In class, 11AM-1PM

Notes

1. See Catherine Redfern and Kristin Aune, *Reclaiming the F Word: Feminisms Today* (London: Zed Books, 2013).
2. Stephenie Meyer, *Twilight* (New York: Little, Brown, 2005).
3. E. L. James, *Fifty Shades of Grey* (New York: Vintage Books, 2012).
4. See especially Butler's work on performativity in Judith Butler, "Performative Acts and Gender Constitution: An Essay in Phenomenology and Feminist Theory," *Theatre Journal* 40.4 (1988): 519–531; Edelman's arguments about the limitations of the child as the only acceptable symbol of the future in the introduction to Lee

Edelman, *No Future: Queer Theory and the Death Drive* (Durham: Duke University Press, 2004); Halberstam's work on anxieties around the monster in J. Jack Halberstam, *Skin Shows: Gothic Horror and the Technology of Monsters* (Durham: Duke University Press, 1995); and Sedgwick's work on triangular desire in the introduction to Eve Kosofsky Sedgwick, *Between Men: English Literature and Male Homosocial Desire* (New York: Columbia University Press, 1985).

5. Sheridan Le Fanu, *Carmilla* (1872; reprint Doylestown, PA: Wildside Press) and Bram Stoker, *Dracula* (1897; reprint New York: Signet, 1992).

6. Le Fanu, 37–38.

7. *Ibid.*, 45–46.

8. Christopher Craft, "'Kiss Me with Those Red Lips': Gender and Inversion in Bram Stoker's *Dracula*," *Representations* 8 (1984): 107–33.

9. Here I recommend students pursuing such topics read Butler, Edelman, Halberstam, and Sedgwick as well as Adrienne Rich, "Compulsory Heterosexuality and Lesbian Existence," *Journal of Women's History* 15.3 (2003): 11–48 and relevant essays from Jeffrey Jerome Cohen, ed., *Monster Theory: Reading Culture* (Minneapolis: University of Minnesota Press, 1996).

10. Stoker, 201.

11. Stoker, 39.

12. *Ibid.*, 149.

13. Craft, 121.

14. *True Blood*, HBO, June 14, 2009–August 24, 2014, written by Alan Ball.

15. This is a very active site of recent scholarship, and students may wish to explore fan sites alongside more traditional scholarship. Recent essays on the topic include Victoria Amador, "The LGBTQ Message in *True Blood* and Charlaine Harris' Sookie Stackhouse Novels," in *The Scourges of the South? Essays on 'The Sickly South' in History, Literature, and Popular Culture*, ed. Thomas Aervold Bjerre and Beata Zawadka, (Newcastle upon Tyne: Cambridge Scholars, 2014), 165–79; Darren Elliot-Smith, "The Homosexual Vampire is a Metaphor for . . . the Homosexual Vampire? *True Blood*, Homonormativity and Assimilation," in *True Blood: Investigating Vampires and Southern Gothic*, ed. Brigid Cherry (London: I.B. Tauris, 2012), 139–54; and Susana Loza, "Vampires, Queers, and Other Monsters: Against the Homonormativity of *True Blood*," in *Fanpires: Audience Consumption of the Modern Vampire*, ed. Gareth Schott and Kirstine Moffat (Washington, D.C.: New Academia Press, 2011), 91–117.

16. Richard Matheson, *I Am Legend* (1954; reprint New York: Tom Doherty, 1995).

17. Dorothea Schuller, "'Something Black and of the Night': Vampirism, Monstrosity, and Negotiations of Race in Richard Matheson's *I Am Legend*," *Inklings-Jahrbuch für Literatur und Ästhetik* 27 (2009): 78–94.

18. I do not assign a reading on intersectionality, a term coined by Kimberlé Crenshaw in 1989 and brought into common parlance in scholarly circles by Patricia Hill Collins throughout the 1990s, but I give a mini-lecture on importance and productive potentials of thinking of identity categories like gender, race, class, sexuality, etc., in terms of how they interact with one another. Most students are already familiar with this concept, although they may not know the term.

19. Matheson, 159.

20. Redfern and Aune, 2.

21. Octavia Butler, *Lilith's Brood* (1987, 1988, 1989; reprint New York: Warner Books, 2000).

22. *Ibid.*, 577.

23. See, for example, foundational essays on this topic such as chapter 10 of Donna Haraway's *Simians, Cyborgs, and Women: The Reinvention of Nature* (New York: Routledge, 1991); Rebecca J. Holden, "The High Cost of Cyborg Survival: Octavia Butler's *Xenogenesis* Trilogy," *Foundation: The International Review of Science Fiction* 72 (1998): 49–56; Naomi Jacobs, "Posthuman Bodies and Agency in Octavia Butler's *Xenogenesis*," in *Dark Horizons: Science Fiction and the Dystopian Imagination*, ed. Raffaella Baccolini and Tom Moylan (New York: Routledge, 2003) 91–111; and Eric White, "The Erotics of Becoming: *Xenogenesis* and *The Thing*," *Science Fiction Studies*, 20 (1993): 394–408.

Creating Visual Rhetoric and the Monstrous

NANCY HIGHTOWER

For an upper division writing and rhetoric course, the monstrous and grotesque yields an especially rich area of study as they share a common and collective history in being relegated to "low brow" or popular culture. The grotesque as an aesthetic was seen as decorous in the 15th century, and the grotteschi discovered in Nero's Domus Aurea (AD 64) in 1480 were simultaneously considered "extraneous marvels of art" and "monsters" since they involved unnatural combinations of human, animal, and plant.[1] In the 15th and 16th centuries monsters appealed to the "learned and barely literate alike," as indicated by the popularity of broadsides that displayed "monstrous" births in conjunction with natural disasters and God's judgments or warnings.[2] Yet the need for classification and categorization of real and unreal monsters by late 16th century scientists and natural historians made the wonder books which replaced the broadsides downplay the supernatural connection. Subsequently, the educated classes withdrew from the "what it perceived as the ignorance and superstition of the folk."[3] One can see the implications of these biases in the way literature has been divided into "fiction," and then "fantasy and science fiction." One subject is worthy of study; the other is a form of escapist literature.

Students have grown up with this paradigm, and so they sign up for my monsters course thinking it will be easy. Such a course is always interesting to today's college student who has grown up with monsters—zombies, vampires, werewolves—each with their own corresponding genre. The first few weeks of class, then, is geared towards reintroducing them to the monsters who cannot be named, the ones that frustrate the linguistic ability to further classify the other into something nameable, knowable. Specifically teaching the monstrous within the aesthetic of the grotesque helps monsters to become marvelous and wondrous again, for while monsters need not be grotesque in order to be effective, the grotesque is always about the body made other.

The grotesque indicts everyone's boundaries, challenging how we think of objects and demanding we see the monstrous as phenomenological beings refusing to be contained by the page, the category, or even by temporality. According to Frances Connelly, "the grotesque is a boundary creature and does not exist except in relation to a boundary."[4] Monsters act in a similar way: they are disparate parts fused together in order to challenge our notions of naming and being known (thereby being relegated to the nomenclature of "monster"), and they reveal something about and to the society in which they are introduced. Within the aesthetics of the grotesque, the monstrous takes a slightly different guise, becoming more interstitial than something that can be named and categorized. The grotesque monster "stand[s] at the margin of consciousness between the known and unknown" and resides "just out of focus, beyond the reach of language."[5] The concept of an aesthetic that resists linguistic certainty and narrative closure is difficult for students to apprehend—this is, after all, the generation that makes up words all the time in their text conversations, and so showing visual examples of where the monstrous combined with the grotesque defies our need for linguistic certainty can help show the pragmatic use of this theory, which tries to categorize the unnamable.

Harpham cites Martin Schöngauer's *The Temptation of St. Anthony* (c. 1470) as a rhetorical focal point: "The spiky snouted figure on the far left, for example, cannot be gathered into a single noun, for it is part porcupine, part anteater, part fish (and part fish-hook in the tail); and, in its limbs, its expression, and its sense of intentionality, part human. The whole is, if not more than, at least very different from the sum of its parts."[6] Now, Harpham goes on to show how we create a sense of comfort when we lob all of these monsters into the category of "temptations"—they are named and, for a moment, de-grotesqued even though they certainly remain monsters.

Erhard Schon's *Der Teufel mit der Sackpfeife* (1535) performs a similar function—when I ask students what to call the creature in the picture, they can come to no consensus regarding a name: "How to describe it? Where to begin? There is a priestly head—awake, obliging, content to be a bladder; and the devil itself—partly vertebrate with strong suggestion of fowl from the neck up, except for the small tusks; and, in the lower belly and genital region, a semi-autonomous, one-eyed grinner."[7] One could argue that we fear something less when we can name it, can wrap boundaries around it, which keep it somewhat contained within the realm of objects. But the grotesque monster resides in an interstitial space that is at once both far and close, inside and outside. The grotesque monster can *roam* because both the grotesque and the monstrous are forms of modality, as Frances Connelly reminds us, that grotesques "may be better understood as 'trans-' ... better described for what they do, rather than what they are."[8] Monsters, Jeffrey Jerome Cohen argues, operate on a similar platform: as a "construct and a projection, the monster exists only to be read: the *monstrum* is etymologically 'that which reveals,' that which warns ... like a letter on the page, the monster signifies something other than itself."[9] Therefore, it is an especially fecund exercise to look at *how* this process takes place. Harpham cites the example of Scylla, whose lower body is horrifically transformed into a pack of dogs. Scylla experiences the "paradox of running both *from* and *with* ... suffering the logically impossible though undeniable recognitions that 'her loins' are also 'dogs gone mad.' The entire sequence could be framed as the death of the theorizing mind, the temporary reign of the senses (or, more accurately, the confusion of theory), followed by a resurrection of theoretical certainty."[10] Within that confusion lies a "paradigm crisis" where enough "anomalies" have loosened the structural integrity of the old system but no new one has arisen to take its place.[11] This explanation can help students reframe the monstrous as a moment rather than an object, as an action rather than thing.

We begin my class on the grotesque with these basic definitions of the monstrous and grotesque, but quickly focus on some of the earliest visual examples from Nero's Domus Aurea and how those *grotteschi* began to spill over and walk into the margins of illuminated manuscripts. My students are delighted and mesmerized with the insolent demons found within Bosch's *Garden of Earthly Delights* or Bruegel's *Mad Meg*, but it is when we arrive at Goya's *Caprichos* aquatint series (1799) that they begin to see some of Harpham's definitions fleshed out. Just what kinds of creatures reside in the shadows of *Swallow It Dog* (Figure 1) or *Blow*, egging on the despicable violence in the foreground? My students cannot find an easy label for them such as zombie, vampire, or werewolf, and besides, they don't quite seem to belong to the classification of the supernatural. Likewise, the human-bird hybrids in *All Will Fall* and *How They Pluck Her* somehow register even more strongly the violence done to them by their human (and semi-human) perpetrators. Perhaps Baudelaire most elegantly captures Goya's gift of drawing the unnamable:

> Goya's great merit consists in his having created a credible form of the monstrous. His monsters are born viable, harmonious. No one has ventured further than he in the direction of the *possible* absurd. All the distortions, those bestial faces, those diabolic grimaces of his are impregnated with *humanity*.... It would be hard to condemn them, so great is the analogy and harmony between all the parts of their being. In a word, the line of suture, the point of junction between the real and the fantastic is impossible to grasp.[12]

It is important that the viewer sees something recognizable, some kind of working logic within the monster in order to give it some kind of validation.

A jumble of things with no kind of order or narrative about it just creates chaos, and chaos, like the obscene, can be dismissed.

Figure 1: *Swallow It Dog*, Goya aquatint series, ca. 1799.

The grotesque monster must, in so many ways, make sense while simultaneously instigating confusion, which Harpham argues can "lead the mind to new inventions."[13] Goya's *Caprichos* questioned the prevailing superstitions of his time; they critiqued the upper classes and systems of education. Even today, they defy any neatly packaged theoretical framework. Patricia Piccinini's sculptures elicit a similar response from viewers. Piccinini's *The Young Family* (2002) presents a creature "which has been bred to provide replacement organs for humans, an idea that springs from the very real prospect of doing so using genetically modified pigs."[14] Yet there is, as in Goya's work, so much humanity infused throughout face and body that it can be classified neither as pig nor human, and in class discussions students have voiced much dissent as to whether killing this monster would also mean killing a sentient being. We then take that question into the realm of bioethics, which holds much interest for Piccinini, as most of her work revolves in some way around ethical issues and technology. Her other work, *Undivided* (2004), features a young child being lovingly cuddled by something that is part mother, part armadillo, and part pig, with protruding mounds in its back, and holds sleeping or erupting young (their positioning can imply either). On first sight of the image, my students shudder and gape, but they cannot take their eyes off the image, nor can they shake the fact that there is real intimacy displayed by the sleeping clasp of surrogate mother and child. Piccinini's work consistently asks viewers to reflect on their relationship with nature, but she also positions her work to ask probing questions about how different cultures also use, abuse, and help the environment.

These are just a few examples of the type of art I show my students, with more reference material on a WordPress blog where I put all class content. From the blog they can click links to the works of Jenny Saville, Kara Walker, the Chapman Brothers, Jonas Burgert, and Tim Noble and Sue Webster, just to name a few. At the same time, having covered the theories of the monstrous grotesque from Geoffrey Galt Harpham, Philip Thomson, and Frances Connelly, we turn to literature that employs different aspects of the monstrous body, starting with sections from Rabelais' *Gargantua and Pantagruel,* "The Lady's Dressing Room" (1732) by Jonathan Swift, and "Where Are You Going, Where Have You Been?" (1966) by Joyce Carol Oates. Showing students how different writers created monstrous bodies to question the prevailing hypocrisies and binaries of their culture encourages them to see monsters as more than entertainment, as more than an aesthetic that in some way they own. The monster that emerges from culture is strong enough to escape, at times, and come to haunt another audience.

Rabelais' "How Grandgousier Became Aware of Gargantua's Wonderful Capacities, When His Son Invented an Ass Wiper" from *Gargantua and Pantagruel* (1534) is a particularly good story to read aloud in class. Their response to the essay falls anywhere from pure delight at the scatological humor running throughout the short chapter to disgust when Gargantua begins using small animals as possible replacements for toilet paper. We go through the rather exhaustive list of all the possible wipes Gargantua used, examining which different societal rules Rabelais was poking fun of by having those objects jammed unceremoniously up a giant baby's bottom. My students begin having more fun now, as we analyze the deeper rhetorical structures to Rabelais' work. However, when we get to the goose which ends the piece, they are still somewhat perplexed, and this is where the monstrous body can leap time periods, can jump from a page into the classroom. I ask the class what images are used in toilet paper commercials today. "Puppies! And bears!" they reply, laughing. I point out these animals are not so different from a goose, and that is the first moment when they experience the grotesque monstrous at an emotional level. The room gets rather quiet. Some will actually shiver as if getting a bit creeped out. But it begins an interesting discussion with students about the "natural" body versus the "normal" body in today's culture. They can talk about their bodies in sexualized codes, referring to one's rear as "booty" and "ass." But when talking about other natural bodily functions, they lose words. They shift their eyes away. And then begins the real conversation about bodies and monsters.

The first formal assignment my upper-division writing students have due is a visual rhetoric paper that employs the theories we foregrounded at the beginning of class. They must create their version of the monstrous grotesque to question a hypocrisy in which *they* participate. The first part of the assignment calls for students to find a very specific issue in American culture that they see is taken as a truth, or has been so normalized we no longer question it. Since my class is interdisciplinary and focused on rhetoric and writing, I encourage them to pick a topic they might have researched before or that applies to their major. The other caveat is that students must choose an issue that they in some way participate in, since it becomes commonplace and easy to look at what someone else does and judge it. Instead, we remember how the grotesque tries to indict all, and the uncanny asks us to see the *other* in ourselves.

My students draft a short description of their issue, looking at it from different rhetorical angles. For example, one of my students had recently become very concerned with the lack of time given to grieve or mourn for the death of a loved one. She was a psychology major, and had concerns about how the DSMV IV's stance towards bereavement and grief could possibly qualify grief as a major depressive episode if lasting longer than two months.[15] Her personal interest in the subject stemmed from the fact that her father had died only five months beforehand, and she felt like society and the academic world pressured her to grieve, but also to "get on with her life." She drew a correlation concerning the brevity of grieving with the recent craze of digital photography, where one can instantaneously document and upload any moment or experience. Her father was a photographer and taught her how to develop pictures in a dark room—the long, arduous, yet calming ritual of watching the pictures develop, as opposed to the current culture of digital pictures taken from phones and iPads. Her exploration, then, became about how art can teach us to slow down, feel pain, and process complex emotions:

> Digital photography offers a quick transition from an average shot to a great shot. It allows any person who owns a camera to change the format, and completely alter the overall image. Instead of reliving a once live action, digital photography takes you out of the moment, and pushes you away from reality. It gives you no time to process the picture. In fact, it gives you no time to process anything. Darkroom photography is the opposite. It's an artistic style of life that must be learned over time in order to achieve a great shot. In the darkroom, you can't simply change the color of a print by clicking sepia, black and white, color, etc. You must conduct several trial runs of the same print, hoping that with each one, you get closer and closer to the desired photograph. Like the darkroom, grieving is a slow process that requires you to go through the same phase repeatedly. You can't easily go from denial to acceptance with the click of a button. You must allow yourself to be alone in the dark in order to see clearly and process death.[16]

The second part of the assignment calls for the student to create a grotesque scene that visually asserts their questions regarding the issue they have already described and rhetorically situated. They must take 12 pictures of this scene from different angles, at different speeds and focus, rearranging the elements. Their ultimate goal is to jolt the audience into a sense of destabilization about its own assumptions regarding the issue, using the aesthetics of the monstrous and grotesque. How my students choose to create the monstrous and grotesque is up to them, but they need to use the rhetorical framework that we established in class for how the grotesque or monstrous manifests itself—i.e., something which is aggressively fantastic, has destabilizing elements of horror/humor/beauty, and combines unlike things, etc. The other limitation is to take pictures of just that one "scene"—all the elements should be the same, although they can be rearranged by time, circumstance, or agency. Finally, they are also not allowed to use Photoshop, since not everyone has access to the program.

They soon discover just how difficult it is to visually create a monster that will intrigue and challenge their chosen audience, and subsequently develop a new respect for authors and artists who use the aesthetics of the monstrous and grotesque in their work. A second, even more profound, aspect to this assignment is that it quickly becomes a community enterprise. Students elicit help from their roommates, friends, and even family to brainstorm the project and participate in the scene they are photographing. This assignment, then, momentarily catapults students out of the classroom and propels them to introduce the monstrous to their own discourse communities. One of the objectives of my upper level writing classes is to prepare students to engage with multiple audiences in a dynamic, authentic way. But students have a hard time visualizing and creating a dialogue as so many have been trained to write "to the teacher." The social aspects of this assignment helps student identify their target audiences while also creating a monster that challenges a hypocrisy in which their own culture participates. My student who wanted to write about mourning and the photographic process discussed possible scenes with both her classmates and me in office hours. Because we were talking about the monstrous, we did not limit what was possible, and so we envisioned combining the ephemeral aspects of the dark room along with the concrete tangibility of a coffin. I had no idea where one could get a coffin, but we kept brainstorming. We went over several possible scenarios, and she seemed to think them good starts. That did not prepare me, as a teacher, for what came next.

She brought the pictures to class a couple of weeks after our discussions; she had borrowed a coffin from her community theatre, *brought it to her house*, and had her sister pose inside it. A twisty, multi-limbed creature that no longer looks female, barely human, and yet recognizably so much a human in anguish greets the viewer (Figure 2). The desperate, clawing monster is both inside the coffin, and getting skewered by it, as it crawls over itself to escape. Another photograph shows a body reminiscent of Hans Bellmer's *Doll* Collection, with multi-leg trunk seemingly autonomous from the torso which now lies outside the coffin (Figure 3). The legs seem to represent different motion: a curtsey for the bottom pair, but is the upper pair in the middle of a handstand, or falling at an awkward angle? My student wrote one word on her sister's body for each photo that correlated both to print development process as well as her own grieving process. The pictures themselves are stunning examples of the monstrous, but the fact that she brought the coffin to her house after her father's death allowed she and her sister to explore their feelings of loss through a participatory process that also honored their dad's creativity. My student posted her paper and pictures on Facebook and later told me how, after months of silently grieving in isolation, she was able to engage with her pain and "mental and emotional distortion of what had recently become [her] new family reality." Monsters have a way of escaping boundaries and walking out of the classroom and into global communities to perform powerful actions of disruption, but never destruction.[17] Like these pictures, and like the grotesques we had been studying, the photographic process itself emphasized broken temporal boundaries, not just spatial ones.

Another student wanted to write about her sleeve tattoo and the struggle she experienced when classmates from her creative writing class asked her if it had any significance. She did not want to be so vulnerable, despite the conversations that tattoo culture generates. I have seen this before in classes, where students who barely know each other will practically strip down to show each other the amazing handiwork of their favorite artist. But that, of course, is different than revealing the deeper narrative the tattoo represents. I asked her to further explore the paradox of living with such visible art that invites curiosity and, possibly, judgment at the same time:

> In part, I avoid sharing to prevent the onslaught of drama from escaping the cage I stuff conflict into. The other part is the fear of being *seen*. My parents see all of me and reject what doesn't meet parental standard. If I volunteer these challenged pieces, the tattooed writer, I am subjugating myself to more abuse. At least, that's what the crying voice in my head believes. Sharing the story of my past experiences, having it associated with me rather than overflow that might occur in fiction, opens the doorway. The idea of being exposed is rarely alluring, but exposing the raw, unhealed portion of myself is mortifying. What if I'm met with rejection again? What if I am misunderstood and frustrated to a breaking point?[18]

Our conversations over the next few weeks involved trying to create a monster that was both held within and escaping the body. While we enjoy, critique, mock, or fear monsters in literature, it is actually quite difficult to create one that employs the aesthetics of the grotesque monsters as defined by Harpham and others.

My student found a model willing to have her back transformed into canvas. The first picture presents a golden door that mimics prison bars, the lock securely fastened from the outside so nothing can escape, and yet so flimsy, what good could it do (Figure 4)? A bony hand then emerges, not quite connected to the more fleshy arm exposed from behind the door. Already, we are warned that something might come out that isn't quite human, despite the human back we see, the human hands that we previously saw hug either side (Figure 5). The creature, then, that begins to emerge is at least somewhat recognizably human, the arm more connected, gender unclear. The lower half of the body is enshrouded in a dress or robe (Figure 6). The creature looks frightened, half mad, even. Is it trying to escape or merely terrified that the door has been opened at last from the outside? The seemingly innocuous questions we pose to people with tattoos regarding their symbolism and even mythic power are recast as an awkward intimate interaction with the grotesque. Tattoo culture—even though it has become widely accepted in American society—is still often seen as low art, as a fad that people have when young and a regret they live with when older. These photos of the monstrous emerging from the human indict the culture as much as they indict the writer who struggles with wanting to be known and seen, and yet remains fearful of judgment.

It's important to note that while this first assignment is an analysis paper, I have my students write in a creative, personal voice rather than focusing solely on an academic audience. The monstrous originally appeal to both popular and scholarly culture, and there is an attempt in this assignment to bring those two worlds back together again. Too often my students have forgotten that rhetoric is the *art* of persuasion. They have learned to rely on the five paragraph essay structure filled to the brim with facts and statistics, believing that evidence is the biggest factor in persuading a reader to accept their viewpoint. The goal of these papers is not to convince anyone that the author is correct in his/her critique of cultural binaries that marginalize others; rather, it is to reinvigorate the particular discourse that is mired in binary oppositions. The scholarly and creative components of the assignment lend themselves to be used by students in ways that further intersect with other academic and pop culture communities. The student who wrote on death and the photographic process expanded on the photo series in her psychology class the next year. Another student sold his pictures to a private collector, one of which is now displayed in a gallery. One junior took the idea of the visual rhetoric assignment and made it the basis for her senior art thesis, using the stories we read from class. And still another student wrote to tell me that she had posted her pictures on Deviant Art and received such positive feedback that she is brainstorming how to use those pictures as a baseline for a new project in her comic book class. I'm not sure such fluid crossover would occur had not the monstrous and grotesque recently returned in force to infiltrate all aspects of culture just as they did in the 16th century.

The assignment also reflects and promotes a kind of carnivalesque participation. One student who was analyzing the health industry had her parents and friends pose in the photo series. And thus, she brought the class dialogue into her home. (I met her parents a few years later and the father, after shaking my hand, said, "I was the bear.") Still others—needing props or extra bodies for their scene—will elicit help from classmates whom they have only known for a few weeks.

Even if students don't use their pictures for other academic purposes, many post their pictures on Facebook, along with their paper, so that it becomes available to their friends, or even the general public, depending on their privacy settings. Sometimes, the monstrous or grotesque pictures influenced the student's choice of topic. For example, I had one history major write a clichéd draft about how we need to save the trees. Now, environmental ethics is a very important issue, but he hadn't employed any of monstrous theories as discussed in class and office hours. I challenged him to create a grotesque monster; the next week he came into class and sheepishly told me, "I redid the pictures, but I'm scared to show them to you." Of course, a statement like that will strike fear into the heart of any teacher. As I looked at the pictures, though, I immediately saw that he had an epiphany. He had created a grotesque scene consisting of a person wearing a George Bush mask being carved up and consumed in a kind of unholy communion. The scene is at once violent and funny; one can't avert their eyes, so beautifully is it constructed. On a deeper level, the sequence of actions presented question our blaming the president for policies we disagree with, and critique how our own lifestyle and privilege help keep different political systems in play. The photos had changed the focus of his paper from environmental ethics to examining how consumer habits help mold and shape the policies of those in office. Perhaps more exciting to me as a teacher, was that the student, who was a loner and very quiet in class, was enthusiastically invited by his peers to discuss the ideas behind his pictures as we passed around his work. This assignment showed me how the classroom morphs into a liminal space where the monstrous can roam free, revealing and reveling in porous boundaries that often students and teacher see as static.

By the end of the semester, my students have a rich lexicon to discuss the monstrous as well the grotesque aesthetics in current art, literature, film, and other media. While some monsters and grotesque works exist to shock and entertain, I would argue that the majority of contemporary artists and writers employ these twisty aesthetics with a higher aim and purpose. Perhaps monsters are still entrenched in low-brow rhetoric because there is no easy equation to apply to them: these creatures hold our unvoiced anxieties, internal judgments, horrific biases, and childhood fears. Often in tandem with the monstrous, the grotesque functions to destroy the boundary between high and low, inside and outside. These aesthetics are, by their very nature, threatening, but by bringing them back into the field of academics, we are perhaps returning to that extraordinary time when academic and popular culture shared equal participation. After all, many of our students do not continue on to graduate school but join the ranks of an industrialized society, filling the better part of their day with full-time jobs. How much more important, then, that they take away analytical tools and an extended vocabulary to untangle the connections between aesthetics and systemic injustices. How much more important that when the term "monster" is thrown onto any politician, judge, criminal, celebrity, or person we loathe, they remember that any monster is *communally* created. These are the rhetorical skills I hope they develop, but as an idealistic teacher in the humanities, I also hope they remember a classroom where walls and chairs and desks melted away into a monstrous, carnivalesque world where everything was questioned, and anything was possible.

Appendix

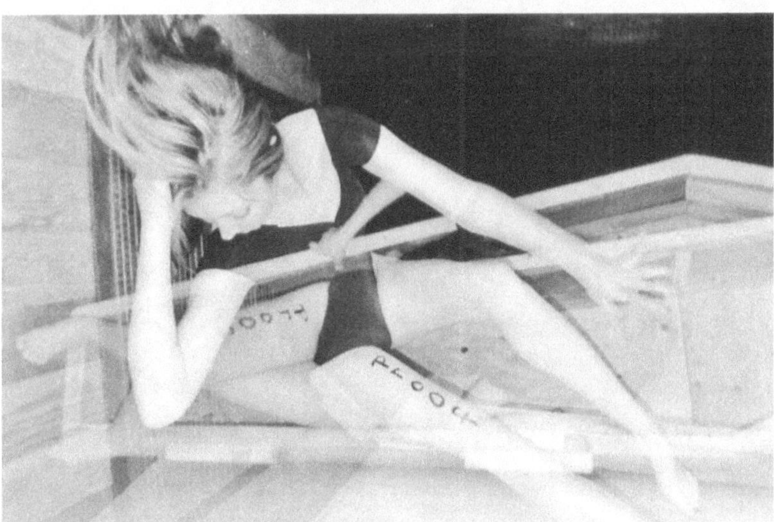

Figure 2: "Dual Process," Bryn Murphy; model Sari Murphy (student work).

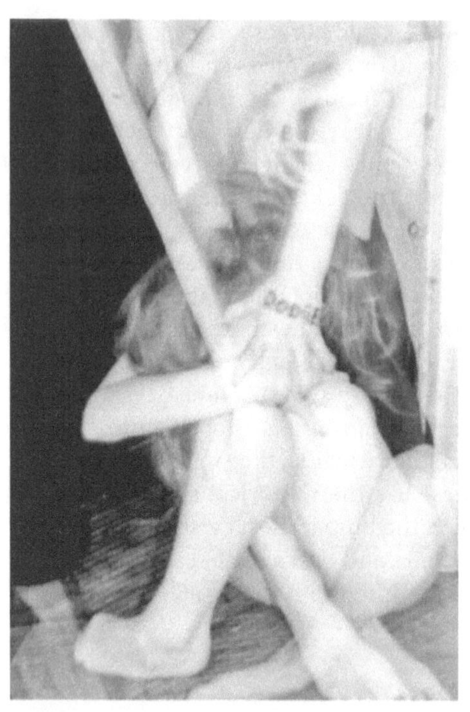

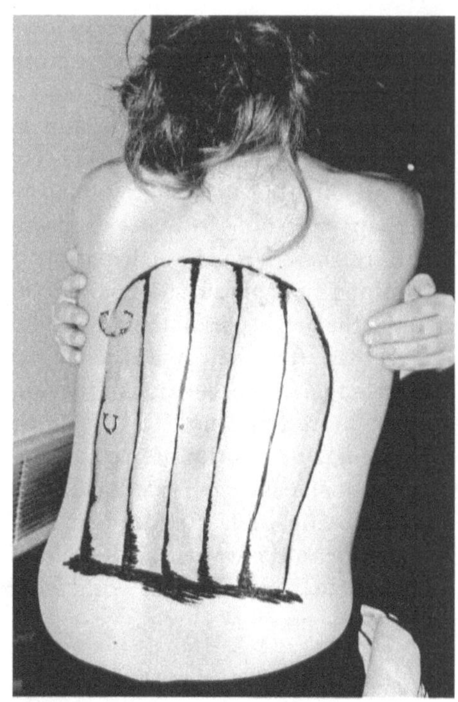

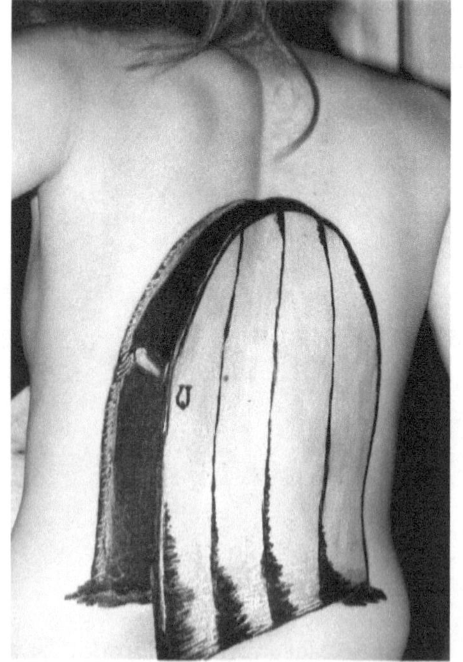

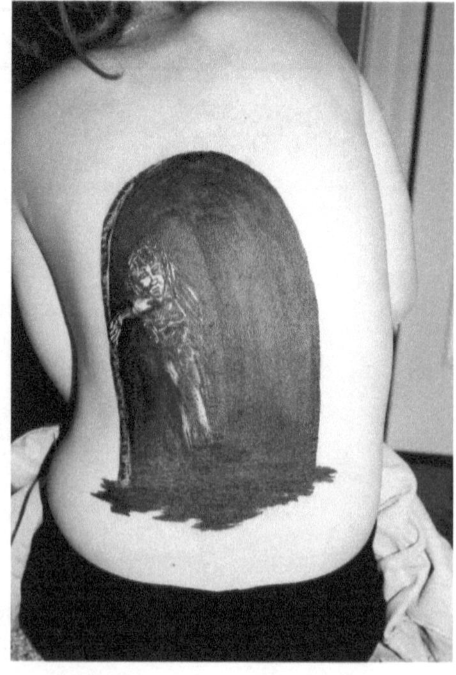

Notes

1. David Summers, "The Archaeology of the Modern Grotesque" in Frances Connelly, ed., *Modern Art and the Grotesque* (Cambridge: Cambridge University Press, 2009), 22–24.
2. Lorraine Daston and Katharine Park, "Unnatural Conceptions: The Study of Monsters in Sixteenth and Seventeenth-Century France and England," *Past & Present* 92 (Oxford: Oxford University Press, 1981), 28.
3. *Ibid.*, 41.
4. Frances Connelly, "Introduction" in Frances Connelly, ed., *Modern Art and the Grotesque* (Cambridge: Cambridge University Press, 2009), 4.
5. Geoffrey Galt Harpham, *On the Grotesque: Strategies of Contradiction in Art and Literature* (Princeton: Princeton University Press, 1982), 3.
6. *Ibid.*, 4–5.
7. *Ibid.*, 6.
8. Connelly, 3.
9. Jeffrey Jerome Cohen, *Monster Theory: Reading Culture* (Minneapolis: University of Minnesota Press, 1996), 4.
10. Harpham, 17.
11. *Ibid.*
12. Charles Baudelaire, *The Mirror of Art* (New York: Doubleday, 1956), 185–86.
13. Harpham, 17.
14. Patricia Piccinini, "The Naturally Artificial World," *Tender Creatures Exhibition Catalogue* (Atrium: ARTIUM of Alva, 2007), (accessed June 2015), http://www.patriciapiccinini.net/printessay.php?id=29.
15. American Psychiatric Association Major Depressive Disorder and the "Bereavement Exclusion" (accessed July 9, 2015), http://www.dsm5.org/Documents/Bereavement%20Exclusion%20Fact%20Sheet.pdf.
16. Bryn Murphy, "Dual Process," student work, 2014. Used with permission.
17. Flannery O'Connor, *Mystery and Manners* (New York: Farrar, Straus and Giroux, 1969), 162.
18. Sara Fardi, "Knock Knock, Go Away!" student work, 2014. Used with permission.

***Opposite: (Top left)* Figure 3: "Dual Process," Bryn Murphy; model Sari Murphy (student work). (*Top right)* Figure 4. (*Bottom left),* Figure 5. (*Bottom right),* Figure 6: "Knock Knock," Sara Fardi; model Martina Kleinova (student work).**

Monsters as Subversive Imagination

Inviting Monsters into the Philosophy Classroom

JESSICA ELBERT DECKER

Intensely fascinating and subversive, monsters capture our attention because they threaten to bring the unruly, irrational dream world to life—a world that does not respect our clean borders and logical conceptualizations but instead manifests prolific imaginative force unfettered from rational consciousness. This essay explores the pedagogical benefits of bringing monsters into the classroom and presents the reader with some practical applications, assignments, and classroom activities using monsters in a variety of philosophy courses. Images of the monstrous can be used to illuminate the symbolic causes of oppression, whether that oppression takes the form of racism, misogyny, or xenophobia. These specific applications of monsters share a common function: they make our human reactions to difference visible. Monsters are hybrid creatures; they often combine categories considered taboo when found together—such as part-animal/part-human creatures, human-machine hybrids. By enacting these breakdowns of border, monsters threaten the identities that have their foundations in those borders—especially the identity of what is "human."

Using monsters in the classroom has multiple benefits: monsters typically originate in popular culture and mythology—these are familiar areas of life to students and present them with an accessible object of study. In addition, using monsters as a working image creates a safe imaginative space where students can grapple with their complex understanding of identity—both of themselves and of others. Monsters can function as a concrete medium upon which students may project their imaginative conceptualizations and fantasies; this is a safe space because it prevents the projection of difference onto classmates and frames the "other" (temporarily) as a creature of fiction. Once students learn to assess critically their understanding of identity and the ways in which we codify "others" in our various cultural narratives, they can begin to extend the conclusions from our fictional analysis of monsters onto real relations between human beings in the social world.

In this essay, I will be exploring the use of monsters in some specific philosophy courses, including Philosophy of Technology, Philosophy and Literature, Feminist Philosophy, Ethics and Environment, and Philosophy of Film. Some of the assignments and objectives will also translate into other classroom settings, and are suitable for use in various courses in the humanities. My focus will be on using monsters to teach students how to understand the meaning of difference—whether it is in the form of race, gender, class, or our relation to animals and other species. First, I will briefly establish the theoretical framework that informs my teaching of monsters, and I will then move on to discussion of specific courses, learning objectives, and assignments.

Theoretical Frameworks

In philosophical discourse, monsters have a very useful function: they present thinkers with a model of difference. Before turning to specific course content, I would like to begin by outlining the theoretical frameworks that lay the foundation for my pedagogical use of monsters. The work of Donna Haraway is especially valuable, since she is concerned with a broad array of philosophical questions, including feminist practice and theory, philosophy of science, and ethical questions regarding the use and meaning of technology. In "The Cyborg Manifesto," Haraway describes her cyborg-monster as a creature that does not respect proper boundaries—especially the borders between human and animal, machine and human, or physical and non-physical.[1] Monsters, like the cyborg, call these conceptual boundaries into question by transgressing them. Generally, these transgressions are both fascinating and horrific to our cultural sensibilities; for this reason, monsters are a common trope in horror stories and films (discussed later in this essay). In approaching questions of identity and difference in the classroom, monsters provide us with a structural model that celebrates hybridity and difference by dissolving clear categories of identity and meaning.

Haraway argues that we have a political responsibility to pay close attention to those "systems of myth and meaning structuring our imaginations."[2] The construction of narratives, including myths, stories, films, and other artifacts of popular culture, often demonstrate our unconscious anxieties about identity and borders; these narratives reflect the structures of thought that give rise to identity politics, the oppression of "others" (racialized, gendered, etc.), and our understanding of what it means to be human. As Haraway and other critical theorists claim, these imaginative structures can make visible the symbolic meanings that underlie political, social, and even economic systems. Many of these symbolic structures reveal our cultural tendency to think in what ecofeminist theorists Mies and Shiva call "antagonistic dualisms": such as man/women, white/non-white, heterosexual/LGBTQ, rich/poor, good/evil, etc. Monsters are unique in their ability to challenge these dualistic constructions by appearing to be "both/and" rather than "either/or."[3]

In the concluding section of her "Cyborg Manifesto," Haraway tells us that the aim of her essay is to encourage both "*pleasure* in the confusion of boundaries and responsibility in their construction."[4] Through this practice of monstrosity, or cyborg consciousness in Haraway's narrative, we can dissolve the oppressive boundaries that pit "us" against "them," and instead, welcome a world "where people are not afraid of their joint kinship with animals and machines, and not afraid of permanently partial identities and contradictory standpoints."[5] Monsters are an antidote for the continual production of 'others' and violent defense of boundaries—whether physical (such as the borders of nations) or psychical (such as misogyny and racism). The narratives that a culture adopts can result in real, concrete oppression of "others," whether these constructed categories are about race, gender, sexual identity, class, or other dividing classifications. While imaginary, these narratives are powerful, and create actual conditions of oppression.

In her study of the monstrous, *Embodying the Monster: Encounters with the Vulnerable Self,* Margrit Shildrick makes a similar point about the function of monsters, with regard to political awareness:

> The point is that monsters can signify both the binary opposition between the natural and the non-natural, where the primary term confers value, and also the disruption within that destabilizes the standard of the same. In other words, they speak to both the radical otherness that constitutes an outside and to the difference that inhabits identity itself. The issue is not so much that monsters threaten to overrun the boundaries of the proper, as that they promise to dissolve them.[6]

Before these boundaries and divisive categories can be dissolved, they have to be made visible. Using monsters as a model emphasizes the nature of our binary thinking, and allows thinkers (including students) to recognize these operations in their own concepts and beliefs. Inviting monsters into the classroom gives students the opportunity to challenge the rigid borders that separate humans from animals or from machines, from gendered or racialized "others," and take responsibility for the construction of these boundaries in their thinking. As Haraway argues, we have a political responsibility to closely examine the symbolic structures that determine our thinking—whether these take the form of concepts, myths, or images from popular culture. The fear of monsters is fear of otherness; the terror and fascination that monsters tend to invoke are responses that students can learn to critically assess in themselves and in others.

Monsters in Philosophy of Technology

In my Philosophy of Technology course, students examine the origins, attitudes, and ethical questions that are raised by our increasing use of technology. In popular culture, there are myriad examples of technological monsters—ranging from dangerous robots or androids, hybrid human-machines, and other technologically-created monsters such as clones or new species. These technological monsters express our cultural anxiety about the precarious control that we have over technology, and our fear that technology can destroy what is "natural." While technology is a human activity, we often experience it as something alien to us because it is so powerful in shaping our perception and our world.

In the literature of Philosophy of Technology, our relation to technology is explored from various perspectives. The position of ancient skepticism perceives technology as *daimonic*, having a will of its own, and inherently destructive. The traditional, optimistic view of technology sees technology as merely an instrument for human use—technology is neither good nor bad in itself, it is the uses that humans devise that make technology destructive or beneficial. The pessimistic model, which is often expressed in popular culture, views technology as a force that exceeds human control; popular films like *Jurassic Park* (1993) and *The Matrix* (1999) and the popular television show *Battlestar Galactica* (2004–09) demonstrate this anxiety about our precarious hold over technology. This "Frankenstein Perspective" emphasizes the dangerous trajectories of technology and our inability to regulate these powerful forces.

In the Philosophy of Technology course, students are assigned an analysis of a popular film that represents our human relation to technology. A list of films is provided, and students have several weeks to watch their chosen film and work on a presentation for class that analyzes the film using the lens of our philosophical readings. Students identify the different attitudes towards technology that we have discussed in the class (skepticism, pessimism, optimism) in their chosen films. For example, students read an essay by Frederick Turner entitled "The Invented Landscape," where Turner argues that human beings ought to embrace our technological skills and employ them whenever possible to create new ecosystems, terra-form other planets, and resurrect extinct species.[7] Turner opposes the common environmentalist argument that human beings are "playing God" when we experiment with technologies, and claims that our technological skill defines us as a species, so it is irrational for us to turn our backs on this special adaptation.[8] Turner's essay represents a very optimistic view of technology, and students evaluate his arguments in defense of this position and construct arguments against his position using other essays that we have read. For example, students might argue from the pessimistic view that these technological experiments can go awry due to our incomplete understanding of science and ecology. Paired with this particular essay, students may choose a film such as *Jurassic Park* (1993) that challenges Turner's position by presenting an apocalyptic scenario caused by the irresponsible use of technology. Rather than take a polemical and extreme position on one "side" or the other, students are encouraged to carefully analyze these positions and evaluate the strengths and weaknesses of both perspectives.

Student learning objectives for this assignment are multiple: students learn how to apply theory to a concrete medium, such as a film, and explore the practical use of philosophical theory in solving real ethical problems (such as the ethical use of genetic engineering, in the case of *Jurassic Park*). Within their chosen film, students identify the "monster" in the story—this can take the form of an actual monster (like Godzilla), genetically engineered creatures (like the dinosaurs in *Jurassic Park*), human-machine hybrids (such as the androids in *Blade Runner* [1982]), or even villainous human beings who unethically manipulate technology for selfish ends (like the creator of the female cyborgs in the 2015 film *Ex Machina*). Once they have identified the monster in their film, students identify the qualities that contribute to its monstrosity—what boundaries does the monster transgress? What concepts does it challenge? What is the relationship between the monster and human beings in the story? How is the monster an object of "difference"? Through this analysis, students are able to apply what they have learned from the fictional medium to the real world, particularly because most of these technological monsters are not entirely fictional, but are based on existing technologies and their possible future trajectories.

Philosophy of Technology is an area of study that has frequent applications to current events and media. Throughout the course, students post in online forums (using Moodle, Blackboard, or other classroom systems) and share news stories, articles, or other relevant media that discusses issues of technology, especially media that raises ethical questions. I maintain a Facebook page for this class, and students are encouraged to share items that they discover while searching the internet—this Facebook page is extremely effective in continuing discussion outside of the classroom, and getting more reserved students to engage in the class discussion. Every semester, students comment on their enjoyment of the Facebook page in the course evaluations; I have found this to be an extremely effective tool.

Since students are often engaged in social media on a daily basis, the use of the Facebook page integrates our classroom studies into their everyday lives. Students share articles about advances in robotics, in cloning, in the creation of genetically modified organisms (GMOs), and in the uses of communication technologies. In these forum post assignments, students are encouraged to examine the attitudes that the media piece represents, both explicit and implicit, and to analyze the ethical questions that the piece raises. For example, a common technological "monster" in our cultural representations is the conscious robot—students analyze articles about advances in artificial intelligence and characterize both the optimistic and pessimistic attitudes that these advances may create. How do people react to the new creation? What anxieties or fears are expressed about it? What possibly could go wrong in this new creation? How can the new creation benefit human beings and the environment?

My "Philosophy of Technology" course also includes a section on environmental ethics and feminist philosophy, and students read the introduction to Elissa Marder's book *The Mother in the Age of Mechanical Reproduction*, where Marder argues that Pandora is a technological creation and a monster.[9] Pandora is created by Zeus and given various gifts by the other gods, according to their abilities and powers, such as charm and feminine wiles from Aphrodite and sneaky cleverness from Hermes. Pandora, then, was never born and is not a human being at all; "in today's parlance, we might call her an android, a robot, or a replicant."[10] This reading picks up several themes that have been under discussion throughout the Philosophy of Technology course, such as the idea that technology is *daimonic* and ambivalent, and the belief that technology is inherently dangerous and deceptive. Marder argues that this myth demonstrates the manner in which women have traditionally been associated with technology, particularly in their reproductive capacities—Pandora, after all, shows up with her jar or box, a metaphor for the womb. Pandora is a monstrous mother and, in bringing with her this box that releases all the evils into the world, a femme fatale.

After reading this essay in class, students watch a film that includes either an image of the monstrous mother, such as *Alien* (1979), or a film that includes a femme fatale, such as *Basic Instinct* (1992). Using the essay, students evaluate the female character in the film and relate her to the image of Pandora. Is the image of the femme fatale a misogynistic one? Why are the mothers in horror films like *Alien* represented as terrifying? What anxieties about maternity and childbirth do these mother-monsters make visible? How do these images of women contribute to the oppression of women in our society? Students work on presentations in teams, after choosing a film to analyze, and share their responses to these questions with the class.

The focus of these assignments is primarily ethical—students examine the meaning of the technological monsters they encounter using the philosophical theory that they have studied in the course. As Haraway argues in her "Cyborg Manifesto," "the machine is not an *it* to be animated, worshipped, dominated. The machine is us, our process, an aspect of our embodiment. We can be responsible for machines, they do not dominate or threaten us."[11] The technological monsters with which students engage in these fictional narratives are aspects of human beings, not alien creatures. We project the aspects of ourselves that we fear onto monsters, and as Haraway argues, we must take responsibility for our creations. The most crucial learning objective in these assignments is learning responsibility for our conceptual constructions, and recognizing that technology and the monsters it creates are not foreign to us, but extensions of ourselves.

Monsters in Philosophy and Literature and Environmental Ethics

Because monsters are creatures of the imagination, literature is a fertile place to find a variety of monsters. I frequently teach a course called "Philosophy and Literature"; the course is structured in such a way that students first read a philosophical piece then read a literary work through that philosophical lens. In literature, there are many classic monster texts such as Mary Shelley's *Frankenstein* and Bram Stoker's *Dracula*; the genre of science fiction also abounds with monsters—the androids in Philip K Dick's *Do Androids Dream of Electric Sheep?* and the strange aliens in Octavia Butler's trilogy *Lilith's Brood* are very different examples of sci-fi monsters. Ancient Greek mythology includes a vast array of famous monsters, including the Minotaur, the Cyclops, Medusa, the Sirens, Scylla and Charybdis, the Furies, the witch Circe, Cerberus, Typhon, the Titans, and many others. In addition to these possibilities, there are a number of literary texts that contain monsters less traditional; for example, Franz Kafka's *Metamorphosis* or Gabriel Garcia Marquez's "A Very Old Man with Enormous Wings."

Before tackling the literary texts, students become familiar with some theoretical frameworks such as Marxism, race theory, feminist theory, and psychoanalysis. We begin the course by studying monsters in Greek mythology, and read these narratives for their symbolic content in the same manner that one might interpret a dream. Students use essays from both Freud and Jung on dream theory in exploring the meaning of the monsters in myth; for example, what aspects of human life does the monster represent? Scylla and Charybdis, for example, are found far out at sea, at the mythical edges of the world—they represent, among other things, our fear of the unknown. Their liminal locations signal their status as border-creatures who haunt the space where two worlds collide. The mythical guardian of the underworld, Cerberus, is another such monster; before the hero is able to traverse the land of the dead, he must grapple with the giant three-headed hound. The monster of the labyrinth, the Minotaur, can represent the hidden aspects of the personality—what Jung calls the Shadow, which the dreamer must confront in order to complete the individuation process.

Students become familiar with the Freudian concept of "latent content" in dream interpretation; the dream contains two layers—the manifest or surface content of the dream and the hidden meaning, its latent content. In addition, Freud outlines several useful mechanisms of dream-creation such as condensation, which refers to the confluence of several meanings in one dream image. In other words, dream images tend to be multiply determined—for example, a person in a dream may be a combination of several real persons known to the dreamer. Students sign up in teams for a particular myth or literary work, and they conduct a close analysis using interpretive tools to read the literary symbols in their chosen work. Monsters are an excellent object of symbolic study because they often reflect unconscious cultural ideas and anxieties, much in the same way that the latent content of the dream expresses the dreamer's unconscious associations. Students work on their analyses together with their team, using class time as well as an online forum, and produce a presentation to share with the class. Each team presents their analysis and then opens up the floor for questions and discussion. This is a very enjoyable activity for the students because it allows them to use their imaginations, and tap into their ability to interpret symbolic meanings. The most prominent learning objective for this assignment is to develop students' ability to recognize the meaning of symbols as products of the unconscious, and to give them practice in exploring the mechanisms of our thinking—a very useful skill for a philosopher, and one that is championed by Socrates himself.

There are also a variety of female monsters in Greek myth: Medusa is a woman who, after she was raped by Poseidon, was made into a monster with serpents for her hair. Medusa the Gorgon is a terrifying monster because she has the ability to turn men to stone with her gaze. The hero Perseus decapitates her though he is only able to defeat her using the reflection of her on his shield (a trick suggested to him by the goddess Athena). Medusa can be read as a terrifying image of what Freud calls "the phallic mother"—a powerful, uncastrated version of Woman. Because of her powerful status, she must be castrated (read: decapitated) by the male hero and reduced to the symbolic state of all women, which is a powerless, castrated and submissive position. Athena, always the champion of patriarchy, assists him in his task. Famously, in the *Orestes*, Athena exculpates Orestes for his matricide in killing Clytemnestra, claiming that she has no mother and will always judge on the side of men in all things.[12] Athena is a powerful goddess because she repudiates her femininity, thus losing her monstrous status and is essentially a male warrior.

Powerful females in Greek myth and tragedy usually end badly—Medea, who heaps vengeance on Jason for betraying her, and Clytemnestra who murders her husband Agamemnon for his sacrifice of their daughter Iphigenia are both strongly vilified in the myths. Characters who devote themselves to the male cause and die for the glory of men are celebrated as "good women"—Alcestis, for example, chooses to die in her husband's place, and Iphigenia consents to her sacrifice for the good of Greece and the success of the Trojan War (a war among men, over the possession of a woman—Helen of Troy). Women who exhibit agency, like Helen, Medea, and Clytemnestra are viewed as monsters for transgressing their "female" roles.

After studying the background feminist theory and psychoanalysis, students study these Greek myths using the theory as a lens. One assignment I often use in this class asks students to identify parallel stories in our culture's myths—in films, literature, video games, and other sources. Students find examples of Medea-like or Helen-like figures from popular culture, and analyze their representation and status as 'monsters' and explain how their characters are transgressive of female roles. For this assignment, students work as teams to search for examples from popular culture that parallel some of the Greek myths. They then post in a discussion forum online, sharing their findings and their analysis of the characters. After reading one another's posts, we spend a class session discussing these mythical figures—each group offers a short presentation of their conclusions: which mythical figures they are exploring, which examples from popular culture that parallel the myths, and their findings in analyzing these narratives together.

In addition to the Greek mythology, students read a variety of texts containing monsters, ranging from Shelley's *Frankenstein* to science fiction stories like Dick's *Do Androids Dream of Electric Sheep?* For each of these texts, students are using theory as a frame (psychoanalysis is very effective for this assignment) and carefully analyze the monster of the text: what makes it a monster? Is the story an allegory? What human aspects or experiences does the monster invoke? How should we read the symbolism of the monster? For example, in reading *Do Androids Dream of Electric Sheep?*, the monsters in the story are the humanoid androids that the protagonist (a bounty hunter) is paid to hunt down and "retire" (i.e., kill).[13] These androids are monsters because they are nearly indistinguishable from human beings, yet they lack empathy. They can only be discovered via a complex "empathy test." They are monsters because they are so much like human beings but lack the quality that, according to the novel, makes us human: empathy. The monsters in this story raise questions about the identity we create for ourselves as human—which qualities do we deem necessary to be a human being?

This novel also raises ethical questions about what counts as "life," and whether or not conscious robots are alive. After reading a selection from Peter Singer about animal rights, students have a debate in class about whether or not these androids are alive, and thus have "interests" in the sense for which Singer argues.[14] Students are given class time to prepare their arguments as teams, then they debate the question using Singer's essay and examples from the novel to support their arguments. The learning objectives for this assignment are twofold: students learn to construct a careful argument using texts and applying theory to the literary work, and students learn to evaluate ethical positions regarding the monsters of the story.

For this debate, students are also asked to think about what traits or qualities we hold as necessary in order to qualify as "human" and/or "alive." Within the debate, they try to argue for their chosen qualities as necessary for life and/or humanity. For example, if we choose empathy as a quality necessary to count as human, then what about sociopaths or human beings with different mental capacities who may not experience empathy in the same way (such as Aspergers)? Would we then have to claim that these people are not human? This class exercise challenges students to think critically about difference, especially the kinds of categories we create in order to divide "us" from "them," whether we are talking about androids, or animals, or other human beings. Historically, philosophical discourse has named reason as the quality that separates humans from animals, men from women, and "civilized" people from "savages"—the novel reverses this traditional principle by making the androids far more rational than human beings, and claiming empathy as crucial to human identity.

In my Philosophy of Technology course, my Philosophy and Literature course, and my Ethics and Environment course, I have used Margaret Atwood's novel *Oryx and Crake* as a way of exploring ethical questions ranging from the uses of biotechnology to human responsibility for mass extinctions.[15] The novel is a dystopian post-apocalyptic story where a somewhat sociopathic genius nicknamed Crake attempts to wipe out the destructive human race and replace them with harmless humanoid creations called the Crakers. The protagonist of the story, Crake's friend Jimmy, struggles with the aftermath of Crake's plan and lives with his creations, the Crakers. The monsters in this story are ambiguous—is Crake the monster, since he tries to cause human beings to go extinct? Or are his not-quite-human creatures the Crakers the monsters, since they are human-like but genetically altered to eat only foliage and lack human experiences like romantic love, religion, art, and writing? We spend several weeks in class discussing this novel, and students contribute to a number of discussion forums, where they analyze elements of the story and respond to ethical questions. After writing their responses, students defend their arguments as teams in a debate forum in class.

Oryx and Crake is a very useful text for discussing the ethical questions raised by monsters, and offers a harsh critique of our current society's values. While it is a work of fiction, the situations and themes of the novel reflect real conditions in our world—for example, the novel contains various grotesque genetically engineered animals created for human use. The society of the novel is violent, starkly divided between the rich and the poor, and aggressively capitalistic at the expense of human health—the Compounds, where the rich and scientific live, produce a variety of dangerous drugs to sell to the poor and even produce diseases so they can then market the antidotes to the poor.

Since I maintain Facebook pages for most of my classes, students in this course also locate news articles that relate to the themes of *Oryx and Crake* and post them to social media throughout the semester. Students also sign up for a class day in the beginning of the semester, and on their assigned day, they present a particular news article that deals with these same themes. One of the questions they are assigned to think about is who or what qualifies as a monster in the story, and why they think so. There are several possible monsters in the novel—Crake himself, the Crakers that he creates as a substitute for human beings, the genetically modified animals in the story, or the violent militaristic organization, the CorpSeCorps. This assignment requires students to analyze the category of monstrosity, and identify the qualities that make something a monster. Students use ethical readings in philosophy to critique various unethical themes of the novel, such as the irresponsible use of technology, the inhumane treatment of animals for human use, and the destruction of our environment for profit.

Monsters in Feminist Philosophy and Film

There is a long history in Western thought of associating women with the monstrous—beginning in the works of Aristotle, who, in his *Generation of Animals* classes females as a kind of original monster, since they fail to resemble the father and represent a deviance from "nature" (despite their obvious necessity in reproduction). Huet describes Aristotle's position in her study *Monstrous Imagination*: "if the monster is nature's disorder, the female instrument for procreation is the cause of all the disorders in nature.... What women hide, what women are, is monstrosity itself."[16] As outlined in the previous section, Greek mythology includes a startling array of female monsters. This close association between women and monsters demands further analysis: why are women, in particular, classed as monstrous?

Since the time of the Ancient Greeks, western culture has understood women to be closer to nature, which means they were perceived as chaotic, uncontrollable, and less rational than men. These images of women are reflected throughout Greek myth and philosophy, and they reveal patriarchal anxieties about women's bodies, particularly in their reproductive capacities. Like other monsters, women are hybrid creatures—they are capable of producing life out of their bodies, and the processes of menstruation, pregnancy and childbirth are all traditionally considered to be "impure," and have historically required rituals that eliminate the dangerous particulars of their bodies.

The very concept of "impurity" depends upon the rigid construction of boundaries between what is clean and proper and what is dirty or corrupted. Historically, many human cultures have been obsessed with "purity" of this kind, manifesting in practices ranging from the murder of brides who are found not to be virgins to outright genocide of others deemed unclean by the dominant group. Blood is necessary for life, but when it is found *outside* of the body, it becomes impure and threatening. This observation is confirmed by the prevalence of blood and gore in horror films; blood becomes monstrous when it ceases to remain in its "proper" place inside the body. In addition, pregnancy and childbirth challenge our understanding of the boundary between life and death; a glance at the controversial debates about abortion and the status of an unborn fetus quickly confirms this anxiety and confusion of boundaries. A pregnant woman is perceived as a hybrid creature—she fails to remain a stable identity and seems to be two people at once. Thus maternity and childbirth are also a common theme of horror films, such as *Rosemary's Baby* (1968) and *Alien*.

For these reasons, horror films provide feminist thinkers with a plethora of material for analyzing the symbolic relation between women and the monstrous. Barbara Creed, in her fascinating study of women and horror, *The Monstrous Feminine*, analyzes the symbolic constellations that manifest in horror films containing female monsters—and there are an alarming number of these films.[17] Her text is a great resource; she arranges her study according to different images of the monstrous feminine, including images of the mother, women as vampires, witches, evil possessed beings, and the femme fatale. These common tropes of horror reflect the (often unconscious) ways of perceiving women in the patriarchal culture of the West, and provide students with vivid imagery of these imaginative structures so they do not only engage with these ideas on an intellectual level, but experience their visceral effect.

The learning objectives and assignments outlined here are relevant to a range of courses; I have used the assignments in feminist philosophy courses cross-listed in Women's Studies, in philosophy of film courses, in psychoanalytic courses, and in introductory courses that had a feminist theme or section. Students read several essays in preparation for watching a film, then analyze the film using the readings. For example, we might read a selection from Barbara Creed that examines the monstrous feminine with a psychoanalytic reading that discusses misogyny and/or the fear of women, like Freud's "phallic mother." I also include a feminist reading about marriage and childbirth as ways in which women are oppressed in patriarchal societies, such as Monique Wittig's *One is Not Born a Woman* or Judith Butler's critique of Freud's work on female sexuality.[18]

The work of Rosi Braidotti is particularly useful in this context; her book *Metamorphoses: Towards a Materialist Theory of Becoming* explicitly deals with questions of the monstrous feminine. In dealing with the association between maternity and horror, she writes:

> [The] preoccupation with the horror of the maternal feminine expresses a deeply-seated postmodern anxiety about the social and symbolic orders. The monstrosity of the female is a sort of paradox, which on the one hand reinforces the patriarchal assumption that female sexuality is evil and abject, on the other hand, however, it also states the immense powerfulness of the female subject … the other side of the coin of the monstrous maternal/material feminine is however the manifest failure of men to maintain paternal authority.[19]

Female monsters tend to be extremely powerful, and often destructive—this theme echoes many of the female monsters of Greek myth. The representation of female monsters in horror reflects male anxiety about the power of women, particularly in their reproductive capacities; for this reason, mothers are a common trope of horror films, as seen in movies like *Alien*, *The Brood* (1979), *Rosemary's Baby*, and *Psycho* (1960).

After getting some theoretical context, we watch a film such as James Gunn's horror-comedy *Slither* (2006), that portrays themes of maternity and the monstrous. In *Slither*, an alien being comes to earth and proceeds to impregnate a woman who later gives birth to many parasitic slugs that turn people into zombies. The film explicitly parallels violence against women with the predominantly male activity of hunting for sport, critiques violence against both women and animals—including the practice of eating meat, and makes very strong critiques of the institution of marriage as oppressive to women. The impregnated woman in the story basically becomes a giant womb with terrifying hunger—a horrific image of the mother.

In studying this film, students are assigned to write a paper that examines the themes of the film through the lens of the philosophical essays that we read. The assignment asks them to identify the monstrous females in the story, and explain some of the critiques of patriarchy made in the film using the feminist readings. Students analyze the female monsters using psychoanalytic tools, and try to carefully express the underlying cultural beliefs about women that these female monsters represent. Why are pregnant women and mothers associated with the monstrous? Students examine the liminal status of maternity, and carefully explain how it is related to monstrosity in the cultural imagination. How do these images of women contribute to the oppression of women in our society? How might we change these images in culture, and what more positive images might we substitute for them?

Conclusions

While the specific monsters with which we engage varies from one course to another, the study of monsters in the classroom includes some consistent themes. Monsters are challenges to all of our conceptual systems and the borders that they entail; they are excellent models of difference that can help students to recognize their own conceptual constructions, unconscious beliefs, and underlying values. The work of monsters is described by Braidotti: "thus by blurring the boundaries of differentiation, the monstrous signifies the difficulty of keeping manageable margins of differentiation of the boundaries between self and other."[20] Monsters help us to see the boundaries that we create in forging our identities; borders that are usually invisible to us are made visible and accessible to critique.

While some of these insights gained from studying monsters appear to be metaphysical, the application of these insights is both political and ethical. If monsters show us how difficult it is to keep our boundaries between self and other clean, as Braidotti suggests, then studying monsters is very effective in allowing us to transform and reimagine those borders. Oppressed groups, whether they are "othered" because of gender, race, class, sexual orientation or being differently-abled, are oppressed because they are categorized outside of what is "normal." The monstrous is precisely that which is not normal; monsters are aberrations that call the norm into question. Whether the monsters we study are relevant to literature, feminism, film, technology, or environmental ethics, they all share in common their function as a model of difference, and present students with the opportunity to critically assess their own understanding of identity and that of others. In this way, students learn to become responsible for their thinking and recognize how our conceptual constructions have an impact on the concrete conditions of oppression.

APPENDIX
Philosophy in Literature Syllabus
Dr. Jessica Decker

We will be engaging in reflective philosophical analysis of several literary pieces, including: Kafka's *Metamorphosis*, Shelley's *Frankenstein*, Borges'

Ficciones, Marquez's *A Very Old Man with Enormous Wings*, Philip K. Dick's *Do Androids Dream of Electric Sheep*, and Octavia Butler's *Lillith's Brood (Book One)*. We will read all of these works through the lens of a particular philosophical perspective, and begin our study with a philosophical selection that will provide a framework for structuring our analysis. Upon completion of this course, you will understand the major areas of study within Western Philosophy, and their basic components and modes of questioning: Ethics, Metaphysics, Epistemology, Existentialism, Idealism, Phenomenology, Socratic Method, and Psychoanalysis. Through close textual analysis, classroom discussion, and writing responses to these texts, you will learn how to skillfully use philosophical methods in analyzing literary selections.

Course Requirements

Attendance: After three unexcused absences, grade reductions will be progressively imposed. *Any student with 7 or more unexcused absences will fail the course.* If you must miss a class, please email me so that we can make arrangements for you to make up the work. Absences will be excused for documented illness, or in other appropriate (documented) situations, which will be determined on a case-by-case basis. Work, including quizzes, can only be made up in the event of an excused absence.

Reading: This course requires a substantial amount of reading per week. In order to pass the course, it is imperative that you keep up with the reading at all times. Make sure you give yourself enough time to complete the weekly readings. We will be reading six literary selections, and each of them will be prefaced by a short philosophical piece.

Reading Quizzes: We will be studying short philosophical selections over the course of the semester, paired with our literary readings. There will be a short in-class reading quiz for each philosophical selection (7 total). Quizzes will be true/false, multiple choice, and short essay response. In addition to these graded reading quizzes, there may be short informal reading quizzes on the literary selections at any class meeting. These informal quizzes are used to determine whether or not students are keeping up with the reading. If the class consistently demonstrates adequate reading, these quizzes may be discontinued. Literary reading quizzes will be graded pass/fail.

Philosophical Analyses: After completing our study of each literary piece, each student will write a philosophical analysis that examines the themes of the novel through the lens of our philosophical readings. There are a total of 6 philosophical analyses due during the semester (see schedule). These analyses will be approximately three pages in length each, and will be submitted via "Turn It In" on Cougar Courses. Guidelines for these assignments will be distributed in class.

Cougar Courses Posts: Over the course of the semester, forums will be created that correspond to our class readings and discussions. Forum posts will be due the night before our class meeting, and will be graded pass/fail. There are 12 forum posts total (see schedule), and you may miss *one post* during the semester with no penalty.

Required Texts

Borges, Jorge Luis. *Ficciones*. Grove Press, 1994.

Butler, Octavia. *Lillith's Brood*. Grand Central Publishing, 2000.

Descartes, Rene. *Meditations*. Hackett, n.d.

Kafka, Franz. *Metamorphosis*. Dover, 1996.

Marquez, Gabriel Garcia. *A Very Old Man with Enormous Wings*. Penguin, 2014.

Shelley, Mary. *Frankenstein*. Dover, 1994.

Additional Readings Will Be Provided on Cougar Courses:

Berkeley, George. *A Treatise Concerning the Principles of Human Knowledge*. Hackett, 1982.

Creed, Barbara. Selections from *The Monstrous Feminine*. Routledge, 1993.

Freud, Sigmund. "The Unconscious" (1915).

Hume, "On Personal Identity" from *Treatise of Human Nature*. Oxford University Press, 2000.

Jung, Karl. Selections from *The Portable Jung*. Penguin, 1976.

Singer, Peter. "Equality for Animals" from *Practical Ethics*. Cambridge University Press, 1979.

Schedule of Reading and Assignments

Class 1: Introduction

Class 2: Descartes' *Meditations 1 and 2*
Quiz on Descartes

Class 3: Descartes Discussion
Forum Post Due (#1)

Class 4: Hume, *On Personal Identity*
Quiz on Hume

Class 5: Kafka's *Metamorphosis*
Forum Post Due (#2)

Class 6: Kafka's *Metamorphosis*

Class 7: Kafka's *Metamorphosis*
Forum Post Due (#3)

Class 8: Shelley's *Frankenstein*

Class 9: Shelley's *Frankenstein*
Forum Post Due (#4)

Class 10: Gabriel Garcia Marquez, "A Very Old Man with Enormous Wings"

Class 11: Monsters in Greek Myth: Selections from Homer's *Odyssey* and Greek Mythology
Forum Post Due (#5)

Class 12: Berkeley, Selections from *Treatise on Human Nature*
Quiz on Berkeley

Class 13: Borges, *Ficciones*

Class 14: Borges, *Ficciones*

Class 15: Borges, *Ficciones*
Forum Post Due (#6)

Class 16: Peter Singer, "Equality for Animals"
Quiz on Singer

Class 17: Philip K Dick, *Do Androids Dream of Electric Sheep?*

Class 18: Philip K Dick, *Do Androids Dream of Electric Sheep?*
Forum Post Due (#7)

Class 19: Philip K Dick, *Do Androids Dream of Electric Sheep?*

Class 20: Philip K Dick, *Do Androids Dream of Electric Sheep?*
Forum Post Due (#8)

Class 21: Freud, "The Unconscious"
Quiz on Freud

Class 22: Octavia Butler, *Lillith's Brood*

Class 23: Jung, Selections
Quiz on Jung

Class 24: Octavia Butler, *Lillith's Brood*
Forum Post Due (#9)

Class 25: Selections from Barbara Creed, *The Monstrous Feminine*
Quiz on Creed

Class 26: Octavia Butler, *Lillith's Brood*
Forum Post Due (#10)

Class 27: Octavia Butler, *Lillith's Brood*

Class 28: Film in Class: *Alien* (1979)
Forum Post Due (#11)

Class 29: Discussion of *Alien*

Class 30: Final Class Discussion
Forum Post Due (#12)

Notes

1. Donna J. Haraway, "A Cyborg Manifesto," in *Philosophy of Technology: The Technological Condition*, ed. Robert C. Scharff and Val Dusek (New York: Wiley Blackwell, 2003), 611.
2. *Ibid.*, 615.
3. Maria Mies and Vandana Shiva, "Introduction to *Ecofeminism*," in *Environmental Ethics: Convergence and Divergence*, ed. Susan J. Armstrong and Richard Botzler (New York: McGraw-Hill Humanities, 2003), 429–437.
4. Haraway, 612.
5. *Ibid.*, 613.
6. Margrit Shildrick, *Embodying the Monster: Encounters with the Vulnerable Self* (London: SAGE, 2002), 11.
7. Frederick Turner, "The Invented Landscape," in *Environmental Ethics: Convergence and Divergence*, ed. Susan J. Armstrong and Richard Botzler (New York: McGraw-Hill Humanities, 2003), 294–306.
8. *Ibid.*, 301.
9. Elissa Marder, *The Mother in the Age of Mechanical Reproduction: Psychoanalysis, Photography, Deconstruction* (New York: Fordham University Press, 2012).
10. *Ibid.*, 9.
11. Haraway, 624.
12. Aeschylus, *Oresteia: Agamemnon, Libation Bearers, Eumenides* (Loeb Classical Library) (Cambridge: Harvard University Press, 2009).
13. Philip K. Dick, *Do Androids Dream of Electric Sheep?* (New York: Del Rey, 1996).
14. Peter Singer, "Equality for Animals?" in *Environmental Ethics: Convergence and Divergence*, ed. Susan J. Armstrong and Richard Botzler (New York: McGraw-Hill Humanities, 2003), 323–330.
15. Margaret Atwood, *Oryx and Crake* (New York: McClelland and Stewart, 2003).
16. Marie-Helene Huet, *Monstrous Imagination* (Cambridge: Harvard University Press, 1993), 59.
17. Barbara Creed, *The Monstrous Feminine* (New York: Routledge, 1993).
18. Monique Wittig, "One Is Not Born a Woman," in *The Straight Mind* (Boston: Beacon Press, 1992) and Judith Butler, *Gender Trouble: Feminism and the Subversion of Identity* (New York: Routledge, 2006).
19. Rosi Braidotti, *Metamorphoses: Towards a Materialist Theory of Becoming* (Cambridge: Blackwell, 2002), 196.
20. *Ibid.*, 215.

Part II

Transforming Space
The Monster Roams

Locating Monsters
Space, Place and Monstrous Geographies

Adam Golub

Monsters draw our attention to place.[1] From the geographies that produce monsters, to the public and private spaces that are breached by them, place is in large part what makes monsters scary. There are many reasons why we may be afraid of a monster—its monstrous body, the deepest fears it represents, the malice it wishes upon us—but our dread is greatly amplified when that monster is *in the closet*. Or *under the bed*. When it approaches the *outskirts of town*. Or lumbers *down the street*. Place and monsters—place and our sense of the monstrous—are inextricably intertwined. Teaching monsters thus requires the teaching of place.

In their book *Mapping American Culture*, Wayne Franklin and Michael Steiner write, "Place is a powerful though often unacknowledged condition of experience. Life does not exist in a vacuum: everything takes place, from sweeping historical events … to the most private occurrences."[2] In a similar vein, monsters "take place." On both macro and micro levels, whether they are destroying a city or lurking under the stairs of your home, monsters shape and are shaped by location. Studying monsters provides students with an opportunity to "acknowledge" place, and—to paraphrase geographer Yi-Fu Tuan—to explore the ways in which undifferentiated space becomes fearful place when endowed with monstrous qualities.[3]

In this essay, I simultaneously make the case that space is an important category of analysis in the study of monsters and that teaching monsters can help students think critically about spatiality. The study of monsters, I argue, leads students to examine the values that underlie spatial culture. As Eric Avila reminds us,

> Space … is an arbiter of social relations, and the identities that we inhabit—race, class, gender, sexuality—are codified within a set of spaces that we describe as neighborhoods,

> homes, cities, streets, suburbs, parks, factories, office buildings, freeways, and so on. More than providing a physical setting for the formation of such identities, space—its organization, construction, destruction, and representation—plays an active role in shaping social consciousness.[4]

To study monsters is to study how monstrous identities are codified in certain spaces (Dracula and Transylvania, for instance, or the Creature from the Black Lagoon). It also compels analysis of the organization, construction, destruction, and representation of monstrous space—analysis of what happens to Tokyo when Godzilla rampages, for example, or to the shopping mall when overrun by zombies. In other words, studying monsters requires the *mapping* of social relations: discovering how identities, ideologies, and power dynamics are inscribed on the landscape and transformed by the presence of imaginary beasts. In what follows, I suggest four ways we might conceptualize and map monstrous geographies when teaching monsters in the classroom: (1) monsters and the imagined community, (2) monsters and nature, (3) monsters and the built environment, and (4) monsters and political geography.

In explicating these four frameworks, I draw heavily on my personal experience designing and teaching an upper-division "American Monsters" course in an American Studies department at a large state university. I have found monsters to be an incredibly rich topic of study for the American Studies classroom. As an area of inquiry, American Studies employs an interdisciplinary approach to analyzing U.S. culture, identity, and everyday life. In American Studies classes, students typically examine "how identities are constructed in the encounter with difference, as well as how identities change over time and in response to historical events."[5] In my particular department, we strive to help students cultivate an interdisciplinary sensibility, gain an understanding of cultural diversity, and think critically about their own culture in the past and in the present. These learning goals are all readily addressed by a monsters class (in fact, in my first semester course evaluations, one student wrote, "I've learned the most I ever have about American Studies because of this course"). The monster is a culturally constructed identity that is the direct product of social ideas about difference and diversity. The monster is also historically determined; it speaks to issues, fears, and anxieties that pervade particular time periods. Further, studying monsters requires students to interact with a range of cultural artifacts—literature, film, television, performance art, folklore—and to interpret them while drawing on a variety of disciplinary and interdisciplinary perspectives, including anthropology, sociology, psychology, history, cultural studies, and—as I discovered when I taught the class for the first time—geography.

I did not originally intend my "American Monsters" course to focus so much on space and place. Initially, my main goal was to create a seminar that gave advanced undergraduates and graduate students an opportunity to analyze monsters as windows onto particular historical moments, from the colonial era to the present, and to see how imaginary creatures resonated with social concerns in the past.[6] However, as my inaugural semester proceeded, I quickly realized that the texts I assigned and the subsequent discussions we had about these narratives repeatedly converged on the theme of spatiality. Where these monsters came from, where they went, the landscapes they threatened and changed—time and again, these details mattered in uncovering what exactly made these monsters scary and what made them resonate in specific historical eras. Halfway through the semester, I decided to focus more intentionally on space and place in order to make "American Monsters" as much a primer on cultural geography as it was a primer on monsters and the monstrous.

The pedagogical strategies offered in this essay reflect both actual classroom practice as well as strategies I have developed for future iterations of the course. I should also note that the frameworks I present in the following pages should not be seen as four discrete analytics, but as overlapping schemas that can be used to teach theories of space and place using monsters. As I hope will become clear, the frameworks interrelate and build on one another in giving students the tools to think critically about spatial culture.

Monsters and the Imagined Community

A guiding premise of my course is that monsters, broadly conceived, are threats to community, however that community may be imagined. If, as Benedict Anderson suggests, communities are imagined places of comradeship, constructed and maintained by shared ideas about what unites all of the members within that community, then monsters are necessarily conceived as antithetical to that image of communion.[7] Indeed, in the 1995 book *Skin Shows*, J. Jack Halberstam writes that the monster "represents many answers to the question of who must be removed from the community at large."[8] Halberstam goes on to argue that "monsters are defined both as other than the imagined community and as the being that cannot be imagined as community."[9] Monsters exist on the borders of community. They are unwelcome, unwanted, and presumably unassimilable. In monster narratives, writes John Edgar Browning, "exteriority (that which is *out there*)" connotes "inferiority (that which is *undesirable*)."[10]

On a fundamental level, then, studying monsters helps students identify criteria for community membership: who or what belongs in a particular place at a particular time? What constitutes the familiar and the strange, the normal and the abnormal, the loyal and the dangerous when it comes to fraternity or residency? Who is native and who is foreign? Who is a "good" citizen? Who is undesirable? Why do monsters belong in certain places and not in others? What kind of threat to the community—local, national, or global—do they embody? Studying monsters can help students think about the policing of places and their boundaries. Through monsters students can interrogate cartographies of belonging.

I introduce students to the concept of imagined communities in the first few weeks of the course, assigning excerpts from Halberstam's book and teaching Anderson's main tenets through short lecture. This provides us with a theoretical framework for analyzing monsters throughout the semester, establishing community as a recurring theme in our inquiry. Of course, laying this foundation also focuses students' attention on space and place from the outset. I find that a community framework for interpreting the meaning of monsters is especially helpful when working to situate monsters in historical context. Whether we are studying sea serpents in the colonial era, the Headless Horseman in antebellum America, reanimated corpses in the progressive era, or giant radioactive ants in the early cold war, focusing on imagined community helps students think about the ways in which specific monsters threaten particular configurations of national identity in different time periods. Whatever monster we study, in whatever era, I ask students to think about how that monster might pose a challenge to certain social, cultural, and political boundaries established by a given imagined community—again, be it local, national, or global.

By way of example, consider the cultural resonance of the monster Dracula in the 1930s. The 1931 film adaptation of Bram Stoker's novel appeared in the midst of profound debates over who belonged in the ideal community of "America" in the 1930s. Though set in Europe, I explain to my students, *Dracula* nonetheless spoke to and for American anxieties about race, class, and ethnicity in the interwar period. When analyzing the cultural work of this film version of *Dracula*, I have students consider the broader historical context of racism and ethnocentrism in the early 20th century: public anxieties over immigration, miscegenation, and declining white birth rates; the nadir of race relations, with widespread racial violence and discrimination against African Americans; and governmental policies directed at eastern and southern European immigrants and other ethnic minorities that were justified by the scientific racism of eugenics. *Dracula*, I tell students, can be read as a commentary on who did and did not belong in the imagined American community of the 1930s.

To help students contextualize *Dracula*, I assign a chapter from Kendall Phillips' book *Projected Fears: Horror Films and American Culture*. Phillips helpfully situates the film within dominant cultural themes of the time period—race, science, religion, economics, and immigration. "Appearing at a moment when virtually all the categories of American life were suddenly uncertain," writes Phillips, Dracula "embodies this uncertainty—the chaos towards which the world seemed to be slipping."[11] Dracula appears in an era when the *imagined* foundations of American national identity—capitalism, Christianity, and whiteness—all seemed to be in crisis in light of the Great Depression, the Scopes Trial and ongoing debates over science and religion, and anxieties about "race suicide" (the fear that Anglo-Saxons were demographically and culturally in decline). Into this "broader cultural turmoil" comes a malevolent, supernatural, foreign bloodsucker who personifies a "rupture in the fabric of civilization."[12]

When discussing *Dracula*, I ask students to think about the multiple ways in which the vampire is depicted as "other" and therefore undesirable as a member of the imagined community. Dracula is coded as "dramatically foreign" through his strange appearance, his extreme dialect, and his peculiar mannerisms.[13] He is from Eastern Europe and he has migrated to England. He is not Christian. He is not interested in assimilating; in fact, he is more focused on converting Londoners to his lifestyle, so to speak. Taken together, these qualities suggest that "Dracula represented a greatly magnified version of the underlying fear of the immigrant other."[14]

In the 1930s, the Prince of Darkness was scary in part because he symbolized monstrous exteriority. Both the film and the monster can be read as what Halberstam calls a "fiction of the foreign, a narrative of who and what is ... not-native."[15] In nearly every conceivable way, Dracula was not-native and therefore he posed a threat to the normative imagined community. The 1931 film clearly suggests that there are national places (England in the film, the United States by proxy) and private spaces (Dracula, after all, enters the bedroom of an unsuspecting white woman to mix his blood with hers) where monsters and the foreignness they embody do not belong and must not be allowed to enter.

Monsters and Nature

Monsters tend to inhabit places we deem "natural," wild, and untouched by human culture. Monsters often live in "lairs deep underground ... or in watery places like marshes, fens, or swamps. Or else they infest distant wildernesses of which people are afraid, like mountain tops, oceans, glaciers, or jungles."[16] Such habitats, of course, make up their own kind of imagined community. As William Cronon observes, nature is not inherently set apart from humanity, it is a "human creation" comprised of the things we *choose* to label as "wilderness."[17] Monsters can therefore help students think about the ways in which "natural" spaces are culturally constructed. Studying how nature creates monsters provides students with an opportunity to consider how humans create nature.

I devote a section in my "American Monsters" course to the topic "Monsters of Nature." As we analyze monsters like Bigfoot, King Kong, the werewolf, and the Creature from the Black Lagoon, I engage students with larger questions about the construction of nature as both mythic and monstrous geography. What exactly makes a place wild or uncivilized? How do we mark certain natural spaces as benign or sublime and others as dangerous? When and how does wilderness become scary? How do we justify the preservation or elimination of natural areas, the taming of "wild" beasts, and the exploitation of natural resources? How do our beliefs about nature shape our assumptions about monstrosity?

I find *King Kong* (1933) to be an especially useful text for considering these questions, in part because it explores (and blurs) the imagined boundaries between civilization and the wild, between the so-called civilized and the primitive. As Cynthia Erb argues, the "nature/culture dynamic" is "central" to the King Kong story.[18] The movement of the plot proceeds from nature (the beaches and jungles of Skull Island) to culture (New York City). Skull Island is uncharted, located somewhere off the coast of Africa, and is home to prehistoric beasts and a "primitive" native tribe. New York, by contrast, is depicted as the apex of civilization, with the film's climactic scene taking place atop the Empire State Building (at the time, the world's tallest building). King Kong is a curiosity of nature, an *exaggeration* of nature, unusual for his size (25 feet tall) and his singularity (he appears to be the only one of his kind). For this reason, the white American filmmaker, Carl Denham, wants to capture him—first on film, and then by force—in order to take him back to the United States and display him in a Broadway theater as the "Eighth Wonder of the World." Denham is presumably the representative of culture, though he is not necessarily an ambassador of high culture. He is more a standard bearer for imperialist mass culture; *King Kong* illustrates the processes through which supposedly uncivilized places, peoples, and creatures are made into ethnographic spectacle for consumption by those who see themselves as superior. In fact, Denham arguably represents what Erb calls an "aggressive Western male gaze" that seeks to conquer and commodify the exotic.[19]

King Kong's depictions of Skull Island and Manhattan—and of Kong and Denham by extension—challenge conventional ideas about the separation between nature and culture. Both landscapes can be read as potentially monstrous, depending on how we interpret monstrosity in the film. Who is the real monster, King Kong or Carl Denham? Is Kong a savage beast or just a mistreated animal? The giant ape's affection for Ann Darrow humanizes him and elicits audience sympathy, but at the same time the film's overtly racialized depictions of Kong suggest that his desire for this white woman is unnatural and he should be punished. Scott Poole points out that the original *King Kong* "readily made use of white supremacist imagery, tapping into centuries of white folklore about Africans and apes and the alleged hypersexuality of black men."[20] Yet, as Erb reminds us, the film also "encourages identification with King Kong as a rather mysterious animal figure, whose domain is violated by an arrogant white male exploration filmmaker."[21] The narrative's main messages about nature, culture, and monstrosity, in other words, are complicated and often contradictory.

In addition to exposing—and helping students interrogate—the constructedness of categories like nature/culture, monsters can be used to examine how humans impose their will upon "natural" environments and their "uncivilized" inhabitants. Tales of frontier monsters in borderline places, be it on earth or another planet, can disclose attitudes about proper use of the land, its inhabitants, and its natural resources. Oftentimes, taming a frontier means containing or eliminating frontier monsters. As Poole argues, "mastery over the monster represents mastery over the … landscape itself."[22] Studying monsters can therefore reveal the ways in which humans not only inscribe ideologies onto landscapes, marking them as natural or not, but also attempt to conquer, control, and exploit these landscapes once they are so-named.

King Kong helps students to think about how humans construct nature through perspective, language, and ideology, and how they subsequently attempt to impose their will on nature depending on how it has been imagined. On the voyage to Skull Island, Denham says, "There's something on that island no white man has ever seen.… If it's there, you bet I'll photograph it." Asked by the ship's first mate, Jack Driscoll, what he will do if the "thing" does not like to be photographed, Denham replies, "Well, now you know why I brought along those cases of gas bombs."[23] In *King Kong*, the "primitive" is wholly a "human creation," constructed by the western imagination, documented by the visual/commercial culture of photography, and subsequently taken by force (guns, gas bombs, and chains). Throughout *King Kong*, first on Skull Island and then in New York City, westerners continually *take aim* at the giant gorilla, both through their cameras and their guns.[24] *King Kong* is the tale of a monster of nature that needs to be disciplined—its image managed, its wildness contained—in order to accommodate the cultural tastes of the "civilized."

I explain to my students that we could similarly study the politics of encounter with monsters in other natural places and spaces. We might consider Jaws and the beachside resort of Amity, for instance, or the genetically engineered dinosaurs on the island of Jurassic Park, or the extraterrestrials and the marines on the planet LV-426 in *Aliens* (1986). Once again, in all of these cases, the monster's place matters, and foregrounding it creates opportunities to contemplate larger cultural questions about environmentalism, exploration, imperialism, and consumerism.

Monsters and the Built Environment

Monsters often *end up* in places they do not belong. Their presence in familiar places—places constructed and inhabited by humans—generates new meanings for those places. Monsters thus provide students with an opportunity to examine the mythography of the built environment. How do we attach value to physical structures and non-natural landscapes? What social, cultural, economic, and emotional capital do we attach to places like the farmhouse, the school, and the shopping mall? What then happens when zombies overrun the farmhouse or the mall, or when vampires live underneath the high school? What changes? How effective are these places at protecting us from our deepest fears? How effectively have we fortified ourselves, and from what?

When discussing the built environment in my monsters course, I explain to students that just as we do with "nature," we inscribe meanings onto the human constructions all around us. The built environment—from fences and roads to houses and skyscrapers to parks and playgrounds—can be read as a "physical projection of ... systems of cultural organization ... the concrete expressions of complex ideologies."[25] When monsters enter and occupy the built environment, familiar systems of social and cultural organization are altered. For instance, the high school in American culture is the concrete expression of ideologies concerning education, opportunity, and coming of age. The high school is the embodiment of a culturally sanctioned rite of passage, a supposedly nurturing space designed by adults to help adolescents acquire knowledge, maturity, and civic responsibility. However, when monsters enter, either as students or as teachers—think *Buffy the Vampire Slayer* (1997–2003), *The Faculty* (1998), or *I Was a Teenage Werewolf* (1957)—the secondary school is transformed from a safe space into a place of danger, a place where "the problems that teenagers face become literal monsters."[26] Adults in school-ground monster narratives are often blamed for "turning innocent teenagers into monsters."[27] Indeed, for teenagers in such stories, the "horror of becoming a [monster] often correlates with the dread of becoming an adult."[28] Monsters, in other words, end up disturbing both the physical space and the ideological function of the school. Reading monsters in relation to the built environment, just like reading them in relation to nature and imagined communities, can help students think more critically about spatiality and how it shapes everyday life.

An especially helpful text for teaching about monsters and the built environment is Richard Matheson's *I Am Legend*. Place is central to this particular narrative. The action of Matheson's 1954 book—about a man who appears to be the sole survivor of a vampiric pandemic—takes place primarily in a suburban home in the outskirts of Los Angeles. As Kyle Bishop observes, the house that Robert Neville barricades himself inside is "the second most important character" in the novel after the protagonist himself.[29] I teach *I Am Legend* by situating it in the context of the rise of the suburbs in the 1950s. In the postwar United States, the suburban home signified middle-class success and cold war security; it was a symbol of the family ideal and the achievement of the American Dream. On the day we discuss *I Am Legend*, I have students read short excerpts from Elaine Tyler May's book *Homeward Bound: American Families in the Cold War Era*, where she writes, "amid a world of uncertainties brought about by World War II and its aftermath, the home seemed to offer a secure private nest removed from the dangers of the outside world."[30] Of course, as I point out, critics like Betty Friedan and William Whyte argued that the suburban home could also be viewed as a source of unhappiness, for housewives who may have felt trapped within the trappings of success (as Friedan argues in *The Feminine Mystique*) or for Americans who may have felt they were sacrificing individuality for the creature comforts of conformity (as Whyte argues in *The Organization Man*).[31] Moreover, the discriminatory real estate covenants that were prevalent in the postwar era ensured that many suburban housing areas remained homogenous enclaves of white residents. Before we even start discussing *I Am Legend*, we explore the ways in which the built environment of suburbia was (and remains) the physical projection of a tapestry of complex ideologies concerning race, gender, family, security, and individualism.

After we have explored this historical context, I ask students to consider how monsters transform suburbia and its attendant meanings in *I Am Legend*. This generates rich discussion about the book's various inversions of suburban stereotypes. For instance, in *I Am Legend*, the suburban home becomes a trap not for a clichéd unhappy wife, but for a miserable, lonely widower. Along similar lines, the self-reliant Neville may have finally achieved individualism in suburbia, but it is by circumstance—he is the last man on earth—not by choice. Furthermore, the suburban home is still depicted as "a secure private nest," but it provides more anxiety than comfort; Neville cannot leave his house at night because the world outside is waiting to kill him. Most significantly, in a majority population that has turned vampire, Neville now stands out as the minority and the "other." He has also become a monster, a menace to the reimagined suburban community—he spends his days, after all, killing nests of sleeping vampires. After the apocalypse, the white male Neville is the one who does not belong in the neighborhood. As Deborah Christie points out, Neville "has become the threat, the virus, the social contaminant that must be removed like a tumor before the social body can re-form and heal."[32] Robert Neville is literally homeward bound because vampires have turned postwar suburbia from the epitome of the American dream into an American nightmare.

By identifying the specific ways in which *I Am Legend* disrupts the traditional meanings attached to suburbia, students not only learn how to analyze the construction of monstrous spaces (what makes familiar places scary?), but to interrogate the larger role of the suburbs as physical place, cultural symbol, and imagined community. *I Am Legend* gives students an opportunity to consider how the built environment can reinforce dominant ideologies and shape social relations in the United States. Once again, learning about monsters becomes a means to examine larger questions about identity, culture, and spatiality.

Monsters and Political Geography

The final way in which monsters can prompt students to think about space and place is through the prism of geopolitics. Certain monsters come from certain nations and are products of those nations' histories and international relations. Monsters can "embody the historical structures and trajectory" of a nation.[33] Through the study of monsters, we can revisit and reexamine global geographies of imperialism and war, of immigration and diaspora, of commerce and trade, of economic development and deprivation. How do monsters reinforce, revise, or subvert what Melani McAlister calls our "moral geographies" of the world, the "cognitive maps" we use to understand various nation-states and to articulate and claim our own national interests?[34] How do monsters, in a sense, memorialize tragedy and acts of violence that have taken place on national landscapes?[35] How do monsters and their meanings travel and change across borders; how are they reimagined and received in different countries and cultures?

Certain monsters, such as Godzilla, connect readily to political geography. The cultural work of Godzilla as a monster cannot be understood properly without locating the creature squarely in the context of Japanese history and the history of U.S.–Japan relations. Godzilla is more than just a scaly, green, fire-breathing behemoth with a distinctive roar; it is an allegory, a "self conscious attempt to deal with nuclear history and its effects on Japanese society."[36] When I teach Godzilla, I make sure students have basic knowledge about World War II, Hiroshima and Nagasaki, *hibakusha* (atom bomb survivors), and the Lucky Dragon (a Japanese finishing boat that was caught in the fallout of a U.S. hydrogen bomb test in 1954). These historical reference points help students analyze Godzilla as a "catastrophic allegory," one that is intertwined with the history of Japan as well as the broader history of war, imperialism, technology, and racism in the 20th century.[37]

When we begin discussing Godzilla, I remind my students that the Japanese director of *Gojira* (1954), the very first Godzilla movie, intended his film to be a political statement about the use of nuclear weapons: "We naively hoped that the end of Godzilla was going to coincide with the end of nuclear testing" he once said in an interview.[38] This helps my students identify the various allusions to geopolitics that can be found in the 1956 U.S. version of *Gojira*, titled *Godzilla, King of the Monsters!* (more on why I assign this version in a moment). For example, the film opens with a thinly veiled reference to the Lucky Dragon incident: the crew aboard a Japanese freighter witness a flash over the horizon that engulfs the boat in flames. Godzilla, we soon learn, is a dinosaur from the Jurassic period that has been "disrupted from its habitat" beneath the ocean floor and "transformed by nuclear testing."[39] The visual depiction of the monster's destruction of Tokyo evokes the destruction of Hiroshima and Nagasaki. Even Godzilla's appearance resonates with Japan's nuclear history: the monster's skin is "thick and furrowed like the keloid scars that afflicted the survivors of Hiroshima and Nagasaki."[40] As Aaron Kerner observes, atomic anxieties "are woven into the visual allegory of Gojira's body."[41]

As I mentioned earlier, I ask students to screen the U.S. version of *Gojira* ahead of our discussion. *Godzilla, King of the Monsters!* was released in the United States two years after the original and it marked the first exposure American audiences had to the monster. *Godzilla* was essentially a heavily re-edited version of *Gojira* containing 30 additional minutes of footage that was shot in a studio in Los Angeles. The U.S. version inserts an American journalist, Steve Martin (played by Raymond Burr), into the story, making him the narrator and privileging his point of view. *Godzilla* splices Martin, often clumsily, into footage from *Gojira* as if he is there with the Japanese characters, talking with them and observing key scenes. In addition to providing new footage, the American version also notably excises some key scenes and dialogue.

Of course, in screening the U.S. version first, my students are unaware of these changes. In class, I show them excerpts from the original *Gojira* to compare and contrast so we can discuss how Godzilla becomes Americanized in the 1956 iteration. For instance, the U.S. version augments Godzilla's reported size; the monster is described as being 150 feet tall in *Gojira*, but it grows to 400 feet in *King of the Monsters!* More glaringly, references to U.S. nuclear testing that appeared in the original film are cut. "Virtually all sections of the original film that might have reflected negatively on the United States, highlighted Japanese resentments arising from World War II, or explored the nuclear issue in any depth," observes William Tsutsui, "were excised or otherwise neutralized in the Americanization process."[42] In *Gojira*, the U.S. exists as the off-screen other, the implied nation state that is responsible for accidentally unleashing the monster because of its nuclear testing. However, in *Godzilla*, Japan becomes the other as a result of the shift in narrative perspective, with the events viewed through the eyes of a white American male. As Kerner writes, "Gojira adopts an allegorical approach to Japan's catastrophic history while American Godzilla films counter that allegory, attempting to neutralize its historical poignancy."[43] When the catastrophic allegory gets in the hands of American filmmakers, "radiation became a gimmick rather than a moral crisis."[44]

"Our monsters register our national traumas," writes Scott Poole.[45] Comparing and contrasting the two versions of the original Godzilla movie helps students consider the ways in which national histories—and national traumas—can shape the cultural production and *reproduction* of monsters. Studying Godzilla also gives students an opportunity to examine space, place, and monstrosity on a global scale, thereby introducing a transnational perspective to our "American Monsters" course. Godzilla was born at the intersection of popular culture and foreign policy; it "embodies both Japan's loss and the United States that inflicted that loss."[46] The atomic monster cannot be fully understood without locating it in this important context of postwar geography and geopolitics.

Conclusion

Monsters redraw maps, and in so doing, draw our attention to geography. Studying monstrous geographies spurs students to *get lost*, to visit places both familiar and strange (as well as places once familiar and now strange), and to theorize and historicize monsters by *locating* them. Studying monsters helps makes visible what Edward Soja calls the "spaciality of social life."[47] Monsters teach students about the meanings we attach to the landscape and the ways in which those meanings circumscribe human relations. Monsters teach students about boundaries, real or imagined, and the consequences of border crossings. Monsters fundamentally help students consider how "culture varies over space."[48] Without question, constructions of monstrosity—our notions of the monstrous body, of monstrous sexuality, of malevolence and monstrous behavior—are all *grounded* and inextricably linked to space and place. Monsters therefore provide us with pedagogical opportunities to explore, map, and critically analyze nature, nations, the built environment, the imagined community, and the politics of international relations. In short, by mapping monsters, we learn to map the contours of our everyday lives.

Appendix
American Studies 428: American Monsters
Fall 2015
California State University, Fullerton

"Dreams and beasts are two keys by which we are to find out the secrets of our nature."—Ralph Waldo Emerson

"There are terrible creatures, ghosts, in the very air of America."—D.H. Lawrence

"The ... monster represents many answers to the question of who must be removed from the community at large."
—J. Jack Halberstam

"In a deeply tribal sense, we love our monsters."—E.O. Wilson

"How many freakin' vampires am I supposed to care about these days?"—Stanley Hudson, *The Office*

Course Description

This upper-division American Studies seminar examines the figure of the monster in American culture. The course provides students with an interdisciplinary framework for analyzing representations of monstrosity in film, literature, television, folklore, popular culture, performance art, and youth culture. Monsters symbolize deviations from the "normal" as it is constructed in American society—they are imagined others who represent transgressions of nature, science, race, gender, sexuality, age, space, place, and/or the body. In this course, we will analyze monsters in context, thinking about the ways in which monsters resonate with broader cultural fears and anxieties in different time periods. In addition, we will consider the ways in which images of monstrosity can reinforce or subvert culturally constructed classification systems (e.g., normal/deviant, natural/supernatural, primitive/civilized). Throughout the semester, we will study how different monsters—and their meanings—have changed over time.

Course prerequisites: AMST 201 or completion of GE section D.3 on American history, institutions, values.

Required Texts

Books

W. Scott Poole, *Monsters in America: Our Historical Obsession with the Hideous and the Haunting*. Waco: Baylor University Press, 2011.

Max Brooks, *World War Z*. New York: Broadway Books, 2006.

Richard Matheson, *I Am Legend*. New York: Tor Books, reissue 2007, orig. 1954.

Charlaine Harris, *Dead Until Dark (Sookie Stackhouse, #1)*. New York: Ace, 2008

There will also be a number of assigned articles for this course, available on Titanium as web links or downloadable PDF files. Consult the course schedule for the list of readings.

Films/TV Episodes

Frankenstein (dir. James Whale, 1931)
The Bride of Frankenstein (dir. James Whale, 1935)
King Kong (dir. Merian C. Cooper, 1933)
Godzilla, King of the Monsters (dir. Ishiro Honda/Terry O. Morse, 1956)
I Was a Teenage Werewolf (dir. Gene Fowler, Jr., 1957)
White Zombie (dir. Victor Halperin, 1932)
Night of the Living Dead (dir. George Romero, 1968)
Dawn of the Dead (dir. George Romero, 1978)
Buffy the Vampire Slayer, Season 1 Episode 1, "Welcome to the Hellmouth" (dir. Charles Martin
Smith, 1997) and Episode 2 "The Harvest" (dir. John T. Kretchmer)
Dracula (dir. Tod Browning, 1931)
Blacula (dir. William Crain, 1972)
True Blood, Season 1 Episode 1, "Strange Love" (dir. Alan Ball, 2008)

You are required to view these films *in advance* of our scheduled discussions [see course schedule]. They are available on reserve in the CSUF library (and many are available in the Fullerton Public Library for free loan), or you may acquire them on your own through DVD-rental or digital streaming services (*Buffy*, *White Zombie*, and *Night of the Living Dead* are all streaming on Netflix). You will be expected to discuss these films in written assignments.

Student Learning Goals

- Analyze and evaluate representations of the monster in American culture, and develop an interpretive framework for connecting these representations to their larger cultural and historical context.
- Synthesize theories of monstrosity and apply to a broader understanding

of the ways in which culture constructs, classifies, and codifies ideas about morality, gender, sexuality, the body, race, age, region, religion, and science.

- Understand and interpret the ways in which culture creates meaning and guides behavior.
- Develop a rigorous concept of culture and cultural process as well as an interdisciplinary sensibility, becoming aware of connections among the social sciences and the humanities.
- Learn reading, writing, and expressive skills to see connections among complex materials and to clearly communicate an understanding of the underlying meanings and causes of cultural/historical events and processes.

Course Assignments and Grading Standards

You will write *three papers* for this course. The papers will challenge you to analyze primary cultural sources and connect them to their historical and scholarly context.

The scholar Gene Wise has written that the practice of American Studies requires one to have a "connecting imagination." Think of each paper as an opportunity to exercise your "connecting imagination."

Each paper should be 6–8 pages in length (8–10 pages for graduate students). All papers should be double-spaced, 12-point font, with 1-inch margins. Acceptable citation styles include Chicago, MLA, APA—whichever you are most comfortable and familiar with. Title pages are not necessary; include a heading on your first page.

Paper #1 Monsters of Science and Nature

Analyze a primary source of your choice that engages with the theme of monsters of science and/or monsters of nature. The source should be a *mainstream popular text*—a film, television show, novel, or video game. Write a paper in which you describe the text you have chosen and explain how it connects to the longer history we have studied of monsters of science and nature. Then, analyze your text as an image of monstrosity, employing *one or more* of the monster theories we've discussed. No additional outside academic research is required. However, you MUST integrate material from *Monsters in America, at least two* of the scholarly articles we read in Unit II, and *at least two* of the films we discussed in Unit II.

Possible mainstream popular texts: *The Blob*, *Sharknado*, *Jurassic Park* (film or novel), *Edward Scissorhands*, any of the Frankenstein films, *Jaws* (film or novel), *The Descent*, *Creature From the Black Lagoon*, *Congo* (film or novel), *The Mist* (film or novella), King Kong remakes, *Teen Wolf*, *X-Files* episodes such as "Post-Modern Prometheus," "Quagmire," "Schizogeny" … and so on.

Paper #2 Zombie Culture

Analyze a primary source of your choice that engages with the theme of zombie culture. The source can either be a *mainstream popular text* (a film, television show, novel, or video game) OR an *ethnographic source* (interview/observation [participation if you so choose] with a performance, fan community, etc.). **If you choose a popular text for paper #2, you MUST chose an ethnographic source for paper #3, and vice versa. For your last two papers, one must analyze a mainstream popular text, and the other must analyze an ethnographic source.** Write a paper in which you describe the source you have chosen and explain how it connects to the longer history we've studied of zombie culture. Then, analyze your source as an image of monstrosity, employing *one or more* of the monster theories we've discussed. No additional outside academic research is required. However, you MUST integrate material from *Monsters in America*, *World War Z*, *at least three* of the scholarly articles we read in Unit III, and at least two of the films we discussed in Unit III.

Possible mainstream popular texts: *The Walking Dead*, any of the Romero sequels or remakes of his films, *iZombie*, the comic book *Afterlife with Archie*, *Fido*, *Warm Bodies*, the film version of *World War Z*, the novel *Generation Dead*, the novel *Dead City*, The *Zombie Survival Guide*, the novel *Zone One* ... endless possibilities here.

Possible ethnographic sources: Go to the Long Beach Zombie Walk Festival; attend a *Walking Dead* season premiere viewing party or observe real-time social media response to it; visit an online fan community related to a specific aspect of zombie culture; interview fans of some aspect of zombie culture; interview someone who writes zombie fan fiction ... and so on ....

Paper #3 Vampires in America

Analyze a primary source of your choice that engages with the theme of vampires in America. The source can either be a *mainstream popular text* (a film, television show, novel, or video game) OR an *ethnographic source* (interview/observation [participation if you so choose] with a performance, fan community, etc.). **If you choose a popular text for paper #3, you MUST chose an ethnographic source for paper #2, and vice versa. For your last two papers, one must analyze a mainstream popular text, and the other must analyze an ethnographic source.** Write a paper in which you describe the source you have chosen and explain how it connects to the longer history we've studied of vampires in America. Then, analyze your source as an image of monstrosity, employing *one or more* of the monster theories we've discussed. No additional outside academic research is required. However, you MUST integrate material from *Monsters in America*, *I am Legend*, *Dead Until*

Dark, *at least one* of the scholarly articles we read in Unit IV, and *at least two* of the films/TV shows we discussed in Unit IV.

Possible mainstream popular texts: any of the Dracula films; *Twilight* (book/s or film/s), *Buffy the Vampire Slayer*, *The Lost Boys*, *Vampire Diaries*, *Salem's Lot*, *Scream Blacula Scream*, *True Blood* (TV series), *Interview with a Vampire* (film or Anne Rice book series) … seemingly infinite possibilities here.

Possible ethnographic sources: attend a *Vampire Diaries* season premiere viewing party or observe real-time social media response to it; visit an online fan community related to a specific aspect of vampire culture; interview fans of some aspect of vampire culture; interview someone who writes vampire fan fiction … and so on …

Additional Assignment for Graduate Students

M.A. students are required to read *one additional book* for the course, selected in consultation with the instructor from the list below, and write a 6–8-page response paper that 1) summarizes AND evaluates the author's main argument and methodology and 2) ties the book into larger themes/issues/questions examined in the course. The paper may be turned in anytime but is due no later than *December 2*.

M.A. Student Reading Options

Carole Clover, *Men, Women, and Chain Saws: Gender in the Modern Horror Film* (1992)

J. Jack Halberstam, *Skin Shows: Gothic Horror and the Technology of Monsters* (1995)

Harry M. Benshoff, *Monsters in the Closet: Homosexuality and the Horror Film* (1997)

James B. Twitchell, *Dreadful Pleasures: An Anatomy of Modern Horror* (1985)

Elizabeth Young, *Black Frankenstein: The Making of an American Metaphor* (2008)

William Tsutsui, *Godzilla on My Mind: Fifty Years of the King of Monsters* (2004)

Eric Greene, *Planet of the Apes as American Myth: Race and Politics in the Films and Television Series* (1996)

Joshua Blu Buhs, *Bigfoot: The Life and Times of a Legend* (2009)

Brian Regal, *Searching for Sasquatch: Crackpots, Eggheads, and Cryptozoology* (2011)

Sarah Juliet Lauro *The Transatlantic Zombie: Slavery, Rebellion, and Living Death* (2015)

Kyle William Bishop, *American Zombie Gothic: The Rise and Fall (and Rise) of the Walking Dead in Popular Culture* (2010)

Course Schedule (subject to revision)

Date	*Topic/Reading Due*	*Paper Due*
W, Aug. 26	**Introduction to Course**	
	I: FOUNDATIONS: THEORY AND EARLY HISTORY	
W, Sep. 2	**Studying Monsters, part 1: Analyzing Monsters in Context** • W. Scott Poole, *Monsters in America*, Preface and Introduction [monsters are born out of history…] • Kendall R. Phillips, "Introduction," *Projected Fears: Horror Films and American Culture* (2005), 1–10. [monsters resonate with cultural anxieties and concerns…] • Heather Urbanski, "The Cautionary Tale," from *Plagues, Apocalypses, and Bug-Eyed Monsters: How Speculative Fiction Shows Us Our Nightmares* (2007), 5–18. [monsters offer a cautionary tale…]	
W, Sep. 9	**Studying Monsters, part 2: Theorizing Monstrous Bodies and Boundaries** • Jeffrey Jerome Cohen, "Monster Culture (Seven Theses)," from *Monster Theory: Reading Culture* (1996), 3–25. [monsters signify…] • John Edgar Browning, "Towards a Monster Pedagogy: Reclaiming the Classroom for the Other," from *Fear and Learning: Essays on the Pedagogy of Horror*, ed. Aalya Ahmed and Sean Moreland (2013), 40–55. [monsters make visible our classification systems…] • J. Jack Halberstam, "Parasites and Perverts: An Introduction to Gothic Monstrosity," from *Skin Shows: Gothic Horror and the Technology of Monsters* (1995), 1–15. [monsters represent threats to the imagined community…]	
W, Sep. 16	**Early American Horrors** • Washington Irving, "The Legend of Sleepy Hollow" (1819) • Nathaniel Hawthorne, "Young Goodman Brown" (1835) • Harriet Prescott Spofford, "Circumstance" (1860) • W. Scott Poole, *Monsters in America*, Ch. 1, "Monstrous Beginnings," and Ch. 2, "Goth Americana"	

Date	*Topic/Reading Due*	*Paper Due*
	II: MONSTERS OF SCIENCE AND NATURE	
W, Sep. 23	**Frankenstein** • Watch *Frankenstein* (1931) • Watch *The Bride of Frankenstein* (1935) • W. Scott Poole, *Monsters in America,* Ch. 3, "Weird Science" • Elizabeth Young, "Here Comes the Bride: Wedding, Gender, and Race in *Bride of Frankenstein,*" in *The Dread of Difference: Gender and the Horror Film*, ed. Barry Keith Grant (1996), 309–337	
W, Sep. 30	**King Kong and Godzilla** • Watch *King Kong* (1933) • Watch *Godzilla, King of the Monsters* (1956) • W. Scott Poole, *Monsters in America*, Ch. 4, "Alien Invasions" • Cynthia Erb, "A Showman's Dream: The Production and Release of *King Kong,*" from *Tracking King Kong: A Hollywood Icon in World Culture* (2009), 21–57. • Aaron Kerner, "*Gojira* vs. *Godzilla*: Catastrophic Allegories," from *Ritual and Event: Interdisciplinary Perspectives*, ed. Mark Franko (2007), 109–124. • Chon A. Noriega, "Godzilla and the Japanese Nightmare: When *Them!* Is Us," from *Hibakusha Cinema: Hiroshima, Nagasaki and the Nuclear Image in Japanese Film*, ed. Mick Broderick (1996), 54–74.	
W, Oct. 7	**The Werewolf and Bigfoot** • Watch *I Was a Teenage Werewolf* (1957) • James B. Twitchell, "Dr. Jekyll and Mr. Wolfman," from *Dreadful Pleasures: An Anatomy of Modern Horror* (1985), 204–227. • Thomas Doherty, "The Horror Teenpics," from *Teenagers and Teenpics: The Juvenilization of American Movies in the 1950s* (2002), 115–144. • Brian Regal, "Crackpots and Eggheads," from *Searching for Sasquatch* (2011), 7–29. • Joshua Blu Buhs, "Camping with Bigfoot: Sasquatch and the Varieties of Middle-Class Resistance to Consumer Culture," *The Journal of Popular Culture* 46:1 (February 2013), 38–58.	
	III: ZOMBIE CULTURE	
W, Oct. 14	**The Transnational Zombie** • Watch *White Zombie* (1932) • Chera Kee, "'They Are Not Men.... They Are Dead Bodies': From Cannibal to Zombie and	**PAPER #1 Due by midnight Friday, October 16,**

Date	*Topic/Reading Due*	*Paper Due*
	Back Again," from *Better Off Dead: The Evolution of the Zombie as Post Human*, ed. Deborah Christie and Sarah Juliet Lauro (2011), 9–23. • Ann Kordas, "New South, New Immigrants, New Women, New Zombies: The Historical Development of the Zombie in American Popular Culture," from *Race, Oppression, and the Zombie: Essays on Cross-Cultural Appropriations of the Caribbean Tradition*, ed. Christopher Moreman and Cory James Rushton (2011), 15–30. • Start reading Max Brooks, *World War Z* for discussion on 10/28	**via TurnItIn on Titanium**
W, Oct. 21	**The Romero Revision** • Watch *Night of the Living Dead* (1968) • Watch *Dawn of the Dead* (1978) • Kendall R. Phillips, "*Night of the Living Dead* (1968)," from *Projected Fears: Horror Films and American Culture* (2005), 81–100. • Kyle William Bishop, "The Dead Walk the Earth: The Triumph of the Zombie Social Metaphor in *Dawn of the Dead*," from *American Zombie Gothic: The Rise and Fall (and Rise) of the Walking Dead in Popular Culture* (2010), 129–157. • Scott Poole, *Monsters in America*, Ch. 7, "Undead Americans" • Continue reading Max Brooks, *World War Z* for discussion on 10/28	
W, Oct. 28	**Zombie Apocalypse Now** • Max Brooks, *World War Z* • Stephanie Boluk and Wylie Lenz, "Generation Z: The Age of Apocalypse," from *Generation Zombie: Essays on the Living Dead in Modern Culture*, ed. Boluk and Lenz (2011), 1–17.	
	IV: VAMPIRES IN AMERICA	
W, Nov. 4	**Americanizing Dracula** • Watch: *Dracula* (1931) • Watch *Blacula* (1972) • Louis Warren, "Buffalo Bill Meets Dracula: William F. Cody, Bram Stoker, and the Frontiers of Racial Decay," *American Historical Review* 107:4 (October 2002), 1124–1157. • Kendall R. Phillips, "*Dracula* (1931)," from *Projected Fears: Horror Films and American Culture* (2005), 11–33.	
W, Nov. 11	**NO CLASS—VETERANS DAY**	**PAPER #2 Due by midnight via**

Date	*Topic/Reading Due*	*Paper Due*
		TurnItIn on Titanium
W, Nov. 18	**Dead and Undead in Suburbia** • Watch *Buffy the Vampire Slayer*, Season 1 Episodes 1 and 2, "Welcome to the Hellmouth" and "The Harvest" (1997) • Richard Matheson, *I Am Legend* (1954) • Scott Poole, *Monsters in America*, Ch. 6, "Haunted Houses"	
W, Nov. 25	*Thanksgiving Recess*	
W, Dec. 2	**Love, Sex, and Coming Out of the Coffin** • Charlaine Harris, *Dead Until Dark* • Watch *True Blood*, Season 1 Episode 1, "Strange Love" (dir. Alan Ball, 2008)	
W, Dec. 9	**Conclusion of Course** • Scott Poole, *Monsters in America*, Epilogue	
F, Dec. 18	**Paper # 3 Due via TurnItIn on Titanium**	**PAPER #3 due by midnight Wednesday, December 16, via TurnItIn on Titanium**

Notes

1. An earlier version of this essay was presented at the Inter-Disciplinary.Net 4th Global "Monstrous Geographies" conference in Lisbon, Portugal, on March 22, 2015. I am grateful to my fellow panelists and conference delegates for their helpful comments and feedback.

2. Wayne Franklin and Michael Steiner, "Taking Place: Toward the Regrounding of American Studies," *Mapping American Culture*, ed. Franklin and Steiner (Iowa City: University of Iowa Press, 1992), 4.

3. Yi-Fu Tuan, *Space and Place: The Perspective of Experience* (Minneapolis: University of Minnesota Press, 2001), 6.

4. Erica Avila, *Popular Culture in the Age of White Flight: Fear and Fantasy in Suburban Los Angeles* (Berkeley: University of California Press, 2004), xiv.

5. Lois P. Rudnick, Judith E. Smith, and Rachel Lee Rubin, eds., *American Identities: An Introductory Textbook* (Malden, MA: Blackwell, 2006), 2.

6. At my university, M.A. students can take 400-level undergraduate electives for graduate credit.

7. Benedict Anderson, *Imagined Communities: Reflections on the Origin and Spread of Nationalism* (New York: Verso, 1983), 5–7.

8. J. Jack Halberstam, *Skin Shows: Gothic Horror and the Technology of Monsters* (Durham: Duke University Press, 1995), 3.

9. *Ibid.*, 15.

10. John Edgar Browning, "Towards a Monster Pedagogy: Reclaiming the Classroom for the Other," in *Fear and Learning: Essays on the Pedagogy of Horror*, ed. Aayla Ahmad and Sean Moreland (Jefferson, NC: McFarland, 2013), 52.

11. Kendall R. Philips, *Projected Fears: Horror Films and American Culture* (Westport, CT: Praeger, 2005), 21.

12. *Ibid.*, 21–22.

13. *Ibid.*, 23.

14. *Ibid.*, 24.

15. Halberstam, 15.

16. David D. Gilmore, *Monsters: Evil Beings, Mythical Beasts, and All Manner of Imaginary Terrors* (Philadelphia: University of Philadelphia Press, 2003), 12–13.

17. William Cronon, "The Trouble with Wilderness; or, Getting Back to the Wrong Nature," in *Uncommon Ground: Rethinking the Human Place in Nature*, ed. Cronon (New York: W. W. Norton, 1995), 69.

18. Cynthia Erb, *Tracking King Kong: A Hollywood Icon in World Culture* (Detroit: Wayne State University Press, 2009), 203.

19. *Ibid.*, 62.

20. W. Scott Poole, *Monsters in America: Our Historical Obsession With the Hideous and the Haunting* (Waco: Baylor University Press, 2011), 98.

21. Erb, 2. Harvey Greenberg describes King Kong as the "quintessential victim of media exploitation" in "*King Kong*: The Beast in the Boudoir, or 'You Can't Marry That Girl, You're a Gorilla!'" in *The Dread of Difference: Gender and the Horror Film*, ed. Barry Keith Grant (Austin: University of Texas Press, 1996), 349.

22. Poole, 43.

23. *King Kong*, directed by Merian C. Cooper (1933; Turner Home Entertainment, 2007), DVD.

24. Cynthia Erb talks about the camera/gun trope in *Tracking King Kong*, 61–64.

25. Peter Bacon Hales, "Topographies of Power: The Forced Spaces of the Manhattan Project," *Mapping American Culture*, 252.

26. Rhonda V. Wilcox and David Lavery, "Introduction," *Fighting the Forces: What's at Stake in Buffy the Vampire Slayer*, ed. Wilcox and Lavery (New York: Rowman & Littlefield, 2002), xix.

27. Don G. Smith, "Teenage Monsters and Their Meaning," in *Images of Youth: Popular Culture as Educational Ideology*, ed. Michael A. Oliker and Walter P. Krolikowski (New York: Peter Lang, 2001), 108.

28. Rhonda Wilcox, *Why Buffy Matters: The Art of Buffy the Vampire Slayer* (New York: I. B. Tauris, 2005), 18.

29. Kyle William Bishop, *American Zombie Gothic: The Rise and Fall (and Rise) of the Walking Dead in Popular Culture* (Jefferson, NC: McFarland, 2010), 105.

30. Elaine Tyler May, *Homeward Bound: American Families in the Cold War Era* (New York: Basic Books, 1988), 3.

31. Betty Friedan, *The Feminine Mystique* (New York: W. W. Norton, 1963); William Whyte, *The Organization Man* (New York: Simon & Schuster, 1956).

32. Deborah Christie, "A Dead New World: Richard Matheson and the Modern Zombie," in *Better Off Dead: The Evolution of the Zombie as Post-Human*, ed. Christie and Sarah Juliet Lauro (New York: Fordham University Press, 2011), 76.

33. Poole, 21.

34. Melani McAlister, *Epic Encounters: Culture, Media, and U.S. Interests in the Middle East Since 1945* (Berkeley: University of California Press, 2005), 4.

35. On landscape, trauma, and public memory, see Kenneth E. Foote, *Shadowed Ground: America's Landscapes of Violence and Tragedy* (Austin: University of Texas Press, 2003).

36. Chon A. Noriega, "Godzilla and the Japanese Nightmare: When *Them!* is Us," *Cinema Journal* 27.1 (1987): 63.

37. Aaron Kerner, "*Gojira* vs. *Godzilla*: Catastrophic Allegories," in *Ritual and Event: Interdisciplinary Perspectives*, ed. Mark Franko (New York: Routledge, 2007), 109.

38. Qtd in William Tsutsui, *Godzilla on My Mind: Fifty Years of the King of Monsters* (New York: Palgrave, 2004), 33.

39. *Ibid.*, 28.

40. *Ibid.*, 33.

41. Kerner, 110.

42. Tsutsui, 40.

43. Kerner, 110.

44. Tsutsui, 41.

45. Poole, 23.

46. Yoshikuni Igarashi, *Bodies of Memory: Narratives of War in Postwar Japanese Culture, 1945–1970* (Princeton: Princeton University Press, 2000), 117.

47. Edward Soja, "Inside Exopolis: Scenes From Orange County," in *Variations on a Theme Park: The New American City and the End of Public Space*, ed. Michael Sorkin (New York: Hill and Wang, 1992), 122.

48. Michael C. Steiner, "Introduction: Varieties of Western American Regionalism," in *Regionalists on the Left: Radical Voices From the American West*, ed. Steiner (Norman: University of Oklahoma Press, 2013), 3.

White Settlers and Wendigos

Teaching Monstrosity in American Gothic Narratives

BERNICE M. MURPHY

"The fiend in his own shape is less hideous than when he rages in the breast of man."
—Nathaniel Hawthorne, "Young Goodman Brown" (1835)[1]

"Monsters are our children. They can be pushed to the farthest margins of geography and discourse ... but they always return."
—Jeffrey Jerome Cohen, "Monster Culture (Seven Theses)" (1996)[2]

Unleashing American Monsters in the Irish Classroom

Antonia Bird's 1998 historical horror film *Ravenous* begins with two quotes which give us some idea of the film's morbid black humor and the ways in which it will mercilessly—and astutely—critique the doctrine of so-called "Manifest Destiny." The first is Nietzsche's famous axiom "He that fights with monsters should look to it that he does not become a monster" (an observation now rather cheapened by the fact that screenwriters seem contractually obliged to deploy the quote in roughly 95 percent of Hollywood-made serial killer movies). The second quote is more succinct, but, like the film's title itself, tells us much about the story that will now unfold: "Eat Me." As these early clues suggest, *Ravenous* is, at heart, a story about monstrosity and a story about greed—both the greed for land, and the greed for human flesh—and the ways in which these desires come to serve as a powerful metaphor for the ruthlessly expansionist tendencies of the mid–19th-century United States itself. *Ravenous* is so effective in doing this because the form of monstrosity that possesses its battling protagonists, F. W. Colqhoun/Colonel Ives (Robert Carlyle) and John Boyd (Guy Pearce), is arguably one of the most distinctively and suggestively North American of all. By the final moments of the film, both men have been transformed into Wendigos, and while Boyle—squeamish from the start about the dirty business of imperial conquest as well as the consumption of human flesh—attempts to cling to his humanity, his rival has no qualms whatsoever about either activity, preferring in fact to combine them.

This film also highlights the ways I have used monstrosity—and in particular, the intriguing and distinctively North American specter of the Wendigo—as a way of encouraging my students to interrogate the doctrine of "Manifest Destiny," and, in a broader sense, the ways in which place and space are represented in North American horror and gothic narratives. In courses such as "Supernatural Literature," "American Nightmares: Horror in Fiction and Film," and "The American Gothic: Landscapes of Fear," I frequently remind students that early European impressions of the North American landscape continue to resonate up until the present day. Our consideration of the ways that the figure of the Wendigo as both a mythological and psychological construct is depicted in texts such as Stephen King's 1977 novel *The Shining* and Stanley Kubrick's 1980 film adaptation as well as *Ravenous*, and Larry Fessenden's eco-horror classic *The Last Winter* (2006), has proven a useful and provocative means of discussing how the landscape can change colonists, even as they attempt to impose their own will upon a landscape perceived as wild and "uncivilized."

Since the beginning of my teaching career, it has been brought home to me time and again that the discussion of horror and gothic themes and tropes can serve as particularly vivid and pedagogically rewarding means of introducing students to complex issues of American identity, history, and racial and cultural contexts in a manner they find both intellectually challenging and engaging. Classroom discussions of monsters and monstrosity have, for me, often served as a kind of "Trojan horse" for the consideration of ideas that Irish freshman students by and large fairly unfamiliar with American history and literary culture might otherwise find—at least initially—somewhat intimidating, or inaccessible, like would-be settlers encountering a seemingly alien landscape for the first time.

One of the keystones of our current Junior Freshman curriculum here in the School of English, Trinity College Dublin, is a team-taught module entitled "American Genres." "American Genres" is a 12-week survey course that is designed to introduce students to the origins and development of American literary culture, with a particular emphasis being placed on 19th-century figures such as Poe, Hawthorne, and Melville. Students will previously have been exposed to a very limited range of pre–20th-century American writers. As the "American Genres" course also has an important contextualizing function, we also try to incorporate the basics of colonial American history and subsequent major historical events into the course on a week-to-week basis, interweaving this historical focus with lecture-based explorations of the core texts, themes, and authors.

I begin my contribution to the course by delivering a lecture on Mary Rowlandson's 1682 captivity narrative, "The Sovereignty and Goodness of God." One of the reasons I have found Rowlandson's harrowing first-person account to be so useful in both this module, and other, more advanced and specifically gothic-focused modules, is because it foregrounds in such a visceral and memorable fashion the often fraught relationship between the white settler and the "howling," wilderness in which they find themselves. Students are always favorably impressed by the immediacy and sheer vividness of Rowlandson's prose style—by the way she economically but effectively conveys, for instance, the horror she felt when the peace and perceived security of her home village of Lancaster, Massachusetts, was suddenly shattered one early morning in February 1676. Indeed, Rowlandson's account has an occasionally lurid, and at times, genuinely poignant intensity that arguably remains as affecting today as it was over three hundred years ago. The text also very usefully opens up discussions of both the practical and psychological effects of the European colonization of the so-called "New World" and foregrounds considerations of the way in which the colonial "other" is represented. It is for this reason I emphasize that Rowlandson, in a very literal sense, genuinely believes herself to be surrounded by monsters from the moment that her settlement is attacked. Indeed, when Rowlandson is taken captive and removed from all that is safe and familiar, she is experiencing the worst-case scenario for the white settler in North America. As she herself recounts, "I had often before this said that if the Indians should come, I should choose rather to be killed by them than taken alive, but when it came to the trial, my mind changed. Their glittering weapons so daunted my spirit that I chose to go along with those (as I may say) ravenous Beasts, than at any moment end my day."[3] It is the reluctant trek into the unknown—and here, the unknown is both a geographical and a psychological state—that terrifies Rowlandson most, and with good reason. As Melanie Perrault notes, "The Puritans who established the Massachusetts Bay colony were particularly concerned about the possibility of becoming wild in the American wilderness. Only a thin veneer separated humans from beasts, they believed, and one must remain ever vigilant to avoid letting the inner beast take over."[4] To experience enforced and prolonged exposure to the "howling wilderness" of the Puritan imagination was therefore to also risk much more than losing one's life: it was to risk losing one's *soul*. As I make clear to my students, I see this fear of losing one's rational, daylight, "civilized" and presumably *white* self as being one of the key components within the development of the American Gothic, which is, as Teresa Goddu effectively puts it, "a historical mode operating in what *appears* to be a historical vacuum."[5]

Rowlandson's account is therefore further potent illustration of the fact that the clash between order and chaos, "civilization" and "savagery," lies at the dark heart of American literary culture. Using Rowlandson as a staring point in both this course, and more specialized, senior-level American Gothic related courses, also provides me with a valuable opportunity to underline significant parallels between anxieties and preoccupations found in early American literature and much more recent depictions of monsters and the monstrous, from the slippery moral allegory of "Young Goodman Brown" (himself of course "the chief horror of the scene"[6]) to the ever-increasing legions of middle-class white folks who invariably take a wrong turn on a bad road in the backwoods horror firms of the 1970s and their numerous sequels, remakes, re-boots and spiritual descendants. Student evaluations for the "American Genres" module in particular have consistently highlighted that our freshmen appreciate the fact that the course contains occasional references to tropes that they already recognize from their own pre-existing engagement with American popular culture. In my experience, these references work because they are considered within the context of a rigorously academic framework that maintains the integrity and historical relevance of the canonical texts under discussion.

Reconsidering Monstrosity in The Village (2004): or, How I became an M. Night Shyamalan Apologist

Monsters are, of course fascinating for many reasons, and one of them is the fact that they can operate on several different levels of comprehension at once. First of all, naturally, there is the simple, practical "It's right behind you!" level of exposure to the monstrous (and here we should perhaps remember that one of the roots of the word "horror" is the term "Horripilation," meaning the physical reaction that takes place when your hair stand on end as a result of external stimuli).[7] Then there is the complex combination of cultural, psychological, sexual and historical, even economic factors which all feed into how we view monsters and the monstrous. After all, our conceptions of monstrosity are always—because they have to be—oddly *intimate.*

While I am always wary of the dangers of positing too simplistic a connection between classic literary texts and the much later narratives from a very different historical and cultural context, I have therefore found that exploring commonalities and congruent themes and tropes from more recent texts does help create a sense that the past continues to impact the ways in which we perceive the present in very potent, and not always immediately obvious, ways. Encouraging students to seek out connections between a text's depiction of monstrosity and its historical/cultural context can also help them see a narrative they had perhaps previously dismissed or, indeed, actively scorned, in a radically different light. As has always been the case, the monster here actively embodies anxieties and preoccupations that may otherwise have remained deeply concealed or overlooked.

To cite one concrete example from my own teaching experience: I have assigned M. Night Shyamalan's 2004 film *The Village* on my Sophister (Senior) level seminar module "The American Gothic: Landscapes of Fear" on several occasions. The course description is as follows:

> This one-term course will explore the relationship between the individual and their physical environment in American horror and gothic texts from the beginnings of an independent American literary culture to the present day. From the seemingly savage wilderness that confronted the first European settlers to the brutal realities of frontier life and, latterly, the rather different variety of terror found in the urban (and then *sub*urban environments), American authors and filmmakers have displayed a notable fascination with the impact that the landscape has upon those who reside there. This course will explore the many reasons why this is the case, and also consider the differing ways in which horror and gothic depictions of specific geographical and architectural settings serve to dramatize some of the most profound anxieties and preoccupations associated with the American way of life and American history.

Without fail, at the beginning of each term in which the film is assigned, there are at least two or three students who good-naturedly but vocally express their disdain for both *The Village* specifically, and Shyamalan's work in general (to be fair, I think in part because many millennials were justifiably aggrieved by his botched 2010 adaptation of *The Last Airbender*). The students who were already predisposed to dislike the film tended to express contempt for the narrative's two pivotal plot twists in particular. However, what has been particularly interesting to witness was the way in which these attitudes tended to evolve as the term progressed. By the time we directly discussed the film, the class had already participated in several weeks of seminar-based discussions about early European conceptions of the North American landscape. They had been encouraged to really think about what wilderness represents on a practical, psychological, and cultural/theological level, and throughout the previous week's classes (and with the extra support supplied by their reading of required background critical material) had been expected to explore the construction of the relationship between "civilized" European settler and supposedly "savage" Native American in a way that has probably not occurred to them before.

The often-tenuous position of the community in the wilderness is a key aspect of the course (and finds echoes in our later discussions of both urban and suburban gothic narratives). *The Village* is always taught the week after we consider seminal small town/village horror stories such as Shirley Jackson's "The Lottery" (1948), H. P. Lovecraft's "The Shadow Over Innsmouth" (1936), and "A Rose for Emily" by William Faulkner (1930). This contextualizing groundwork again means that by the time we begin to discuss the way in which tropes of monstrosity are deployed within Shyamalan's film, students are in a position to re-evaluate the text as a much more potentially interesting and suggestive form of engagement with the nation's very sense of self, and the fact that mechanisms which exclude the perceived "other" are often central to the construction and lasting endurance of the community.

As some readers may be aware, the very existence of a seemingly utopian community featured in *The Village* hinges upon an audacious lie supported by a non-existent "monstrous" threat whose presence is used as a rationale for the settlement's peculiar isolation and insularity. Crucially, for the first half of the film, the viewer, like the community's youngsters, is led to believe that not only is it 1897, but that the "Covington Woods" in which the village lies are inhabited by dangerous creatures referred to, in one of the narrative's many telling euphemisms, as "those we don't speak of."[8] There apparently exists a tenuous truce between the elders of the community and the creatures, which depends upon the strict enforcement of clearly defined territorial boundaries. In an obvious echo of the garrison mentality of the early English settlers in the New World, the woods that tightly enclose the neatly cultivated fields and wooden houses of the settlement are not to be entered under any circumstances, lest an intrusion provoke the creatures to invade and slaughter everyone. There are even occasional animalistic screams heard in the distance, a detail that slyly evokes the "howling wilderness" so feared and loathed by the likes of William Bradford and Rowlandson. Indeed, as Lauren Coats et al. note in their excellent article on the film, "In building his utopia, Professor Edward Walker has chosen to replace Indians—those terrifying lurkers in the woods, those who have language but not one that the dominant white culture understands, those whose primitive responses to bold colors and supernatural ability to sense good and evil intentions frighten us and mark otherness—with monsters."[9]

What might seem to some students as a laughably unconvincing evocation of monstrosity—the "creatures," though initially only briefly glimpsed, are notably unscary and fake looking—is in fact a reflection of the fact that this is, in actuality, a film about the process by which "monstrosity" is strategically manufactured as a means of preserving the status quo, and preserving community identity and cohesion. It is no coincidence either that Edward Walker, both the brains and the money behind the community in the first place, was, in a previous life, a professor of American history. In this notable instance, therefore, the relationship between the community in the wilderness and the "monsters" that supposedly terrorize them is a great deal more interesting—and worthy of critical notice—than may first seem to be the case. At the end of each term in which I have taught this module, the student evaluation forms invariably contain several comments along the following lines: "I really wasn't looking forward to studying *The Village*, but it proved to be a lot more relevant and interesting than I had anticipated." In effect, their pre-existing hostility towards a text has been at least partially eroded, and their take on the film's depiction of monstrosity has definitely been significantly complicated. (Any desire to find a silver lining in Shyamalan's even more critically slammed follow-up, *The Happening* [2008], may prove more difficult to achieve, in that it is, justifiably, widely considered to be one of the worst Hollywood releases of the 2000s. Having said that, however, the plant-related apocalypse posited in the film has in fact come in useful when discussing the current eco-horror renaissance in both this course and my postgraduate "American Nightmares: Horror in Fiction and Film" module. I do not anticipate assigning *Lady in the Water* [2006] anytime soon, however). In this particular instance, then, in-depth and historically-grounded discussion of the specific role that constructions of monstrosity perform within the narrative have invariably encouraged students to reconsider their own preconceived ideas about a text they may well have previously dismissed.

Why Wendigos?

As noted earlier, however, it is the figure of the Wendigo in particular that has proven to be the most interesting American monster featured in my classes. This is in part because the Wendigo conforms so beautifully to so many of the existing critical definitions of monstrosity. As Cohen notes in "Thesis III" of his seminal disquisition on monster culture, "the Monster always escapes because it resists easy categorization.... They are disturbing hybrids whose externally incoherent bodies resist attempts to include them in any systematic structuration. And so the monster is dangerous, a form suspended between forms that threatens to smash distinctions."[10]

The Wendigo has been useful to me in the classroom because it provides such a useful and suggestive means of discussing the relationship between monstrosity and the creation of the United States itself. To begin with, it represents an ideal example of exactly the kind of hybrid, distinction-eroding conception of monster discussed by the likes of Cohen and Asma.[11] Before discussing particular instances in which I have (metaphorically) brought the Wendigo into the classroom, however, it may be useful to very briefly establish just what the Wendigo actually is. The concept has its roots in the folklore of a very distinct subsection of (mainly Northeastern) Native American tribes. As David Gilmore observes, while there are many monsters that haunt the woods of North America, none is more terrible than the specter of the Wendigo.[12] The Wendigo is described in any number of ways in Native American folklore, although some constants do remain: that it is a creature of superhuman size and strength, filled with murderous rage and an unquenchable hunger for human flesh. The Wendigo is vaguely humanlike in appearance, but also overtly monstrous, with bulging eyes and clawed, claw like hands, as well as a heart of ice (one sure way to kill the creature is to melt the heart).[13] The Wendigo is not merely an external threat, however—the most terrifying thing of all about the Wendigo, however, is that humans can, very easily "turn Windigo" themselves—and one sure fire method to achieve this transformation is to eat human flesh.

As Margaret Atwood notes in *Strange Things: The Malevolent North in Canadian Literature*, "Fear of the Windigo is twofold: fear of being eaten by one, and fear of becoming one."[14] Indeed, so-called "Windigo Psychosis" is a controversial and culturally specific psychiatric disorder generally found to be specific to the people of the Northern tribes of the Algonquian-speaking Indians.[15] First studied in detail by anthropologist Morton Teicher in his 1960 monograph *Windigo Psychosis*, the disorder, as Thomas Hay outlines, is marked by the desire to eat human flesh. There were allegedly numerous outbreaks of Wendigo hysteria/melancholia in the Northern United States and Canada right up until the 1950s, and it has been posited that such symptoms derive from the fact that to the Indians, the desire to eat human flesh was seen as incomprehensible except as a result of sorcery or possession by an evil spirit.[16] Having said that, critics such as Lou Marano have also characterized "Windigo Psychosis" as a myth, suggesting that the cases of insanity, murder and cannibalism cited in other accounts of the alleged disorder were in fact motivated by famine and/or other forms of mental disorder.[17] However one chooses to interpret "Windigo Psychosis," there can be no doubt that the folkloric version of the creature offers one of the richest and most suggestive (and distinctively American) visions of monstrosity—and as such, it has proven to be an extremely useful teaching tool.

As a historicist by inclination, I tend to foreground my classes on American horror and gothic texts with critical and historical material that provides a useful context for discussion. When discussing the film *Ravenous* during my "Landscapes of Fear" course, for instance, students will be assigned readings on the historical contexts of Manifest Destiny and the Mexican-American War of 1846–48. In addition, we also spend time discussing the real-life American horror stories that have directly influenced the way in which the Wendigo trope is integrated with the film's historical contexts: the story of opportunistic murderer (and probable cannibal) Alferd [sic] Packer, and the horrific experiences undergone by the Donner Party during their nightmarish enforced sojourn at Truckee Lake during the winter of 1846–70.

The Packer analogue in *Ravenous* is a Scottish prospector named F. W. Colqhoun who shows up at the film's main setting, a run down Cavalry fort, claiming to be a settler who has survived a terrible winter trapped in a cave in the nearby mountains. In an account that also has clear similarities to the fate of the Donner party, Colqhoun claims that his party was led astray by a dastardly guide named "Colonel Ives," whose claim that he knew a shortcut to California led them to become trapped, snowbound for several months. After the increasingly desperate travelers had run out of everything possible that they could eat, Ives, according to this account, murdered and ate two of the party, at which point Colqhoun, who had himself also partaken of human flesh, supposedly fled so that he would not be the next item on the menu. Colqhoun is clearly a figure of some suspicion from the start, not least because George, one of the fort's two Indian servants, insists that Colqhoun is what his tribe (the Objiway) consider to be a "Windigo." George explains in his own language that "a man eats another's flesh and he steals his spirit. And his hunger becomes insatiable. And the more he eats, the more he wants to, and the more he eats the stronger he gets." "George, does this still happen?" the Fort's commander, the affable but skeptical Colonel Hart asks, rather condescendingly, to which George smartly responds, "white man eats the body of Jesus Christ every Sunday." It is not only a fitting response, but an indication of the fact that, in this film, as in several other notable modern versions of the Wendigo tale (such as *The Shining* and the 2013–15 television series *Hannibal*), it is the white man, rather than the Indian, who is seized by outrageous appetites, be they for human flesh, land, or, in recent years in particular, the natural resources contained within the wilderness itself.

Sure enough, after a disastrous trek to Colqhoun's cave, supposedly in order to rescue another survivor from the dastardly Colonel Ives, it becomes clear that the mysterious newcomer is indeed, possessed of an insatiable desire to eat human flesh, and is in fact the murderer of his fellow travelers. What really makes the film fascinating from this point onwards is, as I have already indicated, the way in which the innate monstrosity of the Wendigo becomes a means of explicitly critiquing the aggressive territorial expansion of the United States during the mid–19th century.

It is also interesting to note that Cohen references "Manifest Destiny" both directly and indirectly several times in his definition of monster culture.[18] He also rightly observes that women and nonwhites "have found themselves repeatedly transformed into monsters" by the recorders of the history of the West, who have been "mainly European and male."[19] As noted above, one of the most interesting things about the way the trope of the Wendigo has been used in American horror of the past 40 years in particular lies in the fact that these narratives all feature white men of European descent who are transformed into a distinctively Native American monster. It is a trend that opens up all kinds of fascinating discussions with my students about assimilation, cultural appropriation, and the process of adaptation to the "New World," all of which again come to the fore in Bird's film. Not only does our lead character, Captain Boyd, find himself being forced to drink human blood in order to survive (having been pushed off a cliff by Colqhoun), but Colonel Hart is also transformed into a Wendigo, and when Boyd finally manages to stagger back into the camp, he finds that their new commander is none other than the man who has just tried to kill him, now sporting a cavalry officer's uniform, an American accent and masquerading as the well-respected "Colonel Ives."

In its own distinctively gory and morbidly witty way, *Ravenous* transforms a figure straight out of Indian folklore into an extremely resonant metaphor for the transformation of the United States into an imperial power.[20] "Colonel Ives" intends to transform the fort into a slaughterhouse for the many eager settlers who will pass through the territory on their way to the seemingly endless possibilities represented by the West. Throwing out terms like "Manifest Destiny," and "Westward expansion" as he gazes out at the mountain range that will (literally) provide him and his fellow Wendigos with their new meal ticket, Colqhoun/Ives, makes his greedy agenda clear: "We just need a home. And this country is seeking to be whole. Stretching out its arms, and consuming all it can. And we merely follow."

As *Ravenous* also illustrates, studying the figure of the Wendigo in American horror and gothic narratives further encourages students to consider the relationship between White "civilization" and Native American "savagery" that they will already have encountered in the likes of Rowlandson's captivity narrative, Charles Brockden Brown's 1799 novel, *Edgar Huntly* (in which a seemingly mild-mannered young gentleman farmer is transformed by a stint in a remote cave into a panther eating, tomahawk wielding, Indian-killing renegade so spattered in gore that his own friends fail to recognize him) and, of course, "Young Goodman Brown." Once you start seeking out the Wendigo—or Wendigo-like transformations—in classic American horror texts, it is even possible to read well-known contemporary texts in an enlightening, new manner. Recent horror texts are still rehearsing themes and tropes present at the very beginning of a distinctively American literary culture. In addition to *Ravenous*, the prime example I discuss with my students, in both in my "Landscapes of Fear" and "Supernatural Literature" modules, is Stephen King's novel *The Shining*, as well as Stanley Kubrick's even more widely known film version, both of which can equally be interpreted as Wendigo-related texts.

Reconsidering The Shining and the Wendigo in Contemporary American Horror

From quite early on in the film's critical history in particular, it has been widely acknowledged that *The Shining* is primarily about a very particular vision of American history, with the hotel standing in as a potent metaphor for the nation itself.[21] This reading is also very much apparent in the novel. As I have outlined in much more detail elsewhere, the figure of the Wendigo can in fact be mapped with considerable success onto the transformation—or rather, process of *degeneration*—undergone by Jack Torrance.[22] The novel in particular emphasizes the fact that the Torrance clan, Jack, his wife Wendy, and their son Danny, like many a party of white settlers before them, are traveling from the safe and secure old world of the eastern United States (Vermont) to the uncertain new opportunities presented by Jack's job offer at the Overlook hotel (Colorado). This move West represents a major step down in terms of income and social status when compared to his previous gig as a teacher and aspiring writer at a fancy Vermont prep school, but also a last chance and opportunity for reinvention.

During the course of the novel, King repeatedly has Wendy's anxious thoughts return to the specter of the Donner party, another group (many of whom were family members) who found themselves snowbound amidst an unforgiving Western landscape. Although the sheer abundance of food available in the hotel is underlined from the very beginning of both versions of the story—Kubrick has Dick Halloran give Wendy a guided tour of the kitchen and the extremely well stocked freezers and pantry, for instance—consumption and, indeed, cannibalism are implicitly emphasized throughout King's novel and Kubrick's film. By making reference to contextualizing historical materials on the Donner party, the mythological origins of the Wendigo, and the "real-life," albeit contentious, disorder of Wendigo psychosis, I encourage my students to piece together for themselves the ways in which Jack's journey from well-meaning if latently violent family man to rampaging, axe-wielding, inarticulate ogre actively engages with this most richly suggestive of American monsters.

It also helps that the Wendigo has in recent years had a much higher profile within American popular culture than was the case when *The Shining* was first published or *Ravenous* was released. Perhaps the most fascinating use of the Wendigo since *Ravenous* can be found in the work of Indie horror writer/director Larry Fessenden, for whom the creature has become of particular significance in providing a means of dramatizing the very real sense of ecological crisis that now exists in the face of climate change. The Wendigo first surfaces in his film *Wendigo* (2001), but becomes even more significant in his thematically similar climate change horror movie *The Last Winter* (2006), which deserves to be considered one of the most despairing and politically significant American horror films of the new millennium. (Fessenden also directed a 2008 episode of the horror anthology TV show *Fear Itself* which featured a Wendigo-possessed rancher, and can therefore be seen as a kind of companion piece to the films).[23] In *The Last Winter*, the Wendigo becomes a metaphor for the dire consequences of the kind of greed, resource stripping, and cavalier attitude towards the natural world that has long defined the colonial attitude towards the North American wilderness. Fessenden's recurrent and nuanced use of the Wendigo further illustrates the flexibility and narrative complexity of the trope.

The Wendigo also lurks in the background (more obliquely than in the previous examples, it should be admitted) of Jim Mickle's 2013 remake of the Mexican horror film *We Are What We Are*. Only the original film's core premise—that a family for whom cannibalism is a way of life has been living undetected amongst "normal" society for many generations—is maintained in the remake, but what is particularly relevant here is that in this version, the parallels between flesh-eating and the "pioneer spirit" are, as in *Ravenous*, made resoundingly explicit. The family descends from insular settlers who, again in distinctly Donner party style, were forced to eat one another during a terrible winter of extremity. Now cannibalism has become the foundational ritual of their lives, as well as, it is strongly suggested, a psychological, and perhaps even a supernatural compulsion (although the film is ultimately vague upon that point).

The most prominent depiction of the figure of the Wendigo in contemporary American popular culture, however, can be found in the TV show *Hannibal* (2012–15), show-runner Bryan Fuller's ambitious reimagining of the relationship between Hannibal Lecter (Mads Mikkelsen) and his nemesis, FBI profiler Will Graham (Hugh Dancy). The show manages to be both a prequel to Harris' first Lecter novel, *Red Dragon* (1981)—in that until midway through the third and final season it focused on Lecter's activities before his unique culinary predilections saw him committed to the Baltimore Institute for the Criminally Insane—as well as a mash-up of sorts that both reconfigures and incorporates elements of each of Harris' four Lecter novels to date. In this version of the story, as in previous outings, Lecter is an elegant, poised gourmand who is ultimately defined by his appetite for human flesh.

Yet unlike Jack Torrance or F. W. Colqhoun/Colonel Ives, he is no savage wild-man, but something much more poised, and much more dangerous. Despite his suave and distinctively Old-World courtesy (as is also revealed in the 1999 novel *Hannibal*, Lecter is a Lithuanian aristocrat, although Mikkelsen is himself Danish), the character's monstrosity is underlined by the fact that from quite early on in the first season, subtly at first, he is allied with the figure of the Wendigo. He repeatedly surfaces in Will Graham's subconscious imaginings as a distinctly familiar looking "Stag Man" with antlers—a detail that directly aligns Lecter's horrific "true" self (at least as perceived by Graham) with Native American folk art representations of the monster, which often highlight precisely this merging of man and beast. Lecter's desire to exert absolute power over others by not only killing them, but also transforming them into exquisitely prepared dishes which he often, then, (like Ives/Colqhoun) foists upon unsuspecting guests further associates the character with the themes of monstrous transformation and unchecked appetite seen in the other Wendigo texts mentioned in this essay.

I always begin my first class in "The American Gothic: Landscapes of Fear" by asking my students to consider the following quote: "If we had less imagination, we would feel more secure."[24] The quote—like the second half of the course title, and indeed much of the module's initial inspiration—comes from the seminal human geography text *Landscapes of Fear* (1979) by Yi-Fu Tuan, whose work on the relationship between human beings and the environment has been of immense importance to all of us working within this increasingly significant area of horror and gothic studies. It seems an ideal starting point for a course which is ideally supposed to allow senior undergraduate students to explore, as the rest of the description puts it, "the relationship between the individual and their physical environment in American horror and gothic texts from the beginnings of an independent American literary culture to the present day." As the texts on the course further demonstrate, monsters, of both a metaphorical and a literal nature, have been at the heart of American literary culture since the earliest days of European colonization (if not before). As Asma notes, "To be a monster is to be an omen. Sometimes the monster is a display of God's wrath, a portent of the future, a symbol of moral vice or virtue, or an accident of nature. The monster is more than an odious creature of the imagination; it is a kind of cultural category, employed in domains as diverse as religion, biology, literature and politics."[25] In my American Gothic classes in particular, then, I have found that consideration of the Wendigo as a folkloric, psychological, and fictional construct has consistently opened up fascinating avenues of discussion in a manner that further supports the veracity of Asma's observation and the critical and pedagogical opportunities presented by this uniquely North American monster. The fact that these classes are also well received by students (and generally attract high numbers) also suggests that they themselves have an appetite for monster-related narratives that underlines the powerful emotional attraction/repulsion of these kinds of texts. Whilst discussion of the figure of the Wendigo forms only one component of my classroom time each year, and a wide range of other monsters also manifest themselves in my classes—including zombies, vampires, psychotic motel owners and geriatric Satanists, to name but a few of the usual suspects—it remains my favorite American monster, not just because serves as such a useful teaching tool when considering sinister representations of place and space, but also because the Wendigo's sinister imprint can arguably be detected across such a wide and revealing range of historical and fictional narratives.

NOTES

1. Nathaniel Hawthorne, "Young Goodman Brown," in *Young Goodman Brown and Other Tales*, ed. Brian Harding (Oxford: Oxford University Press, 2009), 119. Page references are from the 2008 Oxford World's Classics edition.
2. Jeffrey Jerome Cohen, "Monster Culture (Seven Theses)," in *Monster Theory: Reading Culture*, ed. Cohen (Minneapolis: University of Minnesota Press, 1996), 20.
3. Mary Rowlandson, "The Sovereignty and Goodness of God," in *The Mayflower Papers: Selected Writing of Colonial New England*, ed. Nathaniel Philbrick and Thomas Philbrick (New York: Penguin, 2007),169.
4. Melanie Perrault, "American Wilderness and First Contact," in *American Wilderness: A New History*, ed. Michael Lewis (Oxford: Oxford University Press, 2007), 28.
5. Theresa Goddu, *Gothic America: Narrative, History and Nation* (New York: Columbia University Press, 1997), 9.
6. Hawthorne, "Young Goodman Brown," 119.
7. Bridget Cherry, *Horror* (London: Routledge, 2009), 46.
8. My personal favorite is "the old shed that is not to be used."
9. Lauren Coats, et al., "Those We Don't Speak Of: Indians in The Village," *PMLA* 123 (2008): 368.
10. Cohen, 6.
11. Although Asma does argue in the latter stages of *On Monsters: An Unnatural History of Our Worst Fears* (Oxford: Oxford University Press, 2009) that "while in earlier paradigms of monsterology, all hybridization and mixing of forms was considered insidious," in the post-Darwinian era, attitudes evolved as "we came to understand that deviation, variation, mixing and even hybridization are mechanisms of all biology" (274).
12. David D. Gilmore, *Monsters: Evil Beings, Mythical Beasts, and All Manner of Imaginary Terrors* (Philadelphia: University of Pennsylvania Press, 2003), 75.
13. *Ibid.*, 79.
14. Cited by Denise Di Marco, "Going Windigo: The Emergence of the Iconic Monster in Margaret Atwood's *Oryx and Crake* and Antonia Bird's *Ravenous*," *College Literature* 38 (2011): 136.
15. Thomas Hay, "The Windigo Psychosis: Psychodynamic, Cultural and Social Factors in Aberrant Behavior," *American Anthropologist* 73 (1971): 1.
16. *Ibid.*
17. Lou Marano, "Windigo Psychosis: The Anatomy of an Emic-Etic Confusion,"

Current Anthropology 23.4 (August 1982), 385–412. For more background information on the mythological roots of Wendigo lore please see the following: Robert A. Brightman, "The Windigo in the Material World," *Ethnohistory* 35.4 (1988): 338–79; Robert John Colombo, *Windigo: An Anthology of Fact and Fantastic Fiction* (Saskatoon, Saskatchewan: Western Producer Prairie Books. 1982); and Carolyn Podruchny, "Werewolves and Windigos: Narratives of Cannibal Monsters in French-Canadian Voyageur Oral Tradition," *Ethnohistory* 51 (2004): 677–700.

18. See Cohen, 8, 16.

19. *Ibid.*, 15.

20. This is a reading that Di Marco in particular explores in much more detail than I have here.

21. It should be noted that King engages with the idea of the Wendigo in even more overt detail in his 1983 novel *Pet Sematary*, in which the creature is this time characterized as "the dead thing whose touch awakens unspeakable appetites" (London: Hodder and Stoughton, 1989), 413. For more, see J.W. Sears, "Postmodern Gothic: Stephen King's *Pet Sematary*," in *Stephen King*, ed. Harold Bloom (New York: Infobase Publishing, 2007), 167–79.

22. Please see my essay "Going Windigo: Civilization and Savagery on the New Frontier," in *The Rural Gothic in American Popular Culture* (Basingstoke: Palgrave Macmillan, 2013), pp. 108–32, for a much more detailed analysis of the Wendigo motif in *Ravenous*, *The Shining* and *The Last Winter*.

23. "Skin and Bones" (*Fear Itself*, Season 1, Episode 8). Aired July 31, 2008. Fessenden's long-standing fascination with the Wendigo now extends to print and video games as well: in 2016, he curated a collection of Wendigo-related writings entitled *Sudden Storm: A Wendigo Reader* for Fiddleback Press, whilst *Until Dawn* (2015), an interactive survival horror game written in collaboration with Graham Reznick, also features Wendigos.

24. Yi-Fu Tuan, *Landscapes of Fear* (New York: Pantheon Books, 1979), 6.

25. Asma, 13.

Meeting the Monstrous Through Experiential Study-Abroad Pedagogy

KYLE WILLIAM BISHOP

I have taught two literature courses on monsters in the past, one at the University of Arizona and another at Southern Utah University (SUU), but I took very traditional pedagogical approaches with both classes, presenting the novels, short stories, and films as cultural artifacts and examples of important popular entertainment, but doing little with the materials beyond that. I lectured, led group discussions, gave quizzes and exams, and required term papers, yet we as a class never really delved beyond the textual surface of the subject matter. When SUU made a deliberate institutional shift to value and promote experiential and project-based learning, however, I decided to take my pedagogical approach to the monstrous in a decidedly different direction, one that more openly and directly embraced engaged active-learning techniques. Rather than simply talking about monsters and the fear responses great literature and film evoke, I chose to encourage those types of physiological responses from my students directly. After all, as Arthur W. Chickering and Zelda F. Gamson famously stated back in 1987, "learning is not a spectator sport."[1] My efforts for this kind of "fear experience learning" are founded primarily on an interactive, space-based pedagogy.

Because we all experience fear at a physiological level, the best way to teach monsters and the monstrous is through environmentally-based experiential engagement. John Loughran advocates such High Impact Practices, proposing instructors adopt "constructivist teaching," a pedagogical approach that requires learning through practice, or "learning by doing," and claims that by following such a guiding principle, teachers may "seek to ensure that teaching and learning are dynamic and responsive to one another."[2] Yet not all spaces easily support the same kinds of experiences, which is why Ken Bain reminds us "the best college and university teachers create what we might call a natural critical learning environment."[3] These environments can simply be a safe space for students to ask questions and to participate in the learning process, but I find great success—especially when it comes to the study of monsters, monstrousness, and fear—in putting students in *un*safe spaces, at least ones that appear so at first glance.

I propose the best way to teach critical thinking and reading skills comes through emersion in a place-based environment with engaged space-transaction experiences, and these pedagogical approaches can most effectively be brought to bear through the study of horror literature abroad. For the past few years, I have regularly taught a class in the Gothic literary tradition as a study abroad course. The students and I spend two weeks in London and Edinburgh studying *The Castle of Otranto* (Horace Walpole, 1764), *The Strange Case of Dr. Jekyll and Mr. Hyde* (Robert Louis Stevenson, 1886), and *Dracula* (Bram Stoker, 1897). We visit key sites from the narratives, with a particular focus on Gothic, frightening, and uncanny spaces, including Highgate Cemetery, Hampstead Heath, and the Greyfriars Kirkyard. We also participate in walking tours, including both a Jack the Ripper tour of London and the infamous "Double Dead" tour in Edinburgh. These interactive environments bring literature to life—as it were—and, potentially, foment tangible fear responses from students, who then explore and analyze their reactions through group discussions, reflection exercises, and hybrid-style critical essays. My pedagogical experiments teaching horror literature have convinced me that the best college "classrooms" are real-world (or realistically-simulated) spaces that result in transformative experiences and foster practice-based critical thinking and learning.

A Horror-Based Theory of Experiential Pedagogy

Traditional lecture- and seminar-based approaches to teaching art, literature, and film certainly have their place in the modern-day university classroom; however, engaged experiential pedagogies afford students the most effective learning opportunities. In many of the science disciplines, for example, teaching approaches regularly link the more theoretical "book learning" of the classroom with practical, task-based educational experiences in the laboratory. In the liberal arts, on the other hand, students are more often than not limited in their engagement with their subject matter because traditional classroom instruction styles relegate the students to the role of consumers and analysts of texts and narratives created by others. But what if it were possible to transport students out of the classroom and *in* to the books and films they are studying? Such experiential engagement with art, literature, and film is indeed possible, even, to some extent, at a local level, although with most texts, a more substantial class "field trip" would be required—hence the inherent value of a study abroad program that focuses on monsters and the monstrous.[4]

Effective instruction requires a positive learning environment, be it the space of a university classroom, an outdoor lecture amphitheater, or the real-world site of a field trip. Faculty support student learning by controlling the environment as much as possible, providing students with not only the resources necessary to understand the presented material, but also a productive, structured space in which students can work through problems and questions. According to Mark R. Young, "faculty create learning environments that impact students' levels of engagement through their decisions on how the material will be presented, which learning activities will be used, and what kinds of feedback will be provided."[5] From this perspective, then, "environment" must be understood as more than just physical space; it includes teacher/student interactions, class discussions and activities, and the syllabus, homework, and assessment methods. Nonetheless, the *physical* environment cannot be neglected, especially when teachers have some measure of control over those spaces. Bain implores the best college teachers to create "a natural critical learning environment," a space in which students "encounter the skills, habits, attitudes, and information they are trying to learn."[6] While Bain's work focuses on how to make the classroom one of these "natural" spaces—a structured space of modular tables and chairs with effective teaching technology that makes learning as easy as possible—he also references the value of practical case studies, interactive role playing, and field work,[7] the latter of which is obviously most relevant to a discussion of study abroad pedagogies.

"Space-based" pedagogical theory generally addresses the physical layout of classrooms. However, the physical spaces in which teachers instruct their students matter little if learning remains limited to abstract or theoretical discussions of the texts and materials under investigation. Students must also engage directly with the subjects they are attempting to understand. Foundational experiential learning theorist David A. Kolb concisely describes the fundamental and ideal process of knowledge acquisition: "immediate personal experience is the focal point for learning, giving life, texture, and subjective personal meaning to abstract concepts and at the same time providing a concrete, publicly shared reference point for testing the implications and validity of ideas created during the learning process."[8] In other words, application of learning must accompany lectures and discussions; in the liberal arts, this kind of application usually takes the low-level form of exams and essays—which can, of course, be "passed" successfully with little more than surface-level contact with the material—but less often in high-level physical engagement with the texts, their content, and their contexts. The best approach to learning is experiential, for as Kolb reminds us, "ideas are not fixed and immutable elements of thought but are formed and re-formed through experience"; learning is a *process* whereby "concepts are derived from and continuously modified by experience."[9]

The ideal process of student learning involves both a conducive physical environment *and* opportunities to engage directly with the subject matter. The best teachers construct this kind of natural learning environment—both physical and psychological—to transcend the boundaries of the campus classroom. However, while these ideals make perfect sense when discussing disciplines such as chemistry, history, political science, and even realist fiction, how exactly are we, as teachers of the Gothic and other horror narratives, supposed to expose students to the environments and experiences of monsters and the monstrous? How do we give students such a practical, engaged experience in the macabre discipline of horror studies—and do it safely? What is *our* laboratory?

Before moving any further in our discussion of pedagogy, we must first understand how human beings experience horror, be it in the real world or through the simulations of art and literature. Noël Carroll, in his influential *The Philosophy of Horror*, differentiates between "horror," or that which is horrific in the natural world, and "art-horror," or those forms of art that replicate the emotional and physiological reactions of horror.[10] One of the defining characteristics of art-horror, then, is that consumers of a monstrous tale must have an emotional response to the narrative, a response that "run[s] parallel to the emotions of the characters."[11] Carroll, using Jonathan Harker's response to Dracula in Stoker's novel as his case study, describes these emotional responses as shudders, recoil, nausea, repulsion, and, above all, disgust.[12] If students are to understand art-horror through intellectual *and* physical engagement, they need to have an understanding of the physiological functions of fear. They must experience the emotions and physical reactions of horror first-hand, all within a natural learning environment constructed by a mindful instructor.

To provide my students with engaged learning experiences related to classic works of Gothic literature, I take them to real-world, physical locations relevant to both the history of Gothic writers and texts, and to those places and spaces directly mentioned in those works of fiction. Additionally, to help my students understand how art-horror functions at a physiological level, I expose them to varying levels of simulated horror, from reading literature, to dramatic performances, to simulated natural and supernatural events and interactions. To assess the students' level of engagement and success at understanding the emotional responses ideally resulting from art- and otherwise simulated-horror, I assign them personal response papers and have them engage in Socratic seminars and discussions, all culminating in hybrid-style term papers. These deliverables, both subjective and objective in nature, reveal the power of experiential and engaged education in a study abroad situation.

A Place-Based Theory of Horror Pedagogy

Place-based pedagogy is about more than simply designing curriculum with real-world locations in mind; it is a very specific educational ideology that embraces *local* places as sites that have inherent value in the learning process. Eric L. Ball and Alice Lai provide a thorough overview of the movement, explaining place-based pedagogy as an ecohumanist approach to education that grew out of the philosophical teachings of Wendell Berry.[13] Those educators who subscribe to this pedagogical methodology believe that "curriculum and learning objectives are … contingent on the place in question,"[14] and they take advantage of local sites—such as historical buildings, noteworthy landmarks, nearby businesses and artists, and other features of the immediate environment. Granted, the primary point of such a theory of teaching is the local, embracing the neighboring environment as relevant to learning as much as those places described and pictured in textbooks and on the internet, and, thanks to this emphasis, "place-based educators … relativize the focus of their pedagogies and the kinds of materials they include for study with respect to … place."[15] Students recognize what they are studying at a potentially less abstract level in the concrete, real-world community that surrounds them.

Yet, if formal place-based pedagogy relies exclusively upon the local environment, how can we teachers of horror possibly take such an approach with romantic, and especially fantastic, texts? The key lies in locating what aspects of those texts can be found in the real world—after all, Walpole's goal was to imbue traditional romance narratives with realistic elements in his creation of the Gothic subgenre. E .J. Clery explains that "Walpole wanted to combine the unnatural occurrences associated with romance and the naturalistic characterization and dialogue of the novel."[16] In the case of *Dracula*, for example, Stoker repeatedly situates his supernatural vampire in the environs of his contemporary London, places that would have been local referents to his original readers, including the zoo at Regent's Park, recognizable buildings along Piccadilly and in the East End, and nearby communities such as Purfleet in Essex. While the physical world of *Dracula* may be anything but "local" to modern readers, at least initially—especially students from the U.S., who are unavoidably removed from the novel in both time *and* place—that world becomes decidedly *local* when those students travel to London and come to recognize the places signified by Stoker's literary signifiers. Taking a place-based approach to teaching a text such as *Dracula* in London, then, realizes Ball and Lai's ideal that "the inclusion of local texts, artifacts, and performances can in itself be a critical move that implicitly confronts the marginalization of place while simultaneously providing one more route—via consideration of the politics of culture—for more explicitly critical inquiry."[17] Content becomes augmented by context, and students more easily understand the subtleties of a text by seeing it as a concrete, local narrative grounded in a real place.

Because Stoker references so many real locations in *Dracula*, that novel benefits particularly well from a place-based pedagogical approach, which is why my Gothic study abroad course focuses heavily on it. Over the years, I have devised a guided walking tour of key London sites for students, and I shepherd them from place to place as a kind of literary tour guide, integrating readings from Stoker's novel with my students' physical interactions and visitations. I begin the tour at the Hyde Park Corner tube station, where we begin a leisurely stroll east along the densely trafficked Piccadilly street. According to Gill Davies and his work mapping *Dracula* onto contemporary maps of London and the surrounding area for *The Literary London Journal*, Stoker located Dracula's house in this part of London at approximately the same location where the Hard Rock Café gift shop is currently found.[18] Although this tourist attraction is hardly a frightening or inherently Gothic location, students begin to see the reality of Stoker's novel because they are standing in the places he references and describes.

After progressing a bit further east along Piccadilly, I have my students pause on the sidewalk across the street from the Japanese Embassy, and I read aloud the following passage from *Dracula*:

> We got up and walked down Piccadilly. Jonathan was holding me by the arm, the way he used to in old days before I went to school.... I was looking at a very beautiful girl, in a big cartwheel hat, sitting in a victoria outside Giuliano's, when I felt Jonathan clutch my arm so tight that he hurt me, and he said under his breath: "My God!"
>
> He was very pale, and his eyes seemed bulging out as, half in terror and half in amazement, he gazed at a tall, thin man, with a beaky nose and black moustache and pointed beard, who was observing the pretty girl....
>
> "It is the man himself!"[19]

After my recitation, I ask the students to discuss the significance of the passage. As in the traditional university classroom, they usually begin by talking about it in terms of plot, story, and even symbolism, completely ignoring the significance of our physical location—likely because those are the types of formal, text-based responses they have been trained to offer. But then I have the group turn around and look into Green Park, and I ask them what might be significant about Stoker's placement of both Dracula's house and his encounter with Jonathan and Mina on that particular stretch of road in that particular part of London. If they do not realize where we are immediately, I take them into Green Park, at least far enough for them to discern how close we are standing to Buckingham Palace. At that moment, the contextual significance of place comes crashing down upon them, and, quite suddenly, all the colonial significance of Dracula as an invading force that threatens the safety of the Crown comes into sharp relief. They begin to understand Jonathan's extreme physiological reaction to seeing Dracula so close to the seat of government, and they, perhaps, experience a bit of that reaction themselves.

From the Green Park tube station, I accompany my students north by subway to the Archway station, and we hike up the steep hill to Waterlow Park on our way to Highgate Cemetery. In Stoker's novel, Dr. Seward writes in his diary concerning Lucy's death and entombment, recording that her body lies in "a lordly death-house in a lonely churchyard, away from teeming London; where the air is fresh, and the sun rises over Hampstead Hill, and where wild flowers grow of their own accord."[20] In their explanatory footnotes to the Norton edition, editors Nina Auerbach and David J. Skal write, "Stoker probably refers to Highgate Hill, which leads to Highgate Cemetery. One of England's glamor burial grounds, Highgate … [is located] in Hampstead Heath, a rural and romantic suburb of London."[21] We walk through the quiet and peaceful park, noting the fresh air and wild flowers of Stoker's novel, occasionally catching glimpses of London proper in the distance through the trees, until we arrive at the imposing iron gates of Highgate Cemetery. Students can't help but experience the rural romance of the location, and, once behind the gates and inside the antiquated cemetery itself, students certainly feel the effects of a decidedly Gothic environment.

While the east side of Highgate Cemetery is open to the public for a nominal fee, the west side, the portion of the facility featuring a dense jungle of family vaults, mausoleums, and dark foreboding catacombs, is only accessible via guided tour, which must be booked in advance. However, the trouble and expense are worth it, as the experienced guides give students access to all the grandeur of the cemetery, along with contextual and historical information and instruction. If Stoker indeed imagined his Lucy entombed in Highgate, Dr. Seward's description of Lucy's "final" resting place comes into stark focus with a tour of the grounds:

> The tomb in the day-time, and when wreathed with fresh flowers, had looked grim and gruesome enough; but now, some days afterwards, when the flowers hung lank and dead, their whites turning to rust and their greens to browns; when the spider and the beetle had resumed their accustomed dominance; when time-discoloured stone, and dust-encrusted mortar, and rusty, dank iron, and tarnished brass, and

> clouded silver-plating gave back the feeble glimmer of a candle, the effect was more miserable and sordid than could have been imagined. It conveyed irresistibly the idea that life—animal life—was not the only thing which could pass away.[22]

While access to the cemetery after dark is prohibited, students can nonetheless imagine themselves navigating its choked pathways with Van Helsing, seeking out the Westenra family mausoleum. Although I have not done it yet, students could be given an assignment to take a photo of the tomb that most thoroughly manifests Stoker's description of "time-discoloured stone, and dust-encrusted mortar, and rusty, dank iron, and tarnished brass, and clouded silver-plating" for later analysis or even a friendly contest. At the very least, though, I do have students write subjective response and reflection essays, exploring how their visit to the cemetery has affected their engagement with and understanding of the novel.

From the famed cemetery, I lead students down Highgate Hill and through an idyllic residential area to the southern tip of Hampstead Heath, a large, verdant park north of London. To enhance *Dracula*'s verisimilitude, Stoker's novel includes a newspaper article attributed to the *Westminster Gazette* titled "A Hampstead Mystery," which reads as follows:

> The neighbourhood of Hampstead is just at present exercised with a series of events.... During the past two or three days several cases have occurred of young children straying from home or neglecting to return from their playing on the Heath. In all these cases the children were too young to give any properly intelligible account of themselves, but the consensus of their excuses is that they had been with a "bloofer lady." It has always been late in the evening when they have been missed, and on two occasions the children have not been found until early the next morning.[23]

The Heath is lush and dense, and students quickly recognize how easily a child might get lost—or worse, abducted—in the thick bushes and wild patches of forest. Ideally, it would be most effective to return to Hampstead Heath after dark to play a game of "bloofer lady" along the dark forest pathways, an activity I hope to facilitate with my next batch of students.

My "*Dracula* Walking Tour" takes most of a day in London, and, after the fact, I ask students to compose two informal response and reflection papers about their engagement with the real-world, "local" places. In these responses, the students generally talk about how the novel "came alive" thanks to their actually being in the places mentioned and described by Stoker. Students are better able to imagine what things might have been like in Stoker's day, giving *Dracula* the kind of realism expected from a Gothic novel in Walpole's tradition. However, as papers are a relatively traditional and potentially bland form of assessment, I will take a new approach in the future. As all my students now carry smartphones with both photographic and cinematic capabilities, a far more engaging and "active" learning activity would be to have students document their day in pictures, be they static or moving. They could spend the evening and next day engaged in "digital storytelling," creating multimedia photo essays to document their experiences and make visual rhetorical arguments about the value of the tour and how their insights into the novel may have changed as a result of the hands-on interaction with the physical world of *Dracula*. I will certainly take such an approach the next time I conduct this monstrous tour.

Space Transaction and Experiential Learning

Because the Gothic is as much about mood, tone, and atmosphere as it is about physical locations—not to mention emotional and physiological responses—the pedagogical emphasis of this kind of interactive study abroad program must not only be on *place*, but also on those *spaces* that include environmental factors beyond simply the relevant sites. Bain explains how "we construct our sense of reality out of all the sensory input we receive,"[24] and, as Carroll has demonstrated above, sensory input is particularly essential in the study of horror narratives. This input comes primarily from our surroundings, and Kolb emphasizes that learning involves a *transaction* between students and their environment, a transaction that "implies a … fluid, interpenetrating relationship between objective conditions and subjective experience, such that once they become related, both are essentially changed."[25] Learning results from such changes; however, since the world of the monstrous—particularly the *supernatural* monstrous in a text such as *Dracula*—doesn't exist in the real world, a monstrous environment must be simulated. Through spatial performative narratives, such as plays and dramatic guided tours, students can gain access to environmental sensory insights into art-horror and the Gothic literary tradition by way of their own fear responses to external stimuli.

Spatial transactions transcend the imaginary confines of a book or even a film by forcing an audience to engage in an actual physical environment; in the realm of horror narratives, this engagement has unavoidable emotional and physiological consequences. For Carroll, art-horror itself *is* an emotion; he explains how "an occurrent emotional state has both physical and cognitive dimensions. Broadly speaking, the physical dimension of an emotion is a matter of felt agitation. Specifically, the physical dimension is a sensation or a feeling. An emotion, that is, involves some kind of stirring, perturbation, or arrest physiologically registered by an increase in heartbeat, respiration, or the like."[26] When students engage in art-horror, they ideally experience emotional and physical reactions, and Carroll emphasizes that this resulting emotional state—primarily fear—must be correlated with some kind of physical agitation.[27] Many of my efforts while abroad seek to have my students better understand the nature of art-horror by exposing them to just this kind of physical—and psychological—agitation.

My most recent group of students was able to attend a performance of Stephen Mallatratt's Gothic play *The Woman in Black*, directed by Robin Herford, at the Fortune Theatre in London's West End, a performance that quite effectively induced a fear response from us thanks to a variety of theatrical conventions.[28] The Fortune Theatre is quite a small space, and my students and I were able to enjoy the intimacy of the second row, from which we could look directly up at the imposingly sloped stage. The action of the play takes place in a mostly deserted old theater; therefore, the physical environment of the performance was identical to the physical environment inhabited by us as the audience. To enhance the antiquated and uncanny mood, the set was sparse, with limited set dressing and a single framed doorway; the rest of the stage was painted black and left unadorned. When Arthur Kipps stepped on stage as Julian Forsyth, he was in our immediate vicinity, and Antony Eden, who played the actor, was initially seated in the audience, enhancing the verisimilitude of the performance and making us feel as if we were watching a real interaction instead of a performance.

Yet the fear responses we experienced (and enjoyed) while watching *The Woman in Black* were facilitated by more than just the excellent acting of the two performers; Herford employed a variety of theatrical conventions to frighten those of us entranced in our seats. The play repeatedly inundated us with dense fog from beneath the stage, sudden assaults on our senses from loud noises and bright lights, and the unexpected appearance of a spectral ghost, despite the fact that no such character was linked to an actor in the playbill. This engagement with our sensory perception startled us—at one point causing one of my students to scream loudly in terror—and imbued us with a real sense of physical danger. Might we, too, be victims of the play's malevolent spirit, her gaunt and diseased face following us home after the performance to murder those closest to us? Carroll argues, "Art-horror is primarily identified in virtue of danger and impurity," and, unlike in the real-world, fiction requires a suspension of disbelief to convince the body that the dangers and impurity are real.[29] In other words, in regards to art-horror, what is feared is merely a *thought*, but the human imagination is enough to induce a physiological response that is essentially indistinguishable from real danger or impurity.[30] Indeed, in their personal responses to the play, my students discussed how they had almost considered the action real and found themselves genuinely frightened on the walk back from the theatre in the dark.

Our experiences with psychological and physiological fear responses were further facilitated by participating in the "Original Jack the Ripper Murders Tour" under the guidance of Lindsay Siviter, an established Jack the

Ripper researcher, author, and member of the historical Whitechapel Society.[31] Primarily, I had the students go on the tour to enhance their understanding of Stevenson's *Dr. Jekyll and Mr. Hyde*, as both deal with monstrous crimes committed at night on the dark streets of London, but the tour in general and Siviter's efforts in particular afforded us a good opportunity to experience Carroll's sense of "physical agitation."[32] Our guide used not only descriptive words to paint a picture of the infamous Whitechapel murders, but she also affected a dramatic tone and used an intense verbal delivery. More importantly, she enhanced the real-world locations with photographs of what the sites had looked like in Jack the Ripper's day, helping us to fuse the "now" with the "then" and complete our immersion in her spatial performance. Most importantly, though, Siviter provided us with historical photographs of the crime scenes and murder victims, one of which she sensationally warned us about before letting us see, due to its abject and disturbing nature. Those on the tour were visibly upset and physical disgusted by the information and visuals as they experienced actual, not just simulated, fear responses.

Our performative walking tour experiences reached a satisfying zenith in experiential (art-)horror when I subjected my students to "The Double Dead Walking Tour" of Edinburgh's South Bridge Vaults, its Covenanter's Prison, and the Greyfriar's graveyard.[33] Unlike the other tour, one steeped in history, the Double Dead tour caused us all to have tangible fear responses thanks to a particularly dramatic set up, a masterful guide, genuinely frightening locations, and some raw theatrics. For starters, the tour's website sets participants up for a fearful experience with its sensational declaration that the tour is "not suitable for pregnant women [or] those with a heart condition."[34] As a tour limited to those over 12 years of age (and the sober), it markets itself as serious adult entertainment.[35] We met Ean, a dashing figure in a weathered black leather trench coat, at dusk outside the imposingly gothic St. Giles Cathedral, and he immediately began working his magic. Ean was a masterful storyteller who shared the horrors of historical Edinburgh with us, stories that included abject sanitary conditions, diabolical crimes against the innocent poor, and unjust executions by the hands of a corrupt city government. He also took us to terrifying locations, including the dank and cramped spaces under the city's South Bridge, where Ean's skills as a storyteller merely augmented the fear we already felt in the dark—especially whenever he would turn out his light or jump out at us from behind obstructing pillars or doorways. His verbal warnings about giant rats and toxic condensation certainly added to our sweaty palms, racing heartbeats, and psychological unease.

One thing the Double Dead tour did, in particular, that surpassed the efforts of all of our other experiences concerning fear was to involve the participants directly in the performance. At the very beginning of the tour, Ean had asked the group if anyone was afraid of the dark, and when one of my students tentatively raised her hand, he gave her a flashlight—and also began targeting her as the focus of his efforts to frighten the entire group. Throughout the tour, he would make her enter dark spaces alone, cut her off from the rest of the group, or suggest she was the likely focus of a nefarious spirit. In one of the tightest and most claustrophobic chambers of the South Bridge Vaults, Ean singled out another of my students, asking her to help him reenact a story of seduction, murder, and infanticide. Her face belied her discomfort at the tale, and her role in it, especially when Ean creepily stroked her hair and made a slashing gesture across her neck with his index finger. By singling out individuals in the tour group, Ean was able to personalize his efforts to frighten us all, for we saw ourselves in the individual on display and recognized any of us could be the "victims" of the night's imagined supernatural terrors.

The climax of the tour was certainly the Covenanter's Prison cell, allegedly haunted by the "Mackenzie Poltergeist," a malevolent entity that, according to Ean, targets women especially, often causing them to faint, throw up, or discover cuts, bruises, and even bites on their body the next day, a story supported by a website with images and testimonials.[36] He escorted us all into a roughly 20-foot by 20-foot cell, and he encouraged all the women to stand near the iron gate at the entrance in case they needed to flee any attacks by the Poltergeist. He then told a dramatic tale about how members of other tour groups had been attacked by the ghost in the past, some even being knocked unconscious. All the while, Ean used his flashlight to project the shadow of his hand along the walls of the cell, affecting the appearance and behavior of a large, black spider. Near the climax of his story, he asked my student with the flashlight to come closer to him in the doorway (to which she initially responded "No thank you!"), and right after she did, a man in a distorted mask jumped around the corner of the vault's entryway, causing everyone in the room to shriek with fright. Although the tactic was essentially a cheap "jump scare," it was extremely effective—a number of my students were visibly shaken, and we had to walk around Edinburgh for some time talking about less troublesome things until they were calm enough to retire for the evening.

By placing my students in the spaces of horror and in proximity to imagined monsters, they came to understand the nature of not only the literary subgenre under investigation but also their real-world engagement with fear. After having participated in a number of performative events and activities that resulted in the physiological responses discussed by Carroll, my students were better able to discuss how readers react to horror texts and find meaning in those reactions as a vital, cathartic engagement with the imaginative. They explored these findings and their significance via additional personal response papers, not to mention the more organic discussions we engaged in as a class, most notably over dinner at the appropriately themed Frankenstein bar and restaurant on George IV Bridge in Edinburgh. Taking my students to the places featured in the Gothic narratives we were studying was one positive result of our study abroad experience; however, putting them in the *spaces* of the monstrous was perhaps even more effective, as they were then forced to personalize the subgenre through actual experience and not merely vicariously through the art-horror of Gothic literature.

Because fear is an emotion people must learn to confront and overcome, it remains an important area of study for the humanities and liberal arts. The monsters produced by a culture or society reveal the most pressing concerns and anxieties of that particular time and place, and such a focus of study teaches students not only about those historical contexts but also about themselves and their engagement with the present world around them. Kolb emphasizes, "*Learning is the process whereby knowledge is created through the transformation of experience*,"[37] and my approach to teaching monsters and the monstrous has certainly transformed my students. However, simply experiencing a place is not enough to engage learning on a deeper, more transformational level.[38] Students also need the guidance of a dedicated and knowledgeable instructor to ensure the effectiveness of the experience, and those experiences must be followed by additional learning activities and more traditional assessment methods. While taking my students to London and Edinburgh to study the local places and Gothic spaces of classic literature was transformative, the learning process is not complete until they have had opportunities to respond to those experiences and I, as their instructor, have been able to assess the measure of their learning. While space limitations prevent me from exploring assessment in this essay, a combination of experiential engagement and traditional assignments and assessments are nonetheless essential to providing students with a rich and rewarding educational experience. But it all begins with the experience, experiences we should be affording our students at every opportunity.

NOTES

1. Arthur W. Chickering and Zelda F. Gamson, "Seven Principles for Good Practice in Undergraduate Education," *AAHE Bulletin*, March 1987, 3.

2. John Loughran, "Pedagogy: Making Sense of the Complex Relationship between Teaching and Learning," *Curriculum Inquiry* 43.1 (2013): 121.

3. Ken Bain, *What the Best College Teachers Do* (Cambridge: Harvard University Press, 2004), 47.

4. I do recognize that study abroad programs require a great deal of planning, coordination, and funding, but many of the teaching methods and activities I share in this essay could be redesigned and reapplied at the local level at minimal cost to the institution and the students.

5. Mark R. Young, "The Art and Science of Fostering Engaged Learning," *Academy of Educational Leadership Journal* 14, Special Issue (2010): 5.

6. Bain, 99.
7. *Ibid.*
8. David A. Kolb, *Experiential Learning: Experience as the Source of Learning and Development* (Englewood Cliffs, NJ: Prentice-Hall, 1984), 21.
9. *Ibid.*, 26.
10. Noël Carroll, *The Philosophy of Horror: Or, Paradoxes of the Heart* (New York: Routledge, 2010), 12.
11. *Ibid.*, 17.
12. *Ibid.*, 17 and 22.
13. Eric L. Ball and Alice Lai, "Place-Based Pedagogy for the Arts and Humanities," *Pedagogy: Critical Approaches to Teaching Literature, Language, Composition, and Culture* 6.2 (2006): 262.
14. *Ibid.*, 273.
15. *Ibid.*, 275.
16. E.J. Clery, "The Genesis of 'Gothic' Fiction," in *The Cambridge Companion to Gothic Fiction*, ed. Jerrold E. Hogle (Cambridge: Cambridge University Press, 2002), 24.
17. Ball and Lai, *Pedagogy: Critical Approaches to Teaching*, 275.
18. Gill Davies, "London in *Dracula*; Dracula in London," *The Literary London Journal* 2.1 (2004), last modified August 21, 2014, http://www.literarylondon.org/london-journal/march2004/davies.html.
19. Bram Stoker, *Dracula*, ed. Nina Auerbach and David J. Skal (New York: W.W. Norton, 1996), 155.
20. *Ibid.*, 159.
21. *Ibid.*
22. *Ibid.*
23. *Ibid.*, 159.
24. Bain, 26.
25. Kolb, 36.
26. Carroll, 24.
27. *Ibid.*, 25.
28. The play is adapted from Susan Hill's 1983 novella, *The Woman in Black* (New York: Vintage Books, 2011).
29. Carroll, 29.
30. *Ibid.*
31. "Jack the Ripper Tour: A Walk Worth Investigating," *Discovery Tours & Events* (accessed June 13, 2015), http://www.jack-the-ripper-tour.com.
32. Carroll, *The Philosophy of Horror*, 25.
33. "The Double Dead Walking Tour," *City of the Dead* (accessed June 13, 2015), http://www.cityofthedeadtours.com/the-double-dead-walk/.
34. *Ibid.*
35. *Ibid.*
36. Jan-Andrew Henderson, "The Mackenzie Poltergeist," *City of the Dead* (accessed June 13, 2015), http://www.cityofthedeadtours.com/the-mackenzie-poltergeist/.
37. Kolb, 28; original emphasis.
38. Young, 4.

Using Zombies to Teach Theatre Students

PHIL SMITH

In past research, practical and theoretical, I have explored how a hybrid viewpoint taken from the fictions of a zombie apocalypse—partly that of an immersed and self-sufficient survivor and partly that of a distanced audience-scholar—might inform a practice of walking. For this practice, I have drawn on the exploratory urbanist wanders of the mostly Paris-based International Lettristes and Situationist International of the 1950s and 1960s and on subsequent developments in walking arts and performance, with a particular interest in developing a "situational-*dérive*" that seeks to transform space through the very act of walking itself.[1] As part of this ambulatory practice, which I have described at length elsewhere, I have developed a walking in relation to the fictional trajectories of the living dead and compiled taxonomies of zombie spaces.[2]

My *dérive*-based walking practices have included informal exploratory wanders of familiar and unfamiliar places, seeking out their multiple layers of materials and meanings and looking for connections to different meshworks of ideas and symbols, as ends and pleasures in themselves. These walks have also served as research tools in making ambulatory performances and as ways of sharing through practice certain skills of observation and methods of analysis and interpretation. Among those I have either taken or joined on such pedagogical walks (or given sufficient techniques for participants to take on their own) have been performance makers, sonic and visual artists, heritage site officers, National Trust visitors, environmentalists, academics from a variety of disciplines and numerous student groups.

Pedagogical Aims

Each year for a decade now I have taken first-year theatre students on walks in order to examine intensely the textures, smells and materials of their immediate urban environment, to consider the ideological implications of the city's symbols and to both enjoy and interpret its ironies, tensions and temporalities. These accompanied walks serve partly as preparation for a task I then set the students for out of class hours. In small groups, they are directed to make a *dérive* of a minimum of four hours across a part of their city or its hinterland with which they are unfamiliar and then devise and deliver to their class a performance-presentation about their findings and experiences.

In the teaching of such a module on site-specific theatre making, my aims in introducing students to the *dérive*'s hyper-sensitized exploring of urban space are to develop their awareness of the resources that the world offers them in even its most abject and everyday spaces, and to encourage an understanding that their performance making can be as much about a dialogue with something that is already there as a fabrication imposed upon it. By adding solo walks and explorations with a relation to a fictional zombie apocalypse, my intentions are to increase the individual student's attention to the fine details, shapes, and relations of their immediate environment, and to get them to "think again" about their assumptions about their world and about "just how things are" through the provocative narratives and transforming lenses of living dead movies and other similarly-themed productions. More recently, I have introduced a collective class engagement with the living dead trope with the aim of developing the students' physical improvisation and ensemble skills and bringing intensity of concentration to situations that also require sensitivity, receptivity, and response to the work of others. One of the advantages of drawing from representations of the living dead is that many students (and others) appear to find the familiarity of these abject bodies offers both an attractive invitation for engagement and also the prospect of relevance and accessibility. They serve as an effective "way in" to ideas and histories of practice, such as those of situationist walking, that require a more challenging research and a greater empathic or imaginative leap.

Who Are the Teaching-Dead?

Skeptical that there is any universal "zombie," I nonetheless seek to impose some cohesion and limitation of the trope in my teaching. In particular, I concentrate on the contradictions and ambiguities of the Romero living dead: those revived and shambling cannibalistic corpse-characters that first appear in George Romero's 1968 movie *Night of the Living Dead*. I characterize them to myself less according to a single overriding and defining principle or a collation of features as in the pseudo-handbooks like Max Brooks' model *The Zombie Survival Guide* (2003), and more from how various products (movies, comics, novels, toys) have shifted their defining characteristics while staying within a still recognizable narrative—all the time and across all manifestations haunted by the hypothesis that the living dead "are the monsters *par excellence* of late-capitalist culture."[3]

A primary quality of this shifting discourse has been how often accounts of the monsters identify zombies as able to represent both "the other" ("an undifferentiated *It*"[4]) and "us" simultaneously: "our tingly entrails tell us that it *matters* who these zombies are that are doing the killing and the eating of people we identify with.... Just because they are dead flesh doesn't mean they aren't also our family and friends."[5] Romero, reflecting on the mythos he had initiated, gave this ambiguity a class twist: "the zombie for me was always the blue collar kind of monster. He was us."[6] This sharp inflection of "us" has recently been broadened by film critic Anne Billson, in line with the idea of the 99 percent that emerged from the Occupy movement, from what "might once have been a metaphor for the dreaded underclass" to "a reminder that we are that underclass, those faceless masses that need to be contained lest they take bites out of the bankers and politicians."[7] At the same time, but from a quite different and opposing point of view, Romero's assessment has been reciprocated by Daniel W. Drezner who, having acknowledged the "disdain of cultural elites ... placing zombies in the derivative, low rent part of the paranormal spectrum" puts himself close to that camp by declaring that his geo-political take on the zombie "project is explicitly prohuman, whereas Marxists and feminists would likely sympathise more with the zombies."[8]

Rather than arguing the validity or otherwise of particular interpretations of the living dead metaphor, general or specific, I instead seek to draw on critical tensions around them. That includes the idea of zombies as being *themselves* both parts, and representations, of an affordant pathology, as identified by Evan Calder Williams in the zombie mythos itself as "structural, shared by all social beings ... who have learned that conflict and urges are mediated by and disseminated throughout all language and discourse, that massive horizontal net of rules and conventions."[9]

The Romero "zombie" (a word never uttered in *Night of the Living Dead*, just as "witches" is never spoken in Shakespeare's *Macbeth*) is mostly slow, mostly impassive in predation, and always with memories in some stage of ruin. Perhaps from the dead Johnny's apparent recognition and targeting of his sister in *Night*, certainly from *Dawn of the Dead*'s 1978 mall grazers through Bub in *Day of the Dead* (1985) to *Land of the Dead*'s Big Daddy in 2005, these characters have been assembling a new consciousness, despite a critical discourse that often seems to wish to see them solely as "blank bodies on an empty march toward absolute massification."[10] Part of their affordance for my walking practices is how they hold these contradictions together: combining an impassive and displaced selflessness and a thoughtfulness on the point of emergence with an excessive, and sharply focused, physical drive and violence.

Within such parameters it is possible to construct a provisional canon of "Romero living dead," from a range of productions and artifacts that would include Robert Kirkman's *The Walking Dead* and *Marvel Zombies* comics and the subsequent *Walking Dead* TV series (2010-), Pat Mills and Leigh Gallagher's *Defoe* strips for *2000 AD* comic (originally serialized 2007–9) and *Batman: Gotham County Line* written by Steve Niles and penned by Scott Hampton, novels by Luke Duffy, Stephen Jones and David Wellington, the *Dead Set* TV mini-series (2008) and monsters and apocalyptic terrains from numerous films and movie episodes. These would include a supermarket sequence from *Messiah of Evil* (1973) that pre-empts the mall scenes in *Dawn of the Dead*, and the monstrous bodies of *Non Si Deve Profanare Il Sono Dei Morti* (1974), *Incubo Sulla Città Contaminata* (1980), *The Return of the Living Dead* (1985) and its sequels (despite the ability of their corpses to shift suddenly from amble to sprint) and Tom Savini's *Night* re-make (1990). The dead of *Les Revenants* (2004), with those of its subsequent TV spin-off series, could also be included on physiological and behavioral grounds, substituting psychological predation for flesh-eating. The canon would range across technical and aesthetic competencies and qualities, and across comic, trash, allegorical, realist and critical genres, accommodating movies as diverse as *La Horde*, *ZMD: Zombies of Mass Destruction* and *Zombie Farm* (all 2009), *Rammbock* (2010), *Juan De Los Muertos*, the movie-within-a-movie in *Kitsutsuki To Ame* and *Extinction: The GMO Chronicles* (all 2011), *Cockneys vs Zombies* (2012), *Before Dawn* (2013), and *[REC] 4 Apocalypse* (2014).

Affordances of the Zombie Trope

The flexibility of the "Romero living dead" narrative, including an openness to repeated reinvention, has been present from its initiation; positively compromised in its originality, connective in its radical and yet only partial break from the colonial Caribbean zombie. It is "original largely because it nails something about 'what we've seen before' and know very well … what seems recognizable … is precisely the point of departure into the uncertain … just like the zombie's obscene parody of the movements and habits of everyday life."[11]

For my own performative walking practices, I draw on certain aspects of this "obscene parody": fixation on everyday things, close study of textures and details, generally very slow pedestrian pace, and then sudden linear drives that access unlikely terrains. I have avoided the lurching gait, moaning, and cannibalism. At the 2012 Performing Monstrosity conference in London, I was challenged about these choices by the performance scholar Carl Lavery, who suggested that I might need to integrate the zombie's violence into my walking if I was to fully realize its subversive potential. Conscious of the ethical problems and challenging legal consequences involved in integrating unrestricted predation within everyday life, however, I fell upon a theoretical interweaving in a hypothesis of Simon Clark's that seemed to offer a hint about how to proceed: "the conflict between humans and zombies … can … be understood as a dramatization of the struggle that exists between civilized individuals and their own repressed instincts … ripped out of the civilized population by repression, and … manifested in a separate body altogether—the Undead corpse."[12]

Clark's suggestion of displaced drives, more diverse than physical appetite, certainly matched the fiction of a zombie that always moves, never seems to digest or shit, and, even when severed from its stomach, continues to hunt and bite. Whatever the living corpse desires, it is clearly something more than physical sustenance. Clark suggests—perversely, perhaps, given its often dead pan predation—that the zombie's overwhelming drive is for and towards pleasure. He compares the stiff, awkward walk of the Romero zombie to a "swollen erection" and its eating to that of a "*vagina-dentata,*" metaphorically distributing a genital-sensitivity across the whole zombie body. Clark argues that Romero, by simultaneously combining drives to reproduce and regress, takes Freud's proposition that "repression squeezes Eros and Thanatos into a destructive union against civilization" and extends it to "its horrific conclusion: … the traditional, hierarchical, and repressive model of civilization … at breaking point."[13]

Generally, all-encompassing interpretations of "the zombie" struggle to do justice to the contradictions that give the monster resonance. Dead labor, the demonized homeless, colonialist racial stereotypes, hyper-consumerism, and heteronormativity have all figured as alternative signifieds. None quite expresses either the illogic of the excessive and vivacious body that rises to repeat itself, or the transgressions of its primary creator, George Romero, who, in Evan Calder Williams' words, is "already screwing around with [its] … rules" even as he is establishing them.[14] By subjecting Clark's Freudian model to a similar "screwing around," I wondered if I could turn the metaphor on itself. I wondered whether by imitating a zombie-body marinated in human instincts, its consciousness in ruins and under re-construction, I could retain its trajectories while displacing those aspects of the living dead which enact the binary of repression and return described by Clark; what Williams calls the "secret communal fantasy of nastiness toward our fellow human."[15] In place of "nastiness," could I put what Lee Miller has described as the "co-operative community" of the living dead, with their sense of "the importance of community.... One zombie will never hide behind another zombie when the shooting starts.... [They] set aside selfish needs, and instead appear to serve a collective need, however accidental that might be"?[16]

By learning the movement scores of the Romero dead, stripping them of the "fantasy of nastiness," and adopting an "accidental ... co-operative community," would it be possible to give free rein to instincts for pleasure focused not on flesh and predations upon it, but instead, redirecting those instincts (and here I was drawing on my taxonomies of zombie space) to the vibrancy of places and things? For "zombieland" is a vital and vibrant place: creaking, hissing, doors flapping, paper yellowing, smoke pluming. There, cities pass into chaos and those things held in artificial stasis begin to shift: food rots, ice melts, power systems begin to seize up and short out. Freed from automation, materials escape from maintenance and refrigeration. New lubrications drip, surfaces rust. In filmic long shots and in the larger panels of comic narratives, vistas shift into unfamiliar darkness and around uncertain contents, every "empty" landscape is full with unseen potential. In this recognizable "zombieland" the celebratory attitude of the hyper-sensitized walker towards the vibrancy of matter becomes everyday.

Preparation

With a view to recruiting such vital terrains, as co-performers in a post-dramatic theatre of zombie movement, I asked the permission of my first year theatre students at Plymouth University's School of Humanities and Performing Arts if they would give over two of their Performance, Space and Environments lessons to an experiment: preparing first in studio space and then exploring in public spaces. They agreed.

We began in a classroom studio, where, after I had reiterated the protocols of the research (the terms in which their work might be identified, students' right to withdraw their participation at any point, and so on), I introduced the idea of a non-aggressive zombie performance. After a general physical warm-up, I rehearsed the 15 students for an hour in solo and group walking. Without any reference to the walk of the living dead, I asked them to draw on their own "natural" walk and to fix their concentration to their own impulses, not communicating with others but staying sensitive to others' movements and impulses. Instructions included variations of speed and energy, walking alone and in pairs and groups, following, mimicking, and attempting to halt and move off as one group without spoken or gestured communication.

After a visualization exercise, aimed at sensitizing the students to the studio space, I asked the students to improvise in groups of five or six (the rest of the class observing) with instructions to allow themselves to be drawn by and to examine fixatedly whatever and wherever attracted them most in the studio, moving on to something else once they felt their interest fade. The students were asked to respond to any other group member's impulse that they felt was stronger than their own and to follow the trajectory of that member until they felt a stronger impulse, either from themselves or from another group member. All this was to be done without any signaling between the members of the group, but they were to remain as sensitive as possible to each other's impulses and movements. The resulting improvisations lasted between ten and 15 minutes.

For a further hour or more (split over two lessons), I then rehearsed the students in a palette of zombie actions: milling, herding when close together, stationary trance, intense fixation on and examination of objects and surfaces, performing everyday actions faintly remembered, being led in a line (like Big Daddy's walkers in *Land of the Dead*), being held as a group at an obstacle such as a fence and then breaking through, sudden targeting of something and moving in a straight line to it, spreading out across a space while walking in the same direction, slack-jawed grazing, and clustering on an object of desire. Most of these actions required very little detailed description or contextualization on my part; in most cases, students were able to immediately reference the actions I described without any need for a detailed description.

One problem arose when I introduced a reaching out with the arms, stretched out in front and parallel to the ground. Perhaps too close to the Boris Karloff monster-walk from James Whale's *Frankenstein* (1931) that Johnny mimics at the start of *Night of the Living Dead*, true to its satirical and superseded qualities, this posture provoked laughter among the students and a comical lapsing into stereotypical zombie character. It was the only time that concentration was lost during this "rehearsal" section; even the clustering upon a target, which I thought might assume a farcical quality and provoke giggles, was performed seriously throughout the class. Before we moved on to the next section, I dropped the Boris Karloff walk from the palette, and I warned the students away from any attempt to "act" a zombie character or scenario or to invent psychological or narrative motivations for their actions. Instead, I urged them, as far as possible, to draw only upon their own immediate impulse, attraction, and enjoyment.

I then directed the students to improvise in groups once more, with the same instructions as before, but now adding the palette of "living dead" actions to their improvisations. Each group, one at a time, had the opportunity to work until they were able to move smoothly from one living dead action to another. This process took the class about half an hour. Once all the groups had become fluent in the movements, I took the entire class to two nearby public spaces in Plymouth (UK). The first was Drake's Place, a spacious, but quiet ornamental garden built in 1891 to celebrate the 16th-century navigator, slaver, and privateer Sir Francis Drake. The second space was a busy atrium in the Roland Levinsky Building, a large modern Arts teaching and administration building opened in 2007 and named after the university's Vice Chancellor who had been electrocuted while walking by high-power cables blown down in a storm.

Improvisation and Feedback

All working at the same time, but in their separate groups, students were invited to follow their subjective attraction to things and places in these new sites. They were encouraged, again, to respond to and join up with any more powerful impulse if they felt one coming from another group member, to draw upon the palette of living dead actions that they had rehearsed, and they were asked not to communicate with each other but to stay co-operatively sensitive to each other's movements. They were also instructed not to engage with members of the public, but, if challenged by a member of the public, or by university staff or students, to explain what they were doing. I watched their improvisations, at times from a distance and at others from close up.

After the improvisations, which in total (on a very cold day) lasted a little under an hour, I asked students to describe their experiences in written form and I received nine responses from the 15 participants. General comments on the overall experiment were positive: "really interesting" (A), "fascinating and unique" (F), "help[ful]" (G). The four students who wrote about the relation of the exercise to zombie fictions felt that it had "altered [their] perspective" (F) or changed or added to their understanding, while three students (B, C & G) saw the exercise as a positive aid to their future study and practice of performance.

The most consistent response, though, was in relation to intensity and immersion. Six of the students described something like an intense engagement: "I instantly began moving and exploring with an intentness inhumane" (D). One noted that their colleagues were "incredibly engaged" (A) and another that after "being able to stay as a group and stay fixated … it took me a couple of minutes to realize that I was out of the zombie zone as I was still walking and having my movements and eyes as a zombie" (C). Another student "found myself getting really lost in the exercise and when Phil told us to stop I couldn't because I was so immersed in what I was doing" (G). Perhaps most striking was this description: "[it] made me feel like the world around me didn't exist anymore.... All the senses in my body had been dimmed ... my arms didn't want to follow what my brain was telling them.... It was like a silent world. You walked in an endless wonder, with no destination, only the urge to continue on with your walk ... everything you had learnt or seen didn't matter anymore" (E).

Five of the nine respondents commented on the cooperative nature of the actions: it "allowed us all to commute to [an] area without having to communicate with each other" (C); the group could "automatically tune into when was a good time" (D) to use particular actions. One student described the ensemble movement: "there was no pushing, just calmness as we made our way.... There was this unspoken communication that we all seemed to have ... we didn't need words because we were all thinking the same thing.... We didn't need to push our way through to get it, we all just gave way to everyone, so everyone could get it" (E). One of the students characterized this as a performance distanced from self: "I found that when I was performing, all of my attention went towards adding to what was already there, rather than creating something new.... I wasn't trying to lead at all, I was just letting the performance take me where it wanted" (H).

Less prevalent, but equally strongly expressed, was a sense of freedom. One student wrote that "I felt that there was no control over what I was able to do ... as if no rules were in place. I found myself knocking on the windows of buildings ... as the task developed, it seemed like I had more of a liberty to explore what I wanted to explore" (F), and another that "I felt no restrictions.... I realized that I could act as strange as I wanted" (H).

There was also mention of participants' sensitization to spaces that they might usually take for granted: "areas in the room that I wouldn't normally engage ... but ... opened up my mind to acknowledge ... simple things that may not be seen normally" (F). Another participant remarked on their discovery of "how many different ways we can view objects simply by focusing upon them" (G).

Where the responses become less consistent is in the different preferences for particular sites; some found the studio more conducive to the exercises, others the gardens, while a number of the students felt they had become "fazed and distracted by the people in [the atrium]" (F), where, despite not "acting" like a zombie at first, the resonance of their movements was quickly reflected in wary glances from students and anxious staff—none of whom, though, seemed able to sufficiently identify what was "wrong" in order to intervene. In contrast to this unevenness, and given the number of participants, and the range of predisposition, articulacy, movement skills and application across the class, the written responses in regard to intensity and immersion, and to subjectivity and collectivity, stand out as being largely consistent with each other. They are also significant in terms of evidence of developing performance skills such as physical application, focus and attention, and sensitivity and spontaneity in ensemble playing.

The students' own accounts of their experiences largely chimed with the field notes that I had written immediately after the class was over, which I described as

> continually "creative" ... never ... becalmed or "stuck" but ... all the time evolving new movements, shifts to places, constructions from things, rearrangements of themselves, dialoguing through things and their bodies.... If an organized intention emerged it was quickly subsumed in a new stimulus or drive.... Extremely pleasurable to watch; an absenting of ego (one student remarked ... "I didn't know what we were doing there") and nervousness, and of that predictability as one sees in the mind of the improviser "where this is going" and then the slavish following of its ... trajectory. Because there was no "where," only the expectation of, eventually, a new drive ... the improvisation was non-organic, the larger body of narrative or structure never predominating over the flows.... Remarkabl[y] free of that ersatz tension and aggression when students attempt to generate dramatic conflict.

Learning through Practice

What I had perceived from the outside and described in my field notes, confirmed by the students' reflections from the inside, was something like a Deleuzo-Guattarian "body without organs": "affective, intensive, anarchist," a "dynamic force field of speeds and intensities 'traversed by a powerful, non-organic vitality.'"[17] Across this "force field" (generated by first invoking the narrative of zombie cannibalism, hollowing it out, then allowing its spectral return in the most formalist and technical of ways) the students' individual flows and drives were followed and morphed by others, but not imitated. These flows operated without, as far as I could see, any clear hierarchy of drives, certainly without representation, and without any observable overarching or organizing principle, other than the instructions for a negative sensitivity to others (to work in the gaps they left) and a responsibility to respond to their own emerging drives or a stronger one shown by another.

I commented in my field notes that "the lack of an obligation to dialogue or fabricate an overall meaning was equivalent to the structural compartmentalizations of happenings." I was referencing the use in 1960s happenings of a structure "based on the arrangement and contiguity of theatrical units that are completely self-contained and hermetic" leaving participants free otherwise to make what they wished within these structures while free from any overarching impulse or meaning.[18] Also, what I had observed in the improvisations had chimed with Michael Kirby's related descriptions of "not-acting" in structuralist theatre where the performer, free from psychological acting, "generally tended to 'be' nobody or nothing other than themselves....

They walked, ran, said words ... and so forth, but they did not feign or impersonate."[19] Similarly, a palette of zombie movements served to reshape the performers through the model of "pseudo-humans," working to inhibit self-display or showmanship: "it [the zombie] demonstrates our limits, it curbs and checks our narcissism."[20] Similarly invoking subtraction and fragmentation, Stephen Barber suggests that when "the body becomes ecstatically inundated with sensory resonances and visual attractions that work to bind corporeal substance to the illuminated urban surface" that it is "the visually self-disassembled body [that] can explore states of resistance to the digital city."[21]

In the students' reflections there is relatively little written about any particular quality of engagement related specifically to particular things or parts of the sites, possibly reflecting their priorities as aspiring performance-makers, or even the priorities of dominant discourses around performance. One student described how in the atrium they had been "flipping the sign outside Peninsula Arts back and forth, the secretary at the desk ... stood up" (H). In the studio the students had dragged objects across the floor, wrapped themselves in clothes and other materials, scratched surfaces, placed themselves in relation to objects, produced equipment from hidden rooms, manipulated lighting, and so on; outside they had kicked a heavy rock along paths, brandished a large bough at the head of a procession and tore up and played with sheets of ice from a concrete channel.

Given their instruction to follow their impulses it was clear that, when in contact with these objects, the impulse often came from the thing; the weight of the bough and the rock partly shaped the mode by which they could be shifted, the cold and reflectiveness of the ice how it might be carried. This suggested a certain *porosity* in the students' actions, an idea expressed elsewhere by Stephen Hodge and myself, partly in relation to walking, as work that is "for others to read into it and connect from it and for the specificities and temporalities of sites to fracture, erode and distress it."[22] Cathy Turner has pointed out that the term porosity, taken from geology, is partly a description of voids in a substance, "it is not in itself a *measure* of interactivity or exchange, nor does it describe what kinds of exchanges might occur. It merely suggests that the structure contains space within it available for occupation," though this space is something that Turner and her co-researcher Duska Radosavljevic thought of "as inviting co-creativity."[23]

What the students could learn from this practice (learning I sought to reinforce in a reflection with the class on their actions) was that they do not need to fill all available space and time with performance or even to finely structure their dramaturgies; rather, the leaving of gaps and breaks can welcome into their performances the vibrancy of things, passersby, weather, and unexpected relations. A certain kind of emptying out (of narrative, mimesis, psychological motivation, violence, and eroticism) in our living dead improvisations had created a void-like space of parallel creativities where "co" meant a negative co-operation. It was not an attempt to arrive at agreements or a physicalized unison, but rather a leaving open or emptying of spaces (voids) where others' impulses and the vibrant materiality of things might take flight and flow through each other—a permeability also cited by Turner as part of a performance understanding of porosity.

Refining the Exercise for Future Teaching

What I felt and had seen, emerging tentatively in the improvisations, was a walk of pleasure, a walk of subjective drives facilitated by a non-communicative and co-operative non-interference. Individuals had responded to others on the basis of the interweaving of their subjective drives, while maintaining the integrity of their impulses. They had separately and collectively fixated on vital objects and spaces that they began, unselfconsciously, to change or challenge, or to involve in physical dialogues. Their improvisations displaced the fiction of predation for a "not-acted" physical and sensual immersion comparable to what Simon Clark has called the zombie's "reactivat[ing] the entire body as an erogenous zone ... tak[ing] the focus away from civilized genital contact."[24]

This walk, the idea of and the instructions for which are simple to transmit (students who missed the first class through illness quickly picked up the ideas at the start of the second), seems to discourage malevolent gazes and elude authority. It is at least partially disguised in plain sight within its ambiguity, while defusing internal inhibitions, the dominance of narrative and psychology, and the fictions of violence and eroticism that, in my experience, often dog unstructured improvisation. The internalized zombie walk, in contrast, offers a means to transforming a theatre student's ability to get beyond self-display or self-conscious concerns and engage more reactively and spontaneously in ensemble work.

Possible future developments of this practice might be created where opportunities were not fully responded to by the participants on this occasion: future participants might work with non-human things and spaces more as partners; they might shift beyond the pleasurable acting out of their subjective drives in a supportive ensemble context to taking more instinctive risks in seeking abstract or shared planes of desire with fellow improvisers, building from the student who found themselves "just letting the performance take me where it wanted" (H) towards more general and more intense "auto-erotic movements of machinic desire" described by Anna Powell as "experienced not by subjectivities, but through intensive states, or 'haecceities': things-in-themselves."[25]

In order to push towards such a *haecceity*, we might take as exemplary the sequence in George Romero's movie *Land of the Dead* when a small zombie band, led by Big Daddy and Jennifer Baxter's Number 9, having subjected the upper classes of the gated community of Fiddler's Green to cannibalistic mayhem, appear to withdraw, by choice, from violence. Rather than continuing their predation among the working class survivors of the besieged city, the living dead set off to traverse their own plane of desire, a haecceity, a journey for the sake of journeying: "just looking for a place to go—same as us" as one survivor describes their departure. They are looking not for a place *to stay* but, significantly, a place *to go*.

Rather swamped by the clumsy class and pseudo-socialist metaphors of *Land of the Dead*, the politics of this Bartlebyesque "zombie strike" has been mostly missed by critical responses to the movie.[26] Kyle William Bishop, in an otherwise brilliant analysis of the zombie, misses its radicalism when he characterizes this moment as prefiguring "an almost utopian future, one where the living and the dead can coexist peacefully."[27] In other zombie products, however, humans have been reciprocating this trajectory in a more extreme way; as early as J. R. Bookwalter's *The Dead Next Door* (1989) humans supporting the rights of the living dead found themselves attacked and infected, while in Max Brooks' *World War Z* (2006) there are the "quislings," uninfected humans who "started moving like zombies, sounding like them, even attacking and trying to eat other people."[28] Complementary to zombies renouncing predation and humans adopting it, there are humans seeking infection or identification with the infected. This rejection of the commonsense of Jeffrey Sconce's "no one wants to be bitten by a zombie, of course" is described by Simon Clark as: "humans lining up in front of their Undead counterparts, happily sacrificing their flesh so that they might be liberated from repression and delivered into a realm of instinctual pleasure … a radical act of self-initiation … a rite of passage into the land of the dead … a realm of pleasure and freedom."[29]

This passage—if taken through the affordances of this experiment, transmitted through the palette of movements and instructions, and realized in a pedagogical process—is not an invitation to imitate zombies (neither in the make-up carnival of zombie walks, nor the kind of role-playing seen in Medea Yarns' film-within-a-film in Bruce LaBruce's *Otto; or Up With Dead People* [2008], nor a disguise for violent predations by the living as in the movie *Mimesis* [2011]). It is a reaching back to Romero's original preoccupations with revolution; an ambulatory way through and beyond the transformative aspirations of the "situational-*dérive*" and other radical walkings, through and beyond their paranoid hypersensitivities, towards an expanded, attentive and tender dramaturgy of the streets to better challenge the morbidities of the shock-capitalist city.

APPENDIX
Assignment Sheet for Zombie Walk

(Message sent by email to class members.)

Dear Performance, Space and Environments class members,

I am looking forward to seeing you all tomorrow at 2pm at RLB 308. We will begin by watching all your short performances with objects/materials.

(IT'S DUE TO BE DRY, BUT COLD—BRING WARM CLOTHES!!!!!)

Then we will begin work on an exercise that will last over this and the next session on Friday. We are going to be working up and learning a series of movement qualities (gait, speed, interactions) taken from the behavior of the "monsters" in zombie movies.

It doesn't take a genius to see that many zombie movies intentionally portray contemporary society in a critical way, depicting ecological and social breakdown, alienation and loss of individuality, the exploitation of workers and the poor, consumerism gone mad, and so on. The "father" of the modern zombie movie, George Romero, said that his 1968 *Night of the Living Dead* is a film about revolution.

But there is something else going on a little more under the surface in zombie movies. Some critics have interpreted the insatiable hunger and relentless seeking of flesh by the living dead as expressions of ordinary but repressed human desires and pleasures suddenly released from social controls like convention, morals, competition, social structures, laws, property and so on.

Using this second level of interpretation we will be learning in the studio how to make a benign "living dead dance" made up of different zombies moves and rules of interaction (milling, tramping, reaching out, and so on) that we can then use in public spaces, not seeking to satisfy a hunger for human flesh (!) but rather to let our pleasure in objects and spaces lead us. This is very much an experiment and we will be gently finding our way together.

After Friday's class I will ask you to produce a short piece of writing about your experience of using the "living dead dance" in a public space…

See you tomorrow,
Phil

NOTES

1. Phil Smith, *Walking's New Movement* (Axminster: Triarchy Press, 2015) and "Pedagogy and the Zombie Mythos: Lessons from Apocalyptic Enactments," forthcoming in Esther Priyadharshini, ed., *Schooling Zombies* (New York: Springer, 2016).

2. See, for example, Phil Smith, *On Walking* (Axminster: Triarchy Press, 2014), or "Performative Walking in Zombie Towns," *Studies in Theatre and Performance* 34.3 (2014): 219–28.

3. Silem K. Mohammad, "Zombies, Rest and Motion: Spinoza and the Speed of Undeath," in Richard Greene and Silem Mohammed, eds., *The Undead and Philosophy: Chicken Soup for the Soulless* (Chicago: Open Court, 2006), 91–102; 101, original emphasis.

4. Jack Morgan, *The Biology of Horror: Gothic Literature and Film* (Carbondale: Southern Illinois University Press, 2002), 175, original emphasis.

5. William S. Larkin, "Res *Corporealis*: Persons, Bodies, and Zombies," in Richard Greene and Silem Mohammed, eds., *The Undead and Philosophy: Chicken Soup for the Soulless* (Chicago: Open Court, 2006), 15–26; 23, original emphasis.

6. Quoted in Ben Hervey, *Night of the Living Dead* (Basingstoke: Palgrave/BFI, 2008), 57.

7. Leon Hunt, Sharon Lockyer and Milly Williamson, eds., *Screening the Undead: Vampires and Zombies in Film and Television* (London: I. B. Tauris, 2014), 1–16; 8.

8. Daniel Drezner, *Theories of International Politics and Zombies* (Princeton: Princeton University Press, 2011), 6, 17.

9. Evan Calder Williams, *Combined and Uneven Apocalypse* (Ropley: Zero Books, 2011), 84.

10. Jeffrey Sconce, "Dead Metaphors/Undead Allegories," in Leon Hunt, Sharon Lockyer and Milly Williamson, eds., *Screening the Undead: Vampires and Zombies in Film and Television* (London: I. B. Tauris, 2014), 95–111; 97.

11. Williams, 76–77.

12. Simon Clark, "The Undead Martyr: Sex, Death, and Revolution in George Romero's Zombie Films," in Richard Greene and Silem Mohammed, eds., *The Undead and Philosophy: Chicken Soup for the Soulless* (Chicago: Open Court, 2006), 197–209; 199.

13. *Ibid.*, 203–04.

14. Williams, 76.

15. *Ibid.*, 84.

16. Lee Miller, "Playing Undead," *Studies in Theatre and Performance* 34.3 (2014): 191–200; 197.

17. Anna Powell, *Deleuze and Horror Film* (Edinburgh: Endinburgh University Press, 2005) 211.

18. Michael Kirby, "Happenings: An Introduction," in Mariellen R. Sandford, ed., *Happenings and Other Acts* (London: Routledge, 1995), 1–24; 4.

19. Michael Kirby, *A Formalist Theatre* (Philadelphia: University of Philadelphia Press, 1987), 3.

20. Stephen T. Asma, *On Monsters: An Unnatural History of our Worst Fears* (Oxford: Oxford University Press, 2009), 191.

21. Stephen Barber, *Projected Cities: Cinema and Urban Space* (London: Reaktion Books, 2002), 158.

22. Wrights & Sights, www.mis-guide.com/about.html (accessed May 5, 2015).

23. Cathy Turner, "Porous Dramaturgy and the Pedestrian," in Katalin Trencsenyi and Bernadette Cochrane, eds., *New Dramaturgy: International Perspectives on Theory and Practice* (London: Bloomsbury, 2014), 199–213; 201–02.

24. Clark, 202.

25. Powell, 212, 93.

26. For interesting parallels, see Claire Fontaine's *Human Strike Has Already Begun & Other Writings* (Luneburg: PML Books, 2013), esp. 29.

27. Kyle William Bishop, *American Zombie Gothic: The Rise and Fall (and Rise) of the Walking Dead in Popular Culture* (Jefferson, NC: McFarland, 2010), 195.

28. Max Brooks, *World War Z: An Oral History of the Zombie War* (London: Duckworth, 2006), 156.

29. Sconce, 106 and Clark, 209, respectively.

Part III

Disrupting Systems
The Monster Attacks

Studying Gods and Monsters

Joshua Paddison

"Religion is never without its monsters," writes religious studies scholar Timothy K. Beal. "Whether demonized or deified or both, no matter how many times we kill our monsters they keep coming back for more."[1] Monsters—whether conceived of as real or imaginary, friendly or terrifying—embody our most desperate hopes and fears about the existence of God, the limits of science, the nature of evil, the afterlife, the natural world, humanity's place in the cosmos, the past, the future, and the Other. This essay explores how bringing monsters into the college or university classroom transforms it into a space where students can conduct unique and profound examinations into religious history, practice, and culture.

My interest in monstrous pedagogy originally arose out of my current research project, which examines a little-known 19th-century spiritualist movement called the Brotherhood of the New Life. This movement operated first in upstate New York, then in England and Scotland, and ultimately in California, and it included white and Japanese members. Members of the Brotherhood of the New Life did not merely communicate with spirits—they also explored the solar system and the heavens, battled demons, spoke with fairies, and entered into erotically charged relationships with heavenly "counterparts" with such names as Lily Queen and Sir Knight Peace.[2] My research into the beliefs and practices of the Brotherhood of the New Life—and the broader transnational spiritualist movement of the 19th century—has sparked an interest in the ways people's beliefs in and ideas about ghosts, demons, and monsters of various types spring from crucial religious concerns.

I currently offer a course called "Ghosts, Monsters, Demons, and Aliens in U.S. History" at Wittenberg University, a Lutheran-affiliated liberal arts institution in Springfield, Ohio. I am trained as a historian but I have taught for Religious Studies and American Studies departments, and I bring an interdisciplinary approach to my teaching. In my "Ghosts, Monsters, Demons, and Aliens in U.S. History" course (see syllabus below), we read books and articles by historians, religion scholars, sociologists, and folklorists as well as examine a wide array of historical primary sources from the 17th century to the 21st: sermons, folk tales, witchcraft trial transcripts, spiritualist poetry, alien abduction narratives, ghost stories, comic books, demonology manuals, "Satanic" rock music, religious tracts, online message boards, and horror movies and television shows. The course is a writing-intensive sophomore-level General Education seminar, capped at 25 students, aimed at non-history majors. It focuses mostly on the United States but this same approach could profitably be applied to other parts of the world.

From my perspective, the many ghosts, monsters, demons, and aliens students encounter in the class are all, at their core, religious manifestations, in the sense that they help people construct existential meaning. Like all things divine, monsters and other supernatural entities resist empirical testing, yet we believe. We need these entities because they help us answer crucial religious questions: Is there a God? What happens after we die? Why is there evil and suffering in the world? What does it mean to be human? Is this mundane life all there is? The monstrous—and its flip side, the wondrous—help us understand and navigate our own existence.

As its title suggests, I divide the course into four units and each unit skips forward through history as we trace Americans' changing attitudes, beliefs, and encounters with each type of supernatural entity. The first unit on demons, for example, starts in late 17th-century colonial Massachusetts. We examine what the outbreak of demonic possession among young people—mostly young women—reveals about Puritan conceptions of gender, race, and selfhood. From there we move forward to the 1970s and the resurgence of a fascination in demonic possession following the popularity of *The Exorcist* novel and film. What did the thousands of Catholics and evangelical Protestants who sought exorcism in the 1970s hope to receive? Finally, we move to the 1980s and widespread concern over "Satanic" rock music. We explore both the appeal of Satanic heavy metal bands like Slayer, Black Sabbath, and Iron Maiden as well as the cultural transgressions that made those bands targets for censorship and repression. The course's other three units—ghosts, monsters (we look at the Jewish golem, Bigfoot, and zombies), and aliens—move similarly through time, allowing us to explore continuities and change in different cultural moments. Along the way, we learn about a wide variety of religious traditions and movements, not just various forms of Christianity but also Judaism, the Lakota Ghost Dance, Hoodoo, Buddhism, Mormonism, the Nation of Islam, Scientology, Heaven's Gate, and the Raëlian movement.

Studying monsters and these sorts of religious entities allows students to approach essential questions in the study of religion in fresh and potent ways. The remainder of this essay will highlight five of these ways. First, the topic itself generates phenomenally high levels of student interest. I have found that a monstrous course title generates strong enrollment numbers as well as an enduring excitement in a way that more traditional courses may not. From a practical perspective, this approach is an effective way to "smuggle" a religion course into the curriculum that attracts plenty of motivated students. A monstrous course is a "fun" class that can also be rigorous, using students' pre-existing interest as a motor to propel them into deeper academic waters.

In my experience, many students interested in a monstrous class are fans of science fiction and horror; many believe that monsters of one kind or another are "real." I make clear in the first week some of the things we will *not* be doing together—we will not be "investigating" the existence of supernatural entities nor will we be spending time discussing or debating their existence in the "real world." Instead, students learn that we will be studying how people in the past and present have conceived of monsters, how and why those conceptions have changed over time, and what people's beliefs in and representations of monsters tells us about larger religious patterns. This approach requires modeling by the professor, but students generally are able to resist the urge to speculate on the "reality" of the supernatural, at least during class, and to focus instead on changing cultural perceptions.

Second, studying the monstrous helps students consider one of the fundamental questions of religious studies—namely, what is "religion" itself? I order my four units strategically so as to help students re-consider the parameters of what is and is not religious. We begin with demons, which everyone sees as clearly arising from people's religious beliefs and texts, and move on to ghosts, which most students recognize as having something to do with religion, and then to monsters and finally aliens. Students come into the class certain that Bigfoot and aliens have nothing to do with religion, but by the end of the semester, they see that in fact people's searches for Bigfoot and aliens are, in important ways, religious impulses. For some Bigfoot hunters, for example, Bigfoot represents the potential for mystery and the unknowable in an increasingly disenchanted world; for others, Bigfoot is an otherworldly visitor with a message of peace and environmental responsibility; and according to Mormon folklore, Bigfoot is Cain from the Book of Genesis, destined to wander the earth seeking to "destroy the souls of men."[3] Through monster studies, students see that religion is not defined simply by a set of sacred texts, institutions, or creeds, but is a fluid process of making meaning that is both individual and social.

Students come to recognize how people's encounters with the monstrous are often described in ways similar to their encounters with God or the divine. In the Book of Job, God visits Job in the form of a whirlwind, demanding,

"Have you an arm like God, and can you thunder with a voice like his?"[4] Job's mixture of dread and awe is characteristic of people's meetings with the monstrous here on earth. To highlight this, I show students the finale of Steven Spielberg's film *Close Encounters of the Third Kind* (1977) in which the characters stare awestruck and terrified as the massive alien "mother ship" slowly moves atop Devil's Tower. As Timothy K. Beal has noted, gods and monsters elicit "a vertigo-like combination of both fear and desire, repulsion and attraction."[5] Religion and horror can both overwhelm our rational mind in a way that is simultaneously awesome and unsettling.

To help students who are more familiar with ideas of a loving rather than a frightening God appreciate this connection, I ask them to write down a description of how it feels—physically, in your body—to be scared. I then ask them to describe how it feels to experience religious ecstasy, based on their lives or imaginations. Comparing what they wrote, students usually find a number of correlations. Both experiences seem to *feel* similarly: your heart races, your muscles tense, your senses seem especially acute, you tremble or shake, you feel "more alive." This short writing exercise helps students who find the notion of a terrible God counter-intuitive to see religion as more than a little horrifying, as it is lived. In this, we follow William James's focus on religion as *experience*, out of which "theologies, philosophies, and ecclesiastical organizations may secondarily grow."[6]

Furthermore, my approach to studying monsters exposes students to a wide range of "strange" or non-normative religious beliefs, from 17th-century Puritanism to 19th-century spiritualism to the 21st-century alien abduction movement. By taking all religious expressions seriously and treating them all respectfully, be it Roman Catholicism, the Lakota Ghost Dance, or the Raëlian movement, students begin to rethink assumptions about what is and is not a "valid" religion. They see that the only things separating a "religion" from a "new religious movement" or "cult" is longevity and mainstream acceptance. My students read Scientology scholar Mikael Rothstein, who writes, "The power of Western society allows the myths of Christianity to flourish as respectable or even true narratives, whereas Scientology's myths have no such status. It is not about the narratives themselves, it is about the *status* they are able to achieve."[7] For students coming from a strong religious background, typically Christianity, this notion helps them see their own religion in a new light, situating it both historically and comparatively among other traditions. For some students, this is a disturbing notion; for others, it is liberating; but all leave class pondering what gets called "religious," what does not, and why.

Third, monsters cross boundaries of medium and category—they are created in folklore, gossip, pop culture, the arts, scientific investigations, theology, and online. According to literary critic Jeffrey Jerome Cohen, "the monstrous is a genus too large to be encapsulated in any conceptual system;

the monster's very existence is a rebuke to boundary and enclosure."[8] As such, they provide rich case studies for understanding diverse religious texts and spaces. Because monsters, by definition, are ineffable, much writing about them falls into the category of esoterica. When students puzzle over esoteric primary sources—such as Thomas Lake Harris' florid spiritualist trance poetry, Elijah Muhammad's cryptic descriptions of the giant "Mother Plane" that carries flying saucers destined to destroy the earth, and writings by members of Heaven's Gate about the "Evolutionary Kingdom Level Above Human"—they appreciate more fully how sacred texts operate. With their great length, lack of conventional narratives, and highly abstracted verbiage, esoteric texts immerse the reader in a specialized worldview. These are truly *religious* texts: they express religious ideas but also enact a religious experience in their reading. Impenetrability, abstraction, and repetition simultaneously confirm these texts' divine origins and render them useful for prolonged study and meditation. As students come to see these sorts of texts as deliberately opaque—in other words, they realize that it's *not their fault* that the reading is so difficult—they begin to consider the uses and appeals of all sacred texts.

Studying monsters also helps students think more deeply about sacred spaces. In my course they encounter a variety of supernatural locales: Lily Dale, New York, the nation's largest spiritualist colony, visited by 25,000 curious "pilgrims" each year; Roswell, New Mexico, the location of a supposed UFO crash in 1947, now decorated with obelisks and a stone monument declaring it a "universal sacred site"; the Bigfoot Museum in Humboldt County, California, celebrating and documenting the first Bigfoot sightings; and the Amityville Horror House, in Amityville, New York, famously haunted in the 1970s. These function as sacred spaces as much as any church, synagogue, or temple—places where visitors deliberately cross a threshold in preparation of meeting the divine. But unlike most churches, synagogues, and temples, these "monstrous" sacred spaces are also tourist destinations, attracting true believers looking to connect, skeptics looking to debunk, and everyone in between. More obviously than traditionally religious structures, monstrous spaces are both sacred and profane.

In my preparations for this course, I discovered that Wittenberg University has its own "sacred space" (other than its Lutheran chapel, that is)—a student dorm called Myers Hall. According to campus legend, during the Civil War, Myers Hall was used as a short-term hospital for wounded soldiers. One general, on his death bed, asked that his beloved horse be brought up to his room on the fifth floor for a final goodbye. The horse was unable to go back down the five flights of stairs, and so perished within the Hall, and his ghost can still be heard and sometimes glimpsed by undergraduates. This story, variations of which seem to exist on many college campuses, is told by guides to all prospective Wittenberg students. It is featured prominently on Wittenberg's website and in its YouTube videos. The Myers Hall ghost horse even has its own Twitter account, @MyersHallGhost, which issues such missives as "Some new activity in my home.... I sense students are about again.... Time to rekindle the flame of the #FellowshipOfTheGhost."[9] It turns out that Wittenberg was never used as a hospital during the Civil War, but my students have explored why the legend lives on. They point out that the ghost horse helps differentiate Wittenberg from similar Midwestern colleges; it connects the campus to a major national event, the Civil War; and the legend of the horse's demise is an appealing mix of tragedy and love between human and beast. Existing in the realms of campus folklore, public relations, sentimental local history, and religion, the ghost horse makes Myers Hall a sacred space of haunted possibility.

Fourth, monsters, as liminal figures, are often *raced* in ways that help students to think about intersections of religion and other co-constitutive categories of identity. As religion scholar Sylvester Johnson has recently pointed out, ideas of the monstrous have long been entangled with transnational processes of colonialism, imperialism, and racism. "Whether describing fanged cannibals, one-eyed giants, or headless monopods," writes Johnson, "[colonial] firsthand accounts disseminated lurid tales of monstrous bodies that promised by the very nature of their physicality to confound any efforts to perceive humanness in the monstrous form."[10]

Throughout American history, Native Americans, African Americans, and other racialized groups have been associated with the monstrous. Puritans viewed Indians as in league with the Devil, and they placed the blame for the Salem witchcraft outbreak on Indian woman Tituba. Two centuries later, Tituba became transformed in public memory as African rather than Native American to fit the racial needs of the 19th century.[11] Historian Mary Renda has shown how white Americans in the 1930s were gripped by fears of Haitian zombies reanimated via "voodoo"—"monstrous, once-dead black men rising up, embodying white fears of black revolt at home as well as abroad."[12] Today, evangelical Protestant "spiritual warfare" handbooks urge Christians to cleanse their home of "demonic" Asian, African, and Native American artworks and objects.[13] Meanwhile, angels are usually imagined as looking white and coming bathed in white light. These and other examples from my course help students to perceive religion and race as mutually constitutive systems, marking certain groups as outside the parameters of what is considered natural, normal, sacred, and human.

These cultural associations continue to have terrible, real-world consequences. As I was teaching this course in fall 2014, headlines became dominated by the killing of African American teenager Michael Brown by white police officer Darren Wilson in Ferguson, Missouri. In his testimony before the grand jury, which declined to indict him, Wilson said that Brown had looked "like a demon" before he shot him.[14] This sort of demonization and dehumanization is a small but important component of much larger processes of racialization, marginalization, and violent oppression in the American past and present. The Ferguson shooting revealed to students how notions of monstrosity and racial inferiority remain intertwined in the American cultural imagination.

Fifth, and finally, monsters help us to consider the question of secularization—that is, religion's supposed loss of authority due to science, modernity, and "rationalization." From Max Weber's "disenchantment of the world" that supposedly followed the Enlightenment to philosopher Charles Taylor's assertion that today "belief in God is no longer axiomatic," secularization has been lamented, championed, and above all assumed to be undeniable.[15] Recent religious studies scholarship, however, has interrogated notions of secularization, emphasizing how those notions in fact depend on and spring from religious (largely Protestant) discourses.[16] Have people truly become "less religious," or have their religious impulses been relocated—as suggested by historian William R. Hutchison—"whereupon we proclaim their disappearance because we are looking for them in the wrong places"?[17]

In fact, by studying monsters, we see how modernization, science, and "secularization" have brought not irreligion but new avenues for the pursuit of awe, mystery, and horror, which are at the heart of the religious experience. Consider, for example, those Americans who claim to have been abducted by aliens. At first glance, at least for my students, aliens and UFOs seem "secular" in the sense that intelligent life could plausibly exist somewhere in the universe. However, as we read the accounts of "abductees," many of which were related during hypnotism, students come to see the abduction experience as fundamentally a religious one. UFO abductions are dream-like: people say they are outside their body, they float and fly, fall, appear naked in public, day becomes night, time shifts, and there are impossibly large structures. Just as God came to Saul on the road to Damascus as a bright light from heaven, UFO abductions often begin with a bright white light from the skies. Like prophets, abductees are often given a message of truth—the importance of world peace and environmentalism, or special knowledge of humanity's origins or a coming catastrophe. Aliens use technology so advanced it seems like magic. Some abductees believe there are two alien races in battle, one good one evil, reminiscent of the "spiritual warfare" that some Protestants believe is going on between angels and demons. Most Americans abducted by aliens are women, just as women have disproportionately been able to communicate with spirits; both alien abduction and mediumship provide routes to spiritual authority outside traditional (and traditionally sexist) churches. In short, UFOs are—to quote Carl Jung—a "modern myth," reflecting fundamental religious anxieties and desires.[18]

Ultimately, abductees are forever changed by the experience; they have gained a broader, deeper, truer conception of the universe. In the conclusion to her firsthand account of alien abduction, Beth Collings writes,

> I have doubts, too, and suspicions and worries and theories. But what I don't have is my old, safe, life. That, clearly, is gone forever.... Once the earth was thought to be the center of the universe; once the earth was thought to be flat; once humankind considered space travel impossible. If we have learned anything from our past philosophies, we should have learned that nothing is impossible, nothing is permanent, and truth lies somewhere in between interpretation and understanding.[19]

This sort of spiritual insight is typical of those visited by aliens (and demons, ghosts, and monsters)—they have come to a new understanding of themselves, the cosmos, and the meaning of life.

However, it should be noted that most UFO abductees—like early spiritualists, Bigfoot hunters, and preppers for the zombie apocalypse—do not consider their experiences to be "religious," or even "spiritual."[20] Part of the appeal of their search for these entities is that many see it as "scientific," although not in the sense that professional scientists use the term. Ghosts, for example, seem to give irrefutable "proof" of God, divine justice, and an afterlife. So when thinking about secularization, studying monsters helps us see the allure—some would say misuse—of scientific discourse even within what I see as being ultimately a religious quest. Religious impulses *are* being "relocated"; they are also borrowing from and adapting to the discourses of modernity in complex ways.

To help students make these kinds of connections across our units, I organize the midterm and final exam around several "big questions" that arise from our discussions. We create a set of these questions as we read, we then grapple with these questions from week to week, and, on exams, students use course materials to answer one or more of them. Previous "big questions" have included: What is the appeal of the monstrous? How have Americans' conceptions of the monstrous changed over time? What specific cultural hopes, fears, and anxieties are addressed by ghosts, monsters, demons, and aliens in different eras? How have Americans' ideas about the monstrous reflected and shaped their racial views? Does what we've learned about Americans' interest in the monstrous support or challenge the notion of secularization? How have ideas of the monstrous reflected Americans' conceptions of nature, animals, and science? How do monsters function as a component of theodicy? Such "big questions" challenge students to make comparisons between course topics, observe historical patterns, and use evidence to support a verifiable claim.

I also guide students as they conduct their own research into an aspect of the American monstrous of their choosing. We talk about this project throughout the semester and practice together various skills that help students write a successful research paper, including practicing close readings of historical sources, using secondary sources to contextualize primary sources, conducting research online and in local archives, forming and evaluating arguments using historical evidence, and writing with clarity, economy, and verve. Students have investigated a wide range of topics, from spiritualist cookbooks to ghost stories on the television show *Supernatural* (2005-), from online communities for Bigfoot hunters to the U.S. government's responses to Roswell-related conspiracies. Even more than exams, this research paper serves as a culmination of the discussions, skill-building, and explorations we've conducted all semester. In addition to these larger-scale exams and projects, I assess students' understanding of day-to-day concepts through short reading responses, group work and presentations, and in-class writing exercises.

The greatest challenge I have encountered while teaching this course is that students, whether they consider themselves religious or not, usually start the semester knowing little about U.S. religious history. More than in other seminars, I have found it necessary to deliver "mini" lectures on such subjects as the religions of the African diaspora, the mainline/fundamentalist split within U.S. Protestantism, the basics of Puritan theology, the rise of the "New Age," and other topics. As a result, the class ends up functioning as something of a U.S. religious history survey. It also functions as an introductory religious studies course in that it exposes students, usually for the first time, to how scholars approach the study of religion critically and respectfully.

Monsters, according to religion scholar John Lardas Modern, "call into question founding assumptions that constitute the true, the good, and the beautiful; they cut across the religious/secular binary; they negate the very act of human meaning-making, confound categorical formations, and make mockery of our epistemic conceits."[21] As a result, the monstrous classroom is a space that is both unsettling and empowering. In it, students can reexamine, with fresh eyes, important issues that frame theological, religious, and historical inquiry.

Appendix
Course Syllabus
Ghosts, Monsters, Demons, and Aliens in U.S. History

Objectives: Using historical primary sources as well as scholarly books and articles, we will investigate what ghosts, monsters, demons, and aliens reveal about Americans' changing religious beliefs and cultural attitudes from the colonial period to the present. It is my intention that students will: consider the ubiquity and importance of horror, the supernatural, and the monstrous in American history, religion, and culture; explore the complexities of a diverse array of American religions, past and present; practice careful reading of diverse textual, aural, and visual primary sources; examine a variety of perspectives and weigh the validity of competing arguments; think "historically" by paying attention to change and continuity over time; and formulate their own arguments using evidence and careful analysis.

Schedule of Topics and Readings

Week One: Course Introduction: Gods & Monsters

- Timothy K. Beal, *Religion and Its Monsters* (London: Routledge, 2002), excerpts

Unit One: Demons

Week Two: Puritan Possessions

- W. Scott Poole, "The Devil Is Come Down in Great Wrath," from *Satan in America: The Devil We Know* (Lanham, M.D.: Rowman & Littlefield Publishers, 2009)
- Samuel Willard, "A Brief Account of a Strange and Unusual Providence of God Befallen to Elizabeth Knapp," 1672
- "Examination of Tituba," 1692

Week Three: Exorcists & Exorcisms

- Michael W. Cuneo, *American Exorcism: Expelling Demons in the Land of Plenty* (New York: Doubleday, 2001), excerpts
- *The Exorcist*, dir. William Friedkin, 1973
- Malachi Martin, *Hostage to the Devil,* 1976

Week Four: Spiritual Warfare

- Jason C. Bivins, "'Runnin' with the Devil': Conservative Evangelical Fear and Popular Music," from *Religion of Fear: The Politics of Horror in Conservative Evangelicalism* (New York: Oxford University Press, 2008)
- Robert Johnson, "Me and the Devil Blues," 1937
- Slayer, "Hell Awaits," 1985
- Petra, "This Means War!," 1987
- Snoop Dogg, "Murder Was the Case," 1994
- Jack T. Chick, "A Demon's Nightmare" tract, 1972
- Chuck D. Pierce and Rebecca Wagner Sytsema, *Protecting Your Home from Spiritual Darkness,* 2004

Unit Two: Ghosts

Week Five: Women & Spirits

- Barbara Weisberg, *Talking to the Dead: Kate and Maggie Fox and the Rise of Spiritualism* (New York: HarperCollins, 2004), excerpts
- "Miss Cora Hatch, the Eloquent Medium of the Spiritualists," *Frank Leslie's Illustrated Newspaper,* 1857
- Thomas Lake Harris, *An Epic of the Starry Heaven,* 1854

Week Six: Race & Ghosts

- Robert S. Cox, "Shades," from *Body and Soul: A Sympathetic History of American Spiritualism* (Charlottesville: University of Virginia Press, 2003)
- Black Elk and John G. Neihardt, *Black Elk Speaks,* 1932
- Zora Neale Hurston, *Mules and Men,* 1935

Week Seven: Haunted Geographies

- Darryl V. Caterine, "Lily Dale: To Wonder Is to Wander," from *Haunted Ground: Journeys Through a Paranormal America* (Santa Barbara, Calif.: Praeger, 2011)
- Ying Chang Compestine, *A Banquet for Hungry Ghosts,* 2009
- "Question: Are ghosts real??!! :(?," Yahoo! Answers message board, 2011

Week Eight: Exam

Unit Three: Monsters

Week Nine: The Golem

- Chayim Bloch, "The Golem," 1919
- Steve Niles and Dave Wachter, *Breath of Bones: A Tale of the Golem,* 2014

Week Ten: Bigfoot

- Joshua Blu Buhs, *Bigfoot: The Life and Times of a Legend* (Chicago: University of Chicago Press, 2009), excerpts
- Julie Scott, *Visits from the Forest People,* 2010
- Bigfoot Discovery Museum, *Newsletter,* 2011
- Lycurgus A. Wilson, *Life of David W. Patten,* 1904

Week Eleven: Zombies

- Kelly J. Baker, *The Zombies Are Coming!: The Realities of the Zombie Apocalypse in American Culture* (Colorado Springs, Colo.: Bondfire Books, 2013)
- *Night of the Living Dead,* dir. George Romero, 1968
- "What Lies Ahead," *The Walking Dead,* 2011

Unit Four: Aliens

Week Twelve: UFOs & Religions

- Christopher D. Bader, F. Carson Mencken, and Joseph O. Baker, *Paranormal America: Ghost Encounters, UFO Sightings, Bigfoot Hunts, and Other Curiosities in Religion and Culture* (New York: New York University Press, 2010), excerpts
- Guy Malone, "Christian UFO Research," alienresistance.org, ca. 2000
- "Vatican Astronomer Cites Possibility of Extraterrestrial 'Brothers,'" *New York Times,* 2008
- Elijah Muhammad, *The Mother Plane,* 1965–1973

Week Thirteen: UFOs as Religion

- John Whitmore, "Religious Dimensions of the UFO Abductee Experience," from *The Gods Have Landed: New Religions from Other Worlds* (New York: State University of New York Press, 1995)
- Beth Collings and Anna Jamerson, *Connections: Solving Our Alien Abduction Mystery,* 1996
- *Close Encounters of the Third Kind,* dir. Steven Spielberg, 1977

Week Fourteen: UFO Religions

- Mikael Rothstein, "'His Name Was Xenu. He Used Renegades…': Aspects of Scientology's Founding Myth," from *Scientology* (New York: Oxford University Press, 2009)
- Heaven's Gate, "'UFO Cult' Resurfaces with Final Offer," *USA Today,* 1993
- Raël, *Intelligent Design: Message from the Designers,* 2005

Week Fifteen: Exam

Notes

1. Timothy K. Beal, *Religion and Its Monsters* (London: Routledge, 2002), 10.
2. See Joshua Paddison, "Disorderly Doctrines: Religion, Race, and the Fountaingrove Sex Scandal of 1891–1892," *Journal of the Gilded Age and Progressive Era* 14 (2015): 475–502.
3. Joshua Blu Buhs, *Bigfoot: The Life and Times of a Legend* (Chicago: University of Chicago Press, 2009); Matthew Bowman, "A Mormon Bigfoot: David Patten's Cain and the Conception of Evil in LDS Folklore," *Journal of Mormon History* 33 (2007): 62–82; Brian Regal, *Searching for Sasquatch: Crackpots, Eggheads, and Cryptozoology* (New York: Palgrave Macmillan, 2011).
4. Job 40:9 New Revised Standard Version.
5. Beal, *Religion and Its Monsters,* 7.
6. William James, *The Varieties of Religious Experience: A Study in Human Nature* (New York: Longmans, Green, and Co., 1903), 31.
7. Mikael Rothstein, "'His Name Was Xenu. He Used Renegades…': Aspects of Scientology's Founding Myth," in *Scientology*, ed. J. R. Lewis (New York: Oxford University Press, 2009), 383.

8. Jeffrey Jerome Cohen, "Monster Culture (Seven Theses)," in *Monster Theory: Reading Culture,* ed. Cohen (Minneapolis: University of Minnesota Press, 1996), 7.

9. Myers Hall Ghost, Twitter post, August 6, 2012, 5:35 a.m., https://twitter.com/myershallghost.

10. Sylvester Johnson, "Monstrosity, Colonialism, and the Racial State," *J19: The Journal of Nineteenth-Century Americanists* 3 (2015): 182.

11. Veta Smith Tucker, "Purloined Identity: The Racial Metamorphosis of Tituba of Salem Village," *Journal of Black Studies* 30 (2000): 624–34.

12. Mary A. Renda, *Taking Haiti: Military Occupation and the Culture of U.S. Imperialism, 1915–1940* (Chapel Hill: University of North Carolina Press, 2001), 225.

13. Sean McCloud, *American Possessions: Fighting Demons in the Contemporary United States* (New York: Oxford University Press, 2015), 47–51.

14. Amy Davidson, "Darren Wilson's Demon," *The New Yorker,* November 26, 2014, http://www.newyorker.com/news/amy-davidson/demon-ferguson-darren-wilson-fear-black-man (accessed March 12, 2015).

15. Max Weber, *From Max Weber: Essays in Sociology,* ed. H. H. Gerth and C. Wright Mills (New York: Routledge, 2009), 155; Charles Taylor, *A Secular Age* (Cambridge: Harvard University Press, 2007), 3.

16. Tracy Fessenden, *Culture and Redemption: Religion, the Secular, and American Literature* (Princeton: Princeton University Press, 2006); Winnifred Sullivan, *The Impossibility of Religious Freedom* (Princeton: Princeton University Press, 2007); John Lardas Modern, *Secularism in Antebellum America* (Chicago: University of Chicago Press, 2011). See also the Social Science Research Council's group blog *The Immanent Frame,* http://blogs.ssrc.org/tif/about/.

17. William R. Hutchison, *Errand to the World: American Protestant Thought and Foreign Missions* (Chicago: University of Chicago Press, 1987), 200.

18. C. G. Jung, *Flying Saucers: A Modern Myth of Things Seen in the Skies* (Princeton: Princeton University Press 1978); Thomas E. Bullard, "UFO Abduction Reports: The Supernatural Kidnap Narrative Returns in Technological Guise," *Journal of American Folklore* 102 (1989): 147–70; John Whitmore, "Religious Dimensions of the UFO Abductee Experience," in *The Gods Have Landed: New Religions from Other Worlds,* ed. James R. Lewis (New York: State University of New York Press, 1995), 65–84; Brenda Denzler, *The Lure of the Edge: Scientific Passions, Religious Beliefs, and the Pursuit of UFOs* (Berkeley: University of California Press, 2001); Christopher Partridge, "Alien Demonology: The Christian Roots of the Malevolent Extraterrestrial in UFO Religions and Abduction Spiritualities," *Religion* 34 (2004): 164–89.

19. Beth Collings and Anna Jamerson, *Connections: Solving Our Alien Abduction Mystery* (Newberg, OR: Wild Flower Press, 1996), 355.

20. On "spiritual" vs. "religious," see Robert C. Fuller, *Spiritual, but Not Religious: Understanding Unchurched America* (New York: Oxford University Press, 2001), 4–7.

21. John Lardas Modern, "Introduction: Duty Now for the Future," *J19: The Journal of Nineteenth-Century Americanists* 3 (2015): 168.

Monsters in the Dark Forest of Japanese Grammar

CHARLOTTE EUBANKS

I had not wanted to teach about monsters. But the monsters, and the monstrous, would not be denied. Every two or three years, at the central campus of my large state institution, I teach an upper-level Japanese language course called "*Gendai Bungaku*" (Modern Japanese Literature). The course is designed for students who have completed at least their fifth semester of the Japanese language, meaning that most of the students come into class with abilities that fall somewhere in the intermediate range of the ACTFL Proficiency Guidelines scale (about which more below). My main goal for the semester is to wean these students from textbook Japanese, and to provide them an "onramp" to reading real Japanese literature. Or, as I put it on the syllabus,

> You've completed five semesters (maybe more) of Japanese, proven yourself the master of [the introductory and intermediate texts] *Genki* and *Tobira*, and probably spent some time living and studying in Japan. You're ready now to move beyond the textbook, to say goodbye to Mary and Takeshi [two characters from *Genki*] and go beyond tales of instant ramen.
>
> おめでとう ["Congratulations!"], and I've got good news for you.... *The stories get better*!

Well, the stories do get better. But they also get a lot creepier. Five or six semesters filled with the innocent flirtations of the international homestay and study abroad (Will Mary and Takeshi *ever* go on a date?) and the quirky affinities for convenience store, vending machine, and instant ramen culture give way, rapidly and ruthlessly (in the reader I have chosen to use), to a haunting tale about what lies buried in a neighborhood sandbox, an erotic account of a young woman abducted and threatened with mummification at the hands of a virile archaeology student, and several stories that question comfortable divisions between the human and the animal. The world beyond the textbook, as we all know, gets infinitely more interesting, but also intricate, complex, troubling, and sometimes downright frightening.

As it turns out, monsters can help. Throughout this essay, I will use the term "monster," and its adjectival form "monstrous," in a capacious sense, not as a nominal category indicating a kind of ontological being (hungry ghost, undead, beast, committed nymphomaniac, alleged criminal, what have you), but rather as a heuristic device, a term indicating a kind of cultural limit case. In this usage, I agree with Jeffrey Cohen's general definition that "the monster is best understood as an embodiment of difference, a breaker of category, and a resistant Other known only through process and movement, never through dissection-table analysis."[1] Monsters, and their larger ecology of the uncanny and the anomalous, serve as a useful cultural diagnostic in which affect (fear, revulsion, horror) precedes analysis (or, indeed, the "dissection" of sentences).

As I help my students find their own twisted paths through the dark forests of advanced Japanese language, grammar, narrative structure, and cultural nuance, I find that, as a class, we also need to grapple with difficult questions of agency, sexual and otherwise, to excavate the intricate interconnections between genre and grammar (horror and the passive voice, for instance), and, perhaps most important of all, to deal with the ways in which linguistic mastery can make, or break, the safety of our own inhabited worlds. Although I was initially reluctant to take it on, I find now that acknowledging the monsters—integrating our fear and discomfort into the fabric of class discussions, homework assignments, free-writing exercises, and class projects—has turned out to be the very thing that allows my students to find the voices they need in order to define, and defend, their own linguistic agency.

The Importance of Monsters for Japanese Literature: A Brief History

Aside from a good electronic dictionary, I require students to purchase one paper-and-ink book for the semester. *Read Real Japanese Fiction: Short Stories by Contemporary Writers* includes the Japanese text of six stories by some of the country's most celebrated contemporary authors.[2] The stories are unabridged and unedited, and are printed in typical Japanese fashion (top to bottom, right to left) on each even-numbered page. Facing, odd-numbered pages provide phrase-length translations of idioms, colloquialisms, and difficult grammar, while a set of notes at the back provides brief English-language accounts of important historical background and cultural knowledge, along with lengthier unpackings of grammatical usage. The book also comes with a CD, so that students can hear a native speaker reading the text at a natural speed, which is useful for gathering information about suspense, pacing, and characters' emotions. The short stories themselves are chock-full of the strange, the anomalous, the creepy and the monstrous. This is not a quirk of the translator.

Monsters, in fact, have long been a mainstay of Japanese literature. They feature prominently, for instance, in the vast compendia of Buddhist explanatory tales (*setsuwa*), which comprised one of the key genres of literary production between the ninth and 13th centuries. Probably the most famous of these compendia is the massive *Konjaku Monogatari* (Tales of times now past, ca. 1120). Tales of the monstrous and the supernatural abound throughout the collection, with some volumes, such as number 27, focusing exclusively on such tales. Perusing the volume, more or less at random, one can find the story of a demon (*oni*) murdering a female traveler (story 17) and another about a demon caught in the act of devouring a court official, leaving only the bloody head behind (story 9), as well as any number of stories about gods (*kami*), ghosts (*rei*), spirits (*sei*), bewitching foxes (*kitsune*) and wild boars (*inoshishi*).[3] Individual stories from the collection have inspired adaptations, remakes, and take-offs right up into the contemporary period, appearing prominently, for instance, as an intertext in Kurahashi Yumiko's *Otona no tame no zankoku dōwa* (Cruel fairy tales for adults, 1984).

In compiling explanatory tales, medieval Japanese authors borrowed heavily from the Chinese tradition of "anomaly accounts" (*zhiguai*), such as Tang Lin's *Ming Pao Chi* (Records of supernatural retribution, ca. 653–655).[4] As with Japanese *setsuwa*, Chinese *zhiguai* have seen a long afterlife, inspiring, for instance, Pu Songling's well-known *Strange Tales from a Chinese Studio* (17th century) which features haunted buildings, humans mating with shape-shifting spirits, ghostly cities, and enchanted objects.[5] *Zhiguai* have also provided the structural matrix for some experimental modern fiction, such as Yu Hua's fantastic short story "*Ci wenxiang gei shaonu Yang Liu*" (This story is for Willow, 1989), which combines a cornea transplant, a tragic car wreck, and an orphaned soul (*guhun*) in a modern twist on an old theme.[6]

As Robert Campany points out, compendia of the anomalous were useful to the Chinese court (and, later, to the Japanese one) because they provided a place to sort events and objects into typical and atypical "with reference to some reigning worldview, system, or ideology."[7] As Campany reminds us, marking the atypical constitutes a way of describing the world, and therefore exploring accounts of the anomalous from particular times and places can help us sketch the contours of that culture's concept of the cosmos and how it works. Not coincidentally, this function of the anomalous proves equally valuable to the language learner who, in tandem with mastering grammar and vocabulary, seeks to understand and navigate an entire cultural system. Monsters are a great diagnostic.

Monsters also sell. As literacy rates rose, the economy boomed, and access to disposable income ballooned in the 17th through the 19th centuries, the Japanese publishing world marketed, heavily and successfully, all sorts of genre fiction: the more sensational (horror, the macabre, "ripped from the headlines"), the better. To take but one example, the popular genre of *kibyōshi* (yellow-backs)—an important precursor to today's manga—combined word and image to satirize aspects of early modern rule-bound life under military (samurai) rule. The wonderfully grotesque *Bakemono no yomeiri* (The Monster Takes a Bride, 1807), for instance, provides a disgustingly funny take on elaborate wedding rituals and makes potshots at etiquette manuals, a competing genre. In the richly illustrated story, Mr. One Eye (a giant, hairy penis) and Mrs. One Eye (a toothy vulva) search for the perfect bride for their son, "the filthier, the better."[8] Artists and townspeople in Edo era Japan found that combining the humorous and the monstrous created just enough room for social critique, a practice carefully monitored, and often suppressed, by the military authorities.

As Sumie Jones notes, many of the "features of Japan's current media culture find their roots in urban Edo during the later 18th century to the mid–19th century," including an intensive relation between word and picture, the crossing of gender and class borders, an intense interest in sexuality and crime, an inclination toward pastiche and parody, and a tendency toward defiance and rebelliousness in self-expression.[9] The publishing practices and predilections of early modern Japan are still very much with us, providing much of the fuel for today's global economies of manga, anime, light novels, video games, and sudden fiction: the foundational elements of what is, arguably, Japan's largest export, its soft cultural "Gross National Cool."[10]

Finally, in addition to their diagnostic and marketing value in the medieval and early modern periods, monsters and monstrosity, broadly speaking, have proven to be a popular place for authors, intellectuals and cultural producers since the late 19th century to think through the opportunities, pressures, and pitfalls of Western modernity, as a number of scholars have noted.[11] Twentieth-century Japan has seen several waves of this cultural phenomenon. One early iteration of this trend is the novelistic genre of confessional literature (*shi-shōsetsu*), whose authors aimed to expose the dark underbelly of modern life, primarily through relaying their own, lightly fictionalized, experimentations with drink, drugs, sex, violence, and behavior dubbed "no longer human."[12] Another variation on the trend can be located in a persistent thematic concern with the human body as pulp and emotion as naked desire (*nikutai bungaku*), as in Tamura Tajirō's 1947 novella *Nikutai no mon* (Gateway to the flesh), which focuses on a group of young women, surviving hand-to-mouth by prostituting themselves, and referred to throughout as "animals" and "beasts." As with much *nikutai* literature, the novella explores the boundaries between the human and the bestial, dilating on that liminal space where the one morphs into the other, where the instinct for survival reigns supreme. More generally, 20th-century Japanese letters has seen an overarching motif of erotic grotesque nonsense (*ero-guro-nansensu*), exemplified by the works of author Edogawa Ranpo (a pen name echoing the Japanese pronunciation of "Edgar Allen Poe").

To gesture toward this long cultural history, I am using "monster" and "monstrous" as umbrella terms in this essay, employing them to demarcate the persistent literary interest in the borderlands of humanity, where sex, violence, and the drive for survival subvert ration, reason, and networks of social obligation. Collectively, this literary history, both ancient and modern, means that the abject, the morally questionable, the socially objectionable, and the hair-raisingly monstrous have a rather large place in Japanese letters, and it is not unusual to find a cluster of stories, such as those included in *Read Real Japanese Fiction*, show up in a teaching text. In fact, omitting stories like these would require cultural contortion. If you are going to teach modern Japanese culture, you have to teach the monsters, even if (perhaps especially because) there is such a gap between this material and the textbook innocence of the beginning and early intermediate Japanese language acquisition texts most often used in North America.

Basic Demographics: Who My Students Are and What They Can Do

Most students who enroll in my course on modern Japanese literature, which is taught entirely in the target language as an advanced language acquisition class, begin the semester with abilities that fall somewhere at the upper level of the intermediate range of the ACTFL (American Council on the Teaching of Foreign Languages) Proficiency Guidelines. The 2012 version of those guidelines describes intermediate level speakers as

> distinguished primarily by their ability to create with the language when talking about familiar topics related to their daily life. They are able to recombine learned material in order to express personal meaning. Intermediate-level speakers can ask simple questions and can handle a straightforward survival situation. They produce sentence-level language, ranging from discrete sentences to strings of sentences, typically in present time. Intermediate-level speakers are understood by interlocutors who are accustomed to dealing with non-native learners of the language.[13]

Consider the adjectives employed here: "familiar," "daily," "personal," "simple," and—somewhat ominously—"survival."

As these descriptors indicate, speakers at this level of fluency may experience language, their primary tool of self-expression, as a precarious enterprise. Aspects of the past and nuances of the future may be fuzzy or imperfectly grasped. Sentences hang together, but lengthy paragraphs and involved narratives may become disjointed. Speakers tend to rely on creatively recombining others' words and phrases, using these to pose simple questions and navigate day-to-day survival. Native speakers may, at times, have trouble understanding them, and so they may seek out primarily people with whom they are already familiar, or with whom they possess some shared social fabric. In the absence of such (even minimally) bicultural interlocutors, intermediate level speakers may become isolated.

Do you feel the anxiety? Couple this basic language acquisition scenario with the fact that many of the students in the classroom have just returned from, or are preparing to depart for, a semester or a year of study abroad, often planning to live in homestays, and you have a highly emotionally-charged classroom situation. I have found that our classroom discussions, as well as the out-of-class essays and homework exercises, can careen from a sense of self-assured adventurousness to outright panic, and from fear to jittery enthusiasm within the space of a few minutes or a couple of sentences. In other words, the "monsters" weren't just in our class readings; they were in our bodies, hardwired into the process of language-learning itself.

I think we forget, too often, that intermediate (and even advanced) language acquisition can feel like the chase scene of a horror flick, a race for survival. Some of the questions my students were dealing with included the following: How do you navigate a romantic relationship, and the topic of birth control, with a homestay sister? Is it appropriate to express concerns with Japan's drinking culture, as the adult child of an alcoholic? You're a committed runner and you want to find a safe place to jog in urban Japan; where do you go and who do you ask? A student in the Reserve Officer Training Corps has just learned she will be posted to Okinawa following graduation; she's nervous about how her language abilities might hold up (or not) in off-base, off-hours communications. I'm queer; who can I safely tell in Japan?[14]

As with most horror, fear or anxiety, talking about and through it is often the best way to overcome it. Responding not only as a language teacher (who wants my students to improve functionally) but also as a human being (who wants them to address their own concerns and explore their own voice), I found myself embracing the monsters and monstrous in my curriculum. And I found myself directing my students to take them on, as well. I wanted them to make full use of the undead, the animal, and the predator—the ways they induce fear, haunt the imagination, defy categorization, mark liminal territory, and critique the cultural status quo. Monsters, I realized, could help my students find their own bearings, define their own territory, lodge their own complaints, and come to terms with their own liminal status as perpetual outsiders to a Japan that, internationalization efforts aside, often remains staunchly (if impossibly) monocultural.[15]

We framed this venture, collectively, as a brave and committed pursuit of advanced level proficiency which, crucially, involves "engag[ing] in conversation in a clearly participatory manner in order to communicate information on autobiographical topics" and other areas of personal interest, as well as "deal[ing] with social situation[s] with unexpected complication[s]."[16] In short, we pursued linguistic agency, not only as a personal tool of survival, but also as a way to create experimental micro-cultures in which we could thrive.

Day Trip with a Bear: The Aloof Way to Be Friendly

The first story we read, Kawakami Hiromi's "Kamisama" (The god, 1994), is something of a soft ball, a relatively gentle way to inaugurate a monster curriculum. To provide a brief summary of the story: a young woman moves into an apartment building and makes the acquaintance of one of her neighbors, an old-fashioned man who is literally a bear—a scrupulously polite bear, who is also enormous, heavy, difficult to plumb emotionally, and possessed of full tooth and claw. The bear and the young woman go on a picnic outing. Other than the main male character being an animal, the story is told in a straightforward, realist style. What seems to be at stake, both for the character (who does not want to upset the admittedly large bear, who may or may not be flirting with her) and for the students (especially those headed out to homestays) is how to negotiate different cultural norms around politeness. In something of a generational rift, the young woman in the story struggles, at times, to maintain the proper register of polite language (*keigo*) that the older, male bear expects, and, as readers, we are privy to some of her musings about intimacy, about how to become friends, and whether that is, indeed, possible for these two strangers.

The question of polite language (*keigo*) is one that vexes many American students of Japanese. More involved than European language distinctions (such as the German *du* and *Sie*, for instance), there are multiple registers of *keigo*, which involve both expressing humility toward the self or members of one's in-group and using honorific and indirect language toward the other or members of one's out-group. So, *keigo* is a complicated dance of belonging or, conversely, of distancing. Too much proximity and you offend; too much distance and you alienate. It really is a bear, so to speak.

Over the first week, I had students read the first half of the story—right up to the point where a child punches the bear in the stomach—and then asked students to speculate on what would happen next. To whom would the young woman speak (The bear? The child? The child's father?), what would she say, at what level of politeness, and with what results? When we collated and compared our answers, then referenced them against the author's continuation of the story, what became immediately apparent was that pretty much every student (except, significantly, the two native speakers of Korean, which employs similar socio-linguistic techniques) had mistaken the bear's politeness and aloofness as social aggression. They thought the bear was mad, or at least annoyed, and perhaps on the edge of violence. But the bear, in Kawakami's telling of the story, just sighed and let the incident pass, essentially without comment. Following this, I asked students to go back through the story and track the places where they thought the bear had been using polite language to hide frustration, anger, or another negative emotion. And I asked them to consider, in a full-class Japanese language discussion, how this misinterpretation had shadowed their understanding of the bear and his character, and their sense of whether the bear and the woman could or should be friends.

One upshot of our discussion, of course, was an increased awareness of our own (largely U.S.-based) cultural norms and expectations around friendliness, facial expression, direct speech, and personal space. But our discussion also elicited a more personal revelation from one of the students, who commented upon his romantic relationship with his homestay sister, and his difficult relationship with her family. He was terribly afraid of his soon-to-be father-in-law, but was now planning on rethinking the relationship, and his transition from out-group to in-group amongst the family more generally. Was his prospective father-in-law really so scary? Or was he just being polite? Either way, he said, their next encounter now seemed somewhat less daunting.

More generally, the take-home for my students and I was the realization that many of us were experiencing a grammatical and cultural feature of the target language (*keigo*, in this case) as a sort of monster. Put the demand for polite language into the room, and it lurks there like a giant bear: too large to be avoided, too menacing to be ignored. I watched as my students approached it: their voices shook, their cheeks flushed, I daresay their heart rates spiked. But, in the end, the bear was not a monster, just a polite old man; and *keigo* was not a threat, just a tool to be negotiated. Embodying the grammatical threat as an enormous omnivore got my students' fears out into the open, where we could talk about them, shine a light in the face of misunderstanding, and regain affective control of the linguistic playing field.[17]

What's in the Sandbox? The Value of Paranoia as a Reading Strategy

If the first story we work through is a gentle awakening, the second proves to be a loud wake-up call. Otsuichi's microfiction "Mukashi yūhi no kōen de" (Long ago, in the park at twilight, 2006; Otsuichi is the pen name of Adachi Hirotaka) starts innocently enough, with an older male narrator recalling an experience he had one summer in elementary school at a neighborhood pocket park. All grown-ups are off-stage; he's a latch-key kid and spends a good deal of time alone, a fairly common phenomenon in urban Japan. The boy finds himself drawn, again and again, to the sandbox, the one source of cool and damp, a refuge from the stifling heat radiating from the asphalt, the high-rises, and the concrete. He sits alone in the sand, looking at a cast-off children's shoe lying in a corner of the park, and begins thrusting his hands deeper and deeper into the gritty grains when he finds something "down so deep that the tip of [his] middle finger could just barely brush against it," something "softly swollen and springy."[18] He tries to remove his hand, but it is stuck fast; something has closed tight around it. There is a girl buried in the sandbox. And she is not dead. In our discussions of this story, my students almost always end up homing in on one topic: when should the boy (or the girl, for that matter) have realized he might have been in danger?

Otsuichi is a master of suspense and exploits the full range of possibilities inherent in Japanese verb forms, which can agglutinate massively into suggestive constructs of passive, causative, and subjunctive inflections. Whereas, as we saw in the Kawakami story, Japanese speakers commonly use passive voice to indicate respect, Otsuichi takes advantage of the spaces of uncertainty that the grammar creates, using these to introduce a sense of hesitation and tentativeness. Further, he fills his narrator's sentences with hedging phrases—"was it perhaps" (*no darō ka*), "mightn't it be" (*no dewa nai ka*), "it seemed something like" (*no yō ni mieru*), and "almost as though" (*maru de ... no yō ni*)—which undermine any sense of reliability and create an atmosphere of self-doubt. In advocating a thorough-going attention to grammar, I help students attune themselves to the sentence, and the narrative, as an event, an encounter in which they engage, first, affectively and, second, analytically.[19]

On our final day of working with this story, we do two in-class writing sessions. In the first, I ask students to imagine or recall a place where they have felt totally comfortable, calm and safe, and I then have them describe that place in a short written paragraph. No action, no characters; just an account of the location. Students have produced descriptions of the seashore, their grandmother's front porch, a treehouse, and the view from a window of a public library. Next, I ask them to rewrite that description, using as much of the grammar of hesitation and uncertainty from the Otsuichi story as they can manage. Students then work in pairs, reading their two descriptions aloud and brainstorming the sorts of stories that might happen in each version of that location. What this exercise does is help students articulate an intense awareness of genre and, crucially, of the ways in which diction and grammar can sculpt a generic expectation rooted in particular landscapes. Seashores, libraries, treehouses and front porches can be warm, comfortable, safe places; but, as even a cursory viewing of any season of *The Twilight Zone* (1959–64) would show, they can also be uncomfortable, vaguely threatening, or even dangerous.

The point of the exercise is to have students experience the ways in which language shapes our affective relationships to place. Take a comfortable place, add scary grammar, and you can end with a monstrous space. Fear and learning. But can you also flip that? Could we find a way to take a monstrous space, subtract out the scary grammar, and end up safe? Paranoia can be a useful reading strategy: not all the time, of course, which would be paralyzing, but *when the genre calls for it*, attending to and expressing hesitation and uncertainty is an important act of self-preservation. I wanted my students to see this aspect of grammatical mastery as well, to experiment with using language to identify sanctuary.

As a follow-up homework assignment, I have students visit the Tokyo Navigator website listing of jogging courses in the metropolitan area and I ask each student to choose one locale to investigate further, bringing to class print-outs of two Japanese language blog entries describing the park or the course.[20] We then work in small groups, dissecting the grammar of these descriptions and making note of linguistic and cultural adverts to hesitation, uncertainty, and indirection. Then, we come up with a ranking of what seem to be, *in terms of genre of description*, the safest and the most dangerous parks.

Finally, we check our results against the most recent edition of the Tokyo Metropolitan Police Department's crime map.[21] Each year, the Police Department posts updated maps, color-coded according to a basic traffic light pattern: green areas are the safest, yellow areas deserve caution, and red areas are the most dangerous. By typing in the address of the park, users can access a map of the neighborhood and, with a few clicks, can get a quick visual sense of which parks have problems with purse-snatchers, which with violent crimes, and which with break-ins. None of these rubrics are a perfect match for "assaults while jogging," and unfortunately the map does not make note of the all-too-frequent sightings of *chikan* (flashers, public masturbators, and the like). But, looking at the statistics, my students and I have been able to note that most crime takes place near train stations and along major roads; parks, as well as temple and shrine grounds, typically have very low crime rates, unless they are located adjacent to train stations or highway transfer centers.

Although our grammatical detective work does not produce a perfect match with the crime statistics maps, on the whole my students' sleuthing does tend to raise red flags where they are warranted, and they learn that attentiveness to language does, indeed, provide them important clues for reading the landscapes in which they find themselves living, learning, and even perhaps enjoying a relaxing run around the park (rather than just a mad dash for survival). The boy in Otsuichi's story recognizes this, too. The narrative reaches a tipping point when the undead girl, tracing letters on the boy's palm deep underground, asks to be let out. For a crucial, unbalanced moment he considers and then, shearing off all the grammar of hesitation and uncertainty, he issues a straightforward, unadorned refusal: "*Dame!*" (No way!). He switches linguistic patterns (from circumspection to command), and this switch saves him. The undead girl stays buried in the sandbox, and the playground reverts to just another urban space.

The Mummy: Interior Monologue and the Active Voice

One of the most complicated stories that we read is Yoshimoto Banana's exquisite "Miira" (The mummy, 2000). The grammar of the story is hard, and working with the affective filters raised by the story is even harder. One narrative summary might go like this: a college-aged woman, walking home after class one evening, runs into another college student who lives in her neighborhood. She finds herself powerfully attracted to him, and they spend the next several days holed up in his apartment having sex. Eventually, she goes home and never sees him again. Years later, she finds his picture in the newspaper and wonders what might have been.

This may sound like a straightforward sexual coming-of-age story, but another summary, supplied with a few more details, complicates this *bildungsroman*-like reading. The narrator, a college-aged woman, is walking home, brooding to herself about how bored she is, when she sees a familiar stranger. Though he is not attractive in any classical sense—and in spite of the fact that he responds to her call of "Good evening" with the non sequitur "There was a murder here last month, you know"—the young woman finds herself deeply erotically interested in him.[22] She consents to follow him home, where he locks her in, smashes her cellphone, and keeps her in a state of confinement. At one point he shows her his pet cat, which he has mummified. She believes he is contemplating killing and mummifying her, too. After several days of intense sex, she attacks him and he allows her to leave. She never sees him again, but she does find herself musing, in future years, about what it may have been like to be a mummy: "Somehow, I simply couldn't convince myself that that would have been such an awful thing."[23]

One of the mind-blowing things about this story is that it is written almost entirely in the active voice. Although we have all the ominous feelings of monstrous location familiar to students from the Otsuichi story, Yoshimoto's first person female narrator speaks clearly and directly of her own desires, thoughts, and actions. In some ways, after all the grammar of hesitation and indirection, and after all the sentences that omit or only loosely imply a subject and end in lengthy passive verb constructions, this directness and candor is refreshing. Finally, a clear subject-verb-object ("I want this") set up![24] But there is a curveball, because what the active speaker actively wants is to fantasize about, and to find sexual liberation in, enforced passivity, bondage, and perhaps even rape.

Written very much in the *nikutai* (human body as pulp and emotion as naked desire) vein of literature discussed earlier, the story asks us to consider that our "animal" aspects (our drives for food and sex, for instance) are, in fact, not animal at all, but are troublingly human. In reviewing her own actions, Yoshimoto's narrator points out that, in contrast to animals who go through periods of estrous and therefore sexual receptivity, "human beings have no rutting cycle, and give in to lust any time they want to" (*ningen wa hatsujōki ga nakute, itsudemo yokujō dekiru*). Furthermore, she argues, animals "listen to their instincts" (*kan ni tayoru*)[25]; they can tell when danger is imminent and they respond by fleeing: a much more rational response than the human tendency to come closer to investigate, out of curiosity. In short, the story raises questions about distinctions between human and animal, civility and indecency, consent and crime, about which side of each of those binaries is preferable, and about human proclivities toward irrational and, indeed, criminal behavior.

For students who have wanted all semester long to work in the active voice, this story is something of an unsettling windfall, providing a cache of grammar for expressing desire, claiming volition, and imagining and accepting consequences. Yoshimoto's narrator thinks through a number of "what if" scenarios, using a grammatical form (*moshi -tara ... darō*) that emphasizes the idea of direct consequences if a contemplated course of action is carried out. She embellishes her interior monologues with candid admissions of risk: "in spite of the fact" (*noni*) that something is dangerous, irrational, counterintuitive, or otherwise not sensible, she "wants to do it anyhow" (*dōshitemo -tai*). Further, she recognizes that her choices are quirky and willful (using the nominal *-narini* construction). She tries on the passive voice (thinking, "If I don't go with him, I'll end up being stalked and killed eventually.... I'd better just hurry up and get it over with"), but quickly rejects this as a cop out ("No, come to think of it, maybe I just wanted to go with him. No matter what, I wanted to have part of my body in contact with his").[26] The story's narrator thus uses strongly agential language and active verbal constructions throughout to claim her own monstrously abject desires.

Lengthy and intense discussions of "The Mummy" often reveal what some students consider to be a cultural flaw in the Japanese language: namely, the ability to compose sentences without an acting subject. Japanese sentences can be entirely comprised of a single inflected verb, which may imply, without directly naming, an agential subject, direct object, or indirect object. This linguistic feature enables many things—polite distancing, indirection, respect, suspense, circumspection, and so on—but, as my students have by now noticed, it also means that it is relatively easy, in Japanese, to express regret without actually taking responsibility. It is both refreshing, and troubling, that the female narrator of "The Mummy" utterly rejects this cultural tool, which could have so easily come to hand. Unusually, she adamantly claims her desires and her actions, consequences and all.

At this point in the class, I often have students examine the transcripts of official apologies in Japanese. We have analyzed, for instance, CEO Akio Toyoda's public comments, in 2010, concerning the massive safety recalls of Toyota automobiles and the allegations that his company was profit-mongering at the expense of consumer safety.[27] We have also examined the official apologies that various Prime Ministers have issued to the so-called "Comfort Women" (*ianfu*, women forced to provide sexual services to members of the Japanese Imperial Army). We comb through these transcripts closely, looking for the grammars of responsibility, volition, and acceptance, as well as the linguistic strategies of hesitation, indirectness, or avoidance.

One semester, a student astonished me by taking this exercise a step further. I mentioned her at the beginning of this essay: the midshipman who had learned that, following her impending graduation, she would be posted to Okinawa. She had been happy at the prospect that she would be able to use her language skills, but, in researching her future post, she had discovered some very unsettling things about relations between the local Okinawan community and members of the U.S. military. In particular, the student wanted to investigate and understand the sustained public outcry over allegations of a recent assault and rape of an Okinawan woman by two U.S. Navy sailors on October 16, 2012. She wanted to know how the apology, offered on behalf of the Navy by Rear Admiral Dan Cloyd on October 23, had been translated in the Japanese language press, and what local activist responses to that apology had been. As both a Marine and a young woman, one who knew she would be spending time in the off-base bars of Okinawa, she felt an understandably compelling need to dissect, translate, and reassemble the at times monstrous languages of both volition and contrition.

Reading "The Mummy" becomes an exercise in considering agency, the ownership we have over our actions, and our abilities to claim that ownership in words. In general, Japanese is a linguistic medium that downplays agency and first-person possessiveness, preferring to initiate utterances with topics ("As for x…") rather than subjects ("I," "you," "she," "he"). My students generally feel this as a lack, but "The Mummy" shows them that chasing this linguistic loose-end can lead down some pretty disturbing rabbit holes: how many of our thoughts and actions are we really prepared to claim? I do not have an easy answer to that question, nor do I think anyone does. We must all decide how to speak with, and of, the monstrous parts of ourselves—an ethical and existential conversation that lies well within the range of advanced language proficiency, one hallmark of which is the move from "description or narration" to "argument or hypothesis." The monster curriculum even pushes students to reach for superior level language skills, including the "construct[ion] and develop[ment of] hypotheses to explore alternative possibilities."[28]

The monster is not an ontological being but, rather, a heuristic device, a cultural limit case: not the bear but the cultural tightrope walk of in-group and out-group, not the undead girl but the landscapes of uncertainty and hesitation that we construct and deconstruct with our words, not the mummified woman but the prospect of confronting our own desires and decisions. As our classroom discussions of "The Mummy" indicates, keeping the monster in sight involves what Melissa Bloom Bissonette has termed a "pedagogy of alienation," in which we "draw attention to the paradox[es] rather than choosing sides."[29] The monster is within. And that is exactly as it should be.

Conclusion: Some Final Thoughts on the Pedagogical Value of the Monstrous

Letting the monsters into the room is the very thing that has gotten my students so engaged in their own learning, so aware of their personal stake in language abilities, as to dig deep and find their voice, reaching for those higher levels of advanced proficiency. Not surprisingly, perhaps, most of our lessons center on confrontations with the passive voice. In part, this is because passive constructions are such a core piece of advanced Japanese grammar, and because indirection provides much of the social lubricant that makes the cultural gears of Japanese life turn smoothly.

But confrontations with the grammars of passive voice, causation, indirection, speculation and hesitation also have deeper connections. They are entangled throughout the structure of language and cultural acquisition, that process of finding, and claiming, one's own voice in another tongue. In some ways, language learning is a process of civilization and, indeed, of policing. As we learn to tame the excesses, to smooth out the deformities, and to polish the nuances of our own language usage, we become human in that other language. And yet, there is a monstrosity in the nature of the language learning enterprise: we become hybrid beings, speaking with two tongues. People talk about being "bitten by the language bug" (foreign language as vampire), or relay anecdotally experiences of "becoming someone else" when they speak a foreign language (bilingual ability as Jekyll and Hyde). My experiences in teaching advanced Japanese language suggest that these metaphors in fact strike quite close to the mark. If, as Jeffrey Cohen argues, "the monster is difference made flesh, come to dwell among us," then the language learner, particularly the learner contemplating study (or life) abroad in a cultural immersion setting, inhabits and inverts this metaphor, sailing heroically into places on the map labeled only "Here there be Native Speakers."[30]

As it turns out, I am a strong believer in learning the rules in order to bend the rules, respectfully but firmly. To be more precise, working with the monstrous has helped me realize that my students' preferential use of active verb structures and sentence constructions with clear subjects is not necessarily a flaw, an artifact of interference from English that is warping and disfiguring their Japanese. Rather, at times, use of the active, agential voice—even when it is culturally not quite fitting—can be a conscious strategy, a way of creating with one's own language a cultural biosphere in which one can, not merely survive, but thrive in complex, open-ended, paradoxical, monstrously human ways.

Notes

1. Jeffrey Jerome Cohen, ed., *Monster Theory: Reading Culture* (Minneapolis: University of Minnesota Press, 1996), x.

2. Michael Emmerich, *Read Real Japanese Fiction: Short Stories by Contemporary Authors* (Tokyo: Kodansha, 2008).

3. Despite its deeply influential role in Japanese letters, the *Konjaku Monogatari* has received only limited treatment English. The best study of the work, consisting of an informative introduction and translations of some representative tales, remains Marian Ury, *Tales of Times Now Past: Sixty-Two Stories from a Medieval Japanese Collection* (Ann Arbor: University of Michigan, 1993). For an introduction to *setsuwa* as a genre, see Charlotte Eubanks, *Miracles of Book and Body: Buddhist Textual Culture and Medieval Japan* (Berkeley: University of California, 2010).

4. See Donald E. Gjertson, *Miraculous Retribution: A Study and Translation of Tang Lin's Ming Pao Chi* (Berkeley: University of California Press, 1989).

5. Pu Songling's collection is often used as an intermediate Chinese language teaching text, as in this popular bilingual version. Linda Hsia and Roger Yeu, *Strange Stories from a Chinese Studio* (New Haven: Yale University Press, 1977).

6. An English translation of the story may be found in Wang Jing, *China's Avant-garde Fiction* (Durham: Duke University Press, 1998).

7. Robert Campany, *Strange Writings: Anomaly Accounts in Early Medieval China* (Albany: SUNY Press, 1996), 3.

8. The story is translated, with English text laid over the original artwork, in Adam L. Kern, *Manga from the Floating World: Comicbook Culture and the Kibyoshi of Edo Japan* (Cambridge: Harvard University Press, 2006). The quote is from page 142.

9. Sumie Jones, *An Edo Anthology: Literature from Japan's Mega-City, 1750–1850* (Honolulu: University of Hawai'i Press, 2013), 38.

10. Douglas McGray, "Japan's Gross National Cool," *Foreign Policy*, http://foreignpolicy.com/2009/11/11/japans-gross-national-cool/ (accessed most recently on 24 June 2015.)

11. Three of the most important and accessible studies on this topic are Michael Dylan Foster, *Pandemonium and Parade: Japanese Monsters and the Culture of Yokai* (Berkeley: University of California Press, 2008); Marilyn Ivy, *Discourses of the Vanishing: Modernity, Phantasm, Japan* (Chicago: University of Chicago Press, 1995); and Gerald Figal, *Civilization and Monsters: Spirits of Modernity in Meiji Japan* (Durham: Duke University Press, 2000).

12. "No longer human," is the title of the most well-known novel in this subgenre, Dazai Osamu's 1948 *Ningen shikaku* (literally, "disqualified from humanity"). Dazai Osamu, *No Longer Human* (New York: New Directions, 1958).

13. "ACTFL Proficiency Guidelines 2012," http://www.actfl.org/publications/guidelines-and-manuals/actfl-proficiency-guidelines-2012 (accessed 15 January 2015).

14. I have omitted names and altered some details in order to preserve students' privacy.

15. For a discussion, see Chris Burgess, "Multicultural Japan? Discourse and the 'Myth' of Homogeneity," Japan Focus, http://www.japanfocus.org/-Chris-Burgess/2389/article.html (accessed 23 June 2015.)

16. "ACTFL Proficiency Guidelines 2012."

17. For a more technical account of the relation of tension, anxiety, and affective filters in the language learning environment, as well as a theorization of a general "amnesty effect," experienced by students once linguistic achievement is marked, see Guy Speilmann and Mary L. Radnofsky, "Language Learning Under Tension: New Directions from a Qualitative Study," *The Modern Language Journal* 85:2 (Summer 201) 259–78.

18. Emmerich, 45.

19. In this, my approaches echo those suggested by Aalya Ahmad and Sean Moreland, who argue that reader-response techniques can be "useful for a historical poetic approach to horror studies. The emphasis upon 'temporal flow' and 'meaning as an event' is also peculiarly suited to horror, which presents its affect as a frightening or shocking 'event' that precedes deeper analysis" in Ahmad and Moreland, eds., *Fear and Learning: Essays on the Pedagogy of Horror* (Jefferson, NC: McFarland, 2013), 9.

20. "Jogguingu kōsu no aru kōen," http://www.tokyo-park.net/park_jogging.html (accessed 14 April 2015).

21. "Hanzai jōhō mappu," http://www.keishicho.metro.tokyo.jp/toukei/annai/map_annai.htm (accessed most recently on 15 April 2015).

22. Emmerich, 77.

23. *Ibid.*, 105.

24. Technically, the Japanese word order is subject (strongly implied)-object-verb, as in the sentence "*Kare to karada no ichibu o fureawaseteitakatta*" (I wanted to have part of my body in contact with his); or, literally, "With him (*kare to*) a part of my body (*karada no ichibu*) wanted-to-have-it-in-contact-with (*fureawaseteitakatta*)."

25. Emmerich, 80.

26. With the passive constructions underlined: "*Tsuiteikanakattara, izure wa tsukemawasarete korosareru.*" Emmerich, 83.

27. Text versions of the various apologies can be found on the official Toyota website. In class, we focus on the February 9, 2010, apology and the follow-up on February 17, 2010, comparing both of these to the English language version presented before the U.S. House of Representatives Oversight and Government Reform Committee, delivered on February 24, 2010. https://www.toyota.co.jp/announcement/100209address.html, https://www.toyota.co.jp/announcement/100217address.html, https://www.toyota.co.jp/announcement/0224_2.pdf (all accessed most recently on 23 June 2015).

28. "ACTFL Proficiency Guidelines 2012," http://www.actfl.org/publications/guidelines-and-manuals/actfl-proficiency-guidelines-2012 (accessed 15 January 2015).

29. Melissa Bloom Bissonette, "Teaching the Monster: Frankenstein and Critical Thinking," *College Literature* 37.3 (Summer 2010): 106–20. Quotes from 108, 111.

30. Cohen, 7.

High School Monsters

Designing Secondary English Courses

BRIAN SWEENEY

In the late nineties, Joss Whedon transformed an unsuccessful film into a successful television show of the same name: *Buffy the Vampire Slayer* (1997–2003). The show's premise centered on "the idea of high school as hell, with various high school problems symbolically represented as various monsters (an abusive boyfriend is a Doctor Jekyll/Mr. Hyde figure, a controlling mother is a witch, and so on)."[1] Of course, because the monsters were all externalizations of the problems that students faced, they frequently appeared as figures of authority, but if Whedon were to remake the show from the perspective of the teachers, different monsters might appear. Most likely, they would all be externalizations of the nightmares of bureaucratic reforms. There would be data collection monsters, standardized testing monsters, value-added rating system monsters, Common Core monsters, college readiness monsters, and more.

In seven years of K–12 teaching, I have witnessed a great deal of despair from educators over the current state of public education, along with the growing sense that the bureaucratic monsters are undefeatable. Before I began teaching, one of my high school teachers warned me of these monsters. "It's over," she said of the profession, "stay away." I cannot say that this despair is unfounded. The levels of incompetence in how a number of reforms have been implemented—in testing, in curriculum design, in funding, in everything—are far worse than have been reported, and the incompetence demonstrated by those demanding impossible levels of excellence from teachers makes it easy to give in to rage and, eventually, apathy.[2]

Despite this, I have found that the business-inspired senselessness that issues forth from local, state, and national mandates on a regular basis can be combatted by a level of creativity in curricular planning. Though the monsters in teachers' nightmares are many, I will restrict my discussion to one in particular: the college readiness monster (the persistent demand that all content from K–12 lead to students being capable of college level work). In spotlighting this topic, it will become clear that a structural reevaluation of traditional English courses will be more likely to result in college readiness than the "return to the text" that the Common Core demands.

To accomplish this, I will look at the dominance of the New Critical method in high school English courses, and propose that breaking its hold over secondary literary study by (deceptively) teaching different theoretical approaches can engineer a firmer bridge between high school and college literary study. As a case study, we will use a course I designed called "Women and Monsters," which structures the junior year English experience around a set of female monsters who continually reappear in the mythical, literary, historical, and popular culture texts under study. Rather than looking at a series of great novels from one time period, tradition, or geographical location, the course moves thematically from monster to monster: there are female monsters who lure men to their doom, monstrous mothers who harm their children, women of power who secretly employ the occult to maintain their rule, and more. In particular, we will explore a unit on those monstrous mothers and see how a careful incorporation of a relevant literary theory (informed by mythological scholarship and new historicism) can offer a different experience of literary study than curricula inspired by the New Critics currently provide.[3]

This is a call for fighting monsters with monsters, and though I do not think that a focus on narratives of the monstrous is the only way to achieve what I believe is possible, the subject of the monstrous has provided me with precisely the level of uncanny, unsettling, and at times, downright weird, content to jolt some life into the dull experience that modern standardized secondary education has, in many places, become.

The College Readiness Monster

When I began teaching middle school in 2008, I soon had to familiarize myself with the "performance indicators" that then defined New York's standardized literacy exams. These indicators give teachers an awareness of just what skills students should develop in anticipation of the exam. Prior to this, I had always assumed that the negative associations surrounding "teaching to the test" were overblown. Shouldn't all teaching build to the final assessment? Isn't that the point of assessment in schools? What I had not considered was the possibility that the test itself would not be worthy of the teaching that built toward it. These performance indicators were my first clue.

Take one of the indicators that bothered me most: "[Students must be able to] determine how the use and meaning of literary devices, such as symbolism, metaphor and simile, alliteration, personification, flashback, and foreshadowing, convey the author's message or intent."[4] In order to prepare students for multiple choice questions that dealt with this "skill," I had to first ignore the complexity behind the questions that my undergraduate and graduate professors frequently raised about authorial intent: can readers deduce an author's intent—if they could, would it matter? More than that, do authors necessarily communicate a definable message in any given work? What kind of message are we talking about here?

The questions on authorial intent at the middle school level often involved merely asking students to recognize that an author writing, say, an op-ed on climate change intends to convince the reader to support government action to combat its effects. Perhaps, I could agree with this training: it may be difficult enough to train young readers to elect to read op-eds, and if we could, it would then be valuable to ensure that they could understand the broad purposes and goals of such texts. But other questions might ask students to apply the same skills to fiction, suggesting that one could divine the message of a fictional work in the same way one would with a non-fiction piece designed to persuade. This glossing over of the nuances that separate types of writing bothered me. Does secondary education require that we knowingly lie about content in the younger grades and slowly reteach the same content with increasing nuance? Do we lie by teaching that the "author's purpose" and hidden message exists somewhere in the text in order to one day be able to explain with more clarity that the endeavor of divining authorial intent can court all sorts of scholarly controversy?

In *The Simpsons*, Apu sits for his U.S. Citizenship Exam and has the following exchange with the examiner:

> EXAMINER: All right, here's your last question. What was the cause of the Civil War?
>
> APU: Actually, there were numerous causes. Aside from the obvious schism between the abolitionists and the anti-abolitionists, there were economic factors, both domestic and inter …
>
> EXAMINER: Wait, wait … just say slavery.
>
> APU: Slavery it is, sir.[5]

This reductiveness defines much of the secondary education experience. We may learn in eighth grade that "slavery" answers the question well enough; textbooks in eleventh-grade classes may side more with Apu's answer; college courses may then seek to question the ability to derive a "cause" or would explore the political ramifications of secondary textbooks that minimize the role of slavery in the Civil War. This progression seems linear, but it feels more like a process that keeps doubling back on itself: really, it is the age-old circle of blame that educators participate in ("What's going on in the middle schools these days? Let me tell you what really caused the Civil War" becomes "What's going on in high schools these days? Let's discuss the problem of those 'causes of the Civil War' lessons"). In other words, we teach by correcting, and we assign blame to the past teacher for incorrectly correcting the previous incorrect teacher.

All of this raises the specter of the College Readiness monster—the consistent demand of the Common Core that we work toward making our students "college ready." If the standards, performance indicators, predictors—or whatever other term we have devised to list what students need to know by college—do not actually match up with the types of literary analyses that college students must be ready to perform, then no amount of rigor in the modern reformed classroom will be able to bridge the gap between high school and college. After all, the authorial intent example is not the only area where the standards end up leading to this constant cycle of re-teaching and blaming earlier teachers for poor teaching. I need not consult my old college professors to know what they would think of most of the standards that the Common Core deems necessary to make a student "college ready."

Consider this standard, coded "CCSS.ELA-LITERACY.RL.9–10.2": "Determine a theme or central idea of a text and analyze in detail its development over the course of the text, including how it emerges and is shaped and refined by specific details."[6] I had few professors who were interested in having me write papers about a text's central idea; I would have been far more likely, however, to have written a paper on whether or not literary texts can be reduced to a central idea.[7] This is the standard for grades nine and ten. In grades 11 and 12 the same standard gets beefed up in the following manner: "Determine two or more themes or central ideas of a text and analyze their development over the course of the text, including how they interact and build on one another to produce a complex account."[8] This is like a bad film sequel—it offers the same thing as the previous version, just more of it. With standards like these, the only thing that formerly straight-A students will be trained for by their first year in college is the C- they are going to get when they hand in their paper on how the "central idea" of Hamlet is that "indecision is bad" (the students—more advanced ones according to the Core—who hand in papers describing how the "two central ideas" of Hamlet are that "indecision is bad and what follows death is uncertain" will get Ds). That is what they will be *trained* to get in college, but they certainly will not be *ready* for it.

All of this is to say that if we are going to be serious about preparing students to get to the highest level of literary analysis then we have to be more careful (and knowledgeable) about how we consider the development of skills from one age to the next. It cannot be as laughably simple as saying that older students should be distinguished by their ability to find *two* central ideas as opposed to *one*. To break the cycle of blame, and to ensure actual college readiness, we need to figure out how to be more nuanced in our teaching at each level. We can do this by teaching what will be taught in college all along, but in a way that is digestible according to the needs of that particular year.

It must be, however, more complicated than simply saying, "let's be more nuanced in our teaching." There is an art to dumbing down, and a knowing deceptiveness that we can skillfully employ in order to successfully translate challenging content to high school minds in a manner that will ensure true college readiness. Before exploring how a course centered on monsters can achieve this, it is first important to explain why the more traditional secondary English course structure quite often cannot accommodate such nuanced teaching.

The Outdated New Critical Classroom

The artful dumbing down that seeks to teach things we can stand behind as educators, but remains on level for secondary students, involves a layer of deception. Rather than directly teaching the overly complex, we must work it into the structure of our courses, our units, and our lessons, so that students experience complex content in a highly digestible fashion. Our job as literacy educators in the lower grades is not to teach the easier content; it is to train students at each level to experience suitable content at a complex level. This means doing more to translate for younger students the various theoretical approaches that dominate higher-level analyses of literature. But just saying that we should "introduce theory" at earlier ages is easier said than done; this is where the deception comes into play.

A level of deception already exists behind the structures of the traditional literature classes that students across the country have experienced for years. The deception involves the way in which traditional literature courses are structured to avoid a multiplicity of theoretical approaches and instead rely upon New Criticism for all theoretical foundations. If this was not officially the case, the Common Core has canonized it by encouraging "close reading" above all else; in some cases, those implementing the Common Core's recommendations have effectively criminalized the use of historical or other theoretical contextualization to meet the demands of a proper close reading.[9] In "Communities of Practice: Bridging the Gap between Methods Courses and Secondary Schools," James Cercone discusses the difficulty that his graduate-level students faced with teaching any form of literary theory while training as educators in the field. Though Cercone's courses encouraged teachers-in-training to draw upon various critical modes of engagement when teaching literature, his students felt the pull of the New Critical methodology to be overpowering:

> In most placement schools, teachers worked to meet the demands of state and national standards, to respond to pressures of high stakes testing, and approach literary texts from the standpoint of New Criticism—a literary theory that has not been prevalent in English departments for many decades.... This resulted in tensions as many preservice teachers began to doubt that the pedagogy they were studying could be of any use in real classrooms.[10]

Indeed, the pull of tradition ensures that the New Critical approach soon appears to the newly-minted teacher to be less a methodology and more the gold standard of a literary education. There is the sense that to teach from the standpoint of the New Critics (with their formalist focus, lack of contextualization, and belief in objectivity—reinforced by worksheets and lists of closed comprehension questions with correct answers) is to teach the basics of literary analysis, and any other theoretical approach would be irresponsible if the standard methodology is not taught first and most frequently. Rather than appearing as one approach among many, New Criticism begins to look like the foundation toward all future study. P. L. Thomas, discussing the prominence of New Criticism in secondary curricula, wrote: "To invite students to consider many thoughtful approaches to literary analysis is much different than instilling in them—often without naming the perspective—New Criticism as the correct way to draw a single meaning from literature."[11]

To be fair, the vision of literary analysis that appears in high school courses is not exactly original flavor New Criticism. Many teachers likely teach these methods without being able to name New Criticism, or describe any of its alternatives. In "Euclid at the Core," Peter Rabinowitz and Corrine Bancroft make the argument that in secondary schools true New Criticism is ignored: "[New Criticism] was a strong position grounded in theoretical claims about the nature of language, the nature of meaning, the nature of poetry—as well as implicit metaphysical claims about the nature of human experience. The "new" New Criticism—what we might call Zombie New Criticism—seems diluted and dehumanized, stripped of that theoretical and metaphysical base."[12] The traditional English course may well offer "Zombie New Criticism." Take, for instance, the aforementioned prominence of standards related to divining authorial intent; worrying over authorial intent is not part of the standard New Critical methodology. Yet, finding a definitive and knowable author's "purpose/message/intent" is a pillar of the Zombie New Criticism. If anything, it would seem that the New Critical devotion to the text itself has retained such a power within the American classroom not because the theory itself is compelling, but because it offers a reductive allure that lends itself to simpler lesson planning.

Legitimately New Critical or not, this privileging of "close reading" above all else in the Common Core (as if theoretical approaches do not allow for close reading to occur), is itself a political move that ensures a conservative reading of both literature and history—one which discourages subjective analysis and promotes the same kind of thinking that leads standardized exams to suggest that the objective meaning of any text is simple, knowable, and profoundly more important than, amongst other things, the actual interaction that readers have with the text. The privilege of New Criticism at the heart of traditional English courses exemplifies precisely the kind of deception that occurs regularly: we conflate the teaching of a particular *method* of reading with the teaching of reading. That deception is encouraged because we leave assumptions about course structure unquestioned, as Thomas suggested. He argues that "to say to students 'Follow this script' without naming the script as New Criticism is narrow and dishonest."[13]

Though I do find an intrinsic dishonesty in the setup of traditional English courses, I *am* comfortable with certain levels of dishonesty in education. If my two-year-old son's playroom is a mess, and it is time for him to learn how to clean it, I could teach him the concept of cleaning, or I could introduce him to a new game. The new game would break down the various forms of cleaning into different activities (this is essentially what Mary Poppins does, just with telekinesis). By turning the chore into a game, the child learns the chore in one form for training purposes.

Likewise, I have no problem with students learning how to be New Critics by breaking down the component parts and giving them experience with those individual parts repeatedly, in different contexts. Often this form of engagement teaches skills better than direct instruction could, and if you have done the work to break down the skills for your students in a series of units and lessons, it is not dishonest to refrain from naming it as New Criticism until a later date ("All year long you've actually been working on a New Critical approach, and now let me teach you about the method and its practitioners and let's discuss how it relates to what we've done this year"—in my experience, this is more effective then the reverse).

Thus, it is precisely the efficacy of the New Criticism swindle that offers us new avenues to teach theory and complexity without having to dumb down the content towards the point of irresponsibility and "college readiness" irrelevance. Yet if we want to provide a nuanced view of literature that avoids the pitfalls of the New Critics and successfully trains students to consider alternative approaches to literature, we need merely adopt the strategies that have made New Criticism the default methodology in the secondary curriculum (but at least be more honest about it once our students are in the midst of putting these theories into practice).

In my monster course, I sought to take control of the New Criticism deception to my own ends by accomplishing two things: (1) replacing the New Critics' theoretical underpinnings with a mythological methodology (using the myths of monsters as the content focus), and (2) replacing the emphasis on the chronological and geographical surveys of texts that dominate most secondary literary course texts/structures with an emphasis on thematic strands. By marrying the desired content with the desired methodological vantage point in the planning process, I was able to teach a vision of literature and its relationship with the mythic that I did not feel was "dumbed down" or a "white lie" version of similar content taught in colleges. More importantly, this approach encouraged students to go deeper in their literary analysis and develop (or at least recognize) complexity within the monstrous texts we read.

Myths and Monsters

If we are going to move beyond the New Criticism deception and begin to offer a model of "college readiness" that we can stand behind, we must translate the expertise of our higher level training into the structures of our core courses in the same way that New Critical assumptions have been woven into traditional courses. My own undergraduate and graduate training centered on exploring the relations between the mythological and the literary; this is the lens through which I wanted to train my students when given the opportunity to design my own course. I thought that a focus on mythical monsters and hybridity would be different enough both to communicate to students that we were approaching literature in a way that stood out from other courses, and to offer a way of viewing the literary tradition that was responsibly comparative and usefully interdisciplinary. I had to structure the class in a manner that would give my students constant practice studying literature and history from the vantage point of the mythologist.[14]

The first step was ensuring I had a firm theoretical foundation to inform all of my planning. This took a summer vacation to accomplish, and it could not have been done on the fly—lesson by lesson during preparation periods in the school year. What counts as the mythological is far more controversial than the topic of authorial intent, and many others might disagree with the underpinnings of my course; nonetheless, by spending the time needed to define the mythological in a way that made me comfortable, the course planning became doable. Defining the monstrous would be the task of the entire course: by putting key figures of monstrosity alongside one another, within and across various units, the ability to define not only what writers code as monstrous but what history and culture has coded as monstrous would become possible for students. The preliminary issue was more a matter of what could be placed alongside one another—of what could be considered mythic.

For many schools (mine included), the textbook for such work remains Joseph Campbell's *The Hero with a Thousand Faces* (1949). Though rarely taken seriously in higher education, Campbell's theory of the "monomyth" and "the hero's journey" appear with great frequency in the curricular materials that schools across the country have published online. The theory, in short, posits that all heroic myths follow roughly the same formula, and some kind of Jungian concept of archetypes embedded in the human mind accounts for this widespread similarity across cultures (rather than cultural diffusion).[15] Literary works that present the formula of the monomyth spring from the same psychological pool and are thus mythological in Campbell's view. This is one of those disconnections between high school and college that I remember experiencing firsthand; as a young student enamored by Campbell's theories taught in my high school, I was angry to see them dismissed so cavalierly by my professors, each of whom saw Campbell as only worthy of the rebuttal because of the popularity provided him by Bill Moyers' exposure. Nonetheless, upon being trained in mythological and folkloric theory at a higher level, my high school training felt less like "beginner's level mythological study" and more like "misguided study provided by poorly written textbooks."

Given this, my goal was to take a more sophisticated theoretical approach to myth and weave it into the high school course structure—ensuring greater continuity between the high school and college level of instruction and truly helping students to be "college ready." For this, I focused on the works of two scholars of myth and religion: Wendy Doniger and Bruce Lincoln.

Doniger's theory is that myth is "a much-retold narrative that is transparent to a variety of constructions of meaning, a neutral structure that allows paradoxical meanings to be held in a charged tension."[16] Whereas other scholars might seek to differentiate between various types of authorless cultural narratives (myths, legends, folktales, fables), Doniger views all such narratives as mythic in their capacity to be retold across time or culture. By grouping the retellings of a mythic narrative alongside one another, a myth becomes not a single story but the collection of all variants of one long-retold story. Each version, when placed alongside one another, allows the reader of what Doniger terms "the macromyth" to see different individual, cultural, and historical responses to the same questions. It is the differences between retellings that make the macromyth interesting; they demonstrate something about the time period that produced the specific variant, and they allow readers of the macromyth to consider why that particular cultural moment might have produced that particular response to the "mythic question."

In many ways, Doniger's views and Lincoln's views themselves would seem to exist as "paradoxical" interpretations that, if forced together, could only co-exist "in charged tension." If Doniger views myth as neutral, Lincoln views myth as inherently ideological. Lincoln writes that "[mythic] narrative packages a specific, contingent system of discrimination in a particularly attractive and memorable form. What is more, it naturalizes and legitimizes it. Myth, then, is not just taxonomy, but ideology in narrative form."[17] In other words, the goal of myth is not to question (as Doniger would indicate) but to answer—and to delude people into believing that the myth's answer is the only possible answer.

Aware of the tension between these ideas, I structured the course with Doniger's theory in mind and planned lessons on individual texts with Lincoln's ideas in mind. Doniger's theories allow for a cross-cultural comparison that does not seek to erase difference (as Campbell's theory does), and if we use her vision of the "macromyth" to construct specific units, we can compare without sacrificing difference. Lincoln's theories provided tools to more successfully explicate those differences. This pairing provided me with an acceptable way to analyze the connections between traditional myths and literary texts that had mythic qualities, and the focus on the topic of monsters made these aims clearer, more focused, and given the richness of the content, more meaningful. In looking at one sample unit, the possibility of communicating this theoretical perspective and the value of using monsters to do so will become clear.

One of the most successful examples of this work came out of a unit focused on narratives of motherhood and violence; the macromyth at the heart of the unit involved monstrous mothers who killed their children. Given certain curricular requirements at my school, the obvious choice for teaching this macromyth would involve linking the monstrous Medea to Toni Morrison's *Beloved*.[18] But why stop at *Beloved*? Morrison based Sethe's story on the life of Margaret Garner, a slave and mother of four children who was caught fleeing slavery, but not before killing one of her children and attempting to kill the others in order to keep them from a life of slavery. A painting by Thomas Satterwhite Noble depicted these events with the title *The Modern Medea* (1867).

The term "Modern Medea," however, exists beyond Garner. It has been applied more recently to news stories of contemporary American women who have killed their children. There is Andrea Yates, a mother of five, who drowned her children in a bathtub in 2001. Deanna Laney stoned her three children to death in 2003. The women have been called "Modern Medeas" and "Medea of Suburbia."[19] The monstrous mother of this macromyth has also come up in debates about abortion. Perhaps the most broad-sweeping usage occurred in a 2007 article by conservative actor Michael Moriarty. Declaring the 2000s "Medea's Millennium," Moriarty argued that "this millennium will never be released from Medea's ownership until the Roe v. Wade decision legalizing abortion, and the Supreme Court which authored it, are de-fanged."[20]

The Campbellian approach would have me teach *Beloved* but use *Medea*, historical sources on Garner, and news coverage of Yates and Laney as supplementary materials (we would ignore the abortion examples as too tangential). Our discussions would be reduced to this sort of analysis: "You see? This kind of thing happens again and again. Let's look at the similarities between each case. We will make a chart on their similarities and perhaps source this common tragedy to some broadly philosophical observations of the human condition, tragedy, and the problems of self-actualization."

With Doniger's vision, however, the curricular structure would place each text (or set of articles/primary sources about the real life events) equally alongside one another (in a manner that is clearly inspired by the methods of the New Historicists and their notion of the "co-text").[21] The goal would not be to see how each text shows "the same thing," but to question the differences in how each time period, each culture, and each individual responded to the same monstrous scenario of a mother murdering her children. In this instance, Doniger's theory informs the unit structure without it necessarily needing to be taught explicitly. I could teach a lesson on what macromyths are and how Doniger discusses neutral variants of the same narrative, but I would rather purposefully structure the unit with the seemingly minor but crucial shift that moves *Beloved* from being the "centerpiece" text to it being a text that exists alongside other sets of texts that we must confront with equally serious purpose. In other words, reject the typical New Criticism English course unit with a focus text that we seek to understand by spending weeks reading it page by page and chapter by chapter. If *Medea*, Garner, and other examples of murderous mothers entered the traditional unit, they would only do so as "enrichment" texts.

This shift away from historical enrichment texts that provide context is important because *Beloved* was not written in 1856, when Margaret Garner killed her children (or in 1873, when much of the novel is set). Too often we confuse the depiction of a literary setting with its historical time period. We have not necessarily "covered slavery" and its literature because we read a 1987 text that depicts it. But how do we ensure that our students recognize the difference between reading Morrison as a product of 1987 and understanding Garner's life as a product of 1856? Enter Lincoln.

By using Lincoln's methodology within individual lesson plans, we can begin breaking down into its component parts the analytical approach I wanted my students to master. Merely having them read *Medea*, *Beloved*, and nonfiction accounts about various real life murderous mothers as equally valid texts achieves a structural shift in perspective, but teaching how to responsibly analyze these connections is another matter entirely. To just seek similarities and pat ourselves on the back for finding them would create the gap between college perspectives and high school teaching that I wanted to avoid: the similarities are not where the real analysis would be found in a college course.

One thing I wanted students to discover, for example, was the ideological implications of naming any woman a "modern Medea." What are we really saying when we call Andrea Yates a "modern Medea"; what are we saying by calling Garner one? Can we really say that Sethe is a "Medea"? What is the meaning and effect of applying the monstrosity of one figure to another person or character? These are questions that exist outside of each of the texts read, and answering them takes us away from the typical New Criticism format. Still, a successful analysis of these questions must depend upon a strong close reading of each text.

In Lincoln's view, myths take an ideology and mask it in narrative in a manner that makes the ideology itself appear authorless, timeless, and natural. He gives the example of Queen Medb of Irish myth, who fails to lead her troops into battle because she unexpectedly gets her period before the battle and is incapacitated; the narrative links the cultural supposition (women cannot lead, much less lead in battle) with a natural scenario (the arrival of Medb's period); the natural scenario provides the text that legitimizes the subtext.[22] Ascribing the term "Modern Medea" to women who are not Medea helps perform a similarly sinister magic act: it takes suppositions about Medea herself, a mythical monster, and links them to real acts—and because the real acts are so similar to the monstrous acts, we implicitly accept their connection.

But what are the suppositions about Medea that we are imposing on the other non-mythical, non-monstrous individuals? To answer this, there are a number of analytical moves we must make: first, Medea herself is complex. Medea exists outside of the *Medea* that is Euripides' tragedy (the version most frequently, if not exclusively, taught in classes). In certain versions, she does not kill her children. If we can be sure that the Medea being referenced is the Medea of Euripides' telling, even there, scholars are divided as to how we should take Medea's infanticide. Was the text being sympathetic to the oppression of women at the time by depicting the psychological effect of Jason's degradation of Medea with such shocking brutality? Or was it holding up Medea as a symbol of all that should be feared about women—a "hell hath no fury" kind of monster? Does it need to have been either of those exclusively?

The simple, unlikely-to-be-questioned linking of a real mother who commits infanticide with Medea, then, brings up a host of potential interpretations. Are we saying, "Here is another woman scorned who seeks revenge when confronted with her man's failings"? Are we saying, "Here is another woman who is fundamentally unhinged and finally gave into her insanity"?

Are we saying, "Here is another woman who was broken by an oppressive culture"? By calling someone a "Medea" we are saying *something distinct* even if the original text itself says multiple things. By then forcing students to try to unpack something as basic as calling Andrea Yates a "Modern Medea," we give them the experience of doing precisely the opposite of what the Common Core asks—settling on one or two central ideas in a text. We practice seeing how there may be multiple valid interpretations of what kind of monster Medea was, and how the term in headlines or clever titles breaks down when it is analyzed. We can ensure a deeper experience of reading cultural texts and a more "college ready" mind.

By first analyzing what it means to use Euripides' Medea to describe these other women we can go even further later. I wanted my students to read *Beloved* and *Medea*, but I did not want them to explain why the two texts are connected—I wanted them to question whether or not *I* should have them read the texts alongside one another. A number of the best discussions witnessed in class involved students explaining why Medea, Sethe, and Margaret Garner should *not* be compared to one another, or categorized as a monster, so easily. Doing so required students to apply their understanding of each text, their understanding of each historical moment, and their own emotional responses to each act of horrific violence. The monstrosity of infanticide ensured their engagement (the stakes for debate were high), and the political decision to ascribe the term monster to three women they had gained varying degrees of sympathy for and empathy with resulted in some controversial analyses. By constantly assessing and arguing over the validity of the mythical connections we make (with all of the monsters in each unit), individual texts gain clarity for students and historical moments have weight and reality.

Additionally, these frequent assessments of various figures and texts in relation to one another deepened our overall appreciation of how the monstrous functions as a cultural category in literature and society. Just as I could have been more direct about the theoretical underpinnings of the course, I could have started the course by lecturing on how monsters have been defined in various contexts. Instead, it was through comparison that this course's vision of the monstrous took shape. By analyzing key monsters more as labels that could be applied to wider contexts, the course ultimately presented monsters as a kind of "otherizing" agent that cultures depend upon and reuse repeatedly. If mythical theory underscored the structure of the course, this view of the monstrous informed its content. The seriousness with which my students explored this content represents a key reason why those hesitant about focusing on a seemingly silly topic like "monsters" in a core course should reconsider. Coming to this definition of monsters as an otherizing agent required connections to be made across units throughout the year.

Euripides' Medea is a monstrous figure in multiple traditional senses of the term. She is an outsider, wields supernatural powers, acts freakishly different from other wronged women—and she commits multiple immoral acts with full awareness of their evil. Yet, when we see the term "Medea" used as a weapon, and we see contexts in which the so-called "Modern Medeas" of the real world are capable of gaining our empathy, our view of the monstrous moves from representing some kind of literary/fantasy stock figure to a concept that cultures employ to provide a shorthand for describing what it considers to be unacceptable. It is this shorthand that itself can often be used to morally monstrous ends, and in studying it, our questions became less "what is a monster?" and more "why do cultures need to classify the monstrous?" The latter is a question with far greater applications than the former, and whereas some might balk at centering a core English course on something as specific as the monstrous, any course that can train students to tackle such grand overarching questions will make them "college ready."

Later in the course, we focused on the topic of women and power (rather than violence and motherhood); to do so, we looked at various power-seeking monstrous women in different contexts and eventually found our way to *Macbeth.* Lady Macbeth may be more of a moral monster than a supernatural one, and though there are certainly witches elsewhere in the play, in one famous scene Lady Macbeth does seem to perform a kind of spell. She calls on spirits to "unsex" her and keep "visitings of nature" from stopping her from doing the violence she needs to commit to achieve her ends (1.7.30–44).

As we did with Medea and the "Modern Medeas," we were able to see multiple instances in which real life female politicians were described as "Lady Macbeths." Given that Lady Macbeth herself clearly views the monstrous acts she is going to commit as more male than female, it seemed strange to the class that those who call scheming politicians Lady Macbeths associated that scheming, plotting cruelty with the worst traits of women. In other words, if Lady Macbeth defines her acts as being male in nature (or, at least, not feminine), then wouldn't we associate her name with male politicians who behave badly? On the day we were studying this text in class, Hillary Clinton had just made headlines, and we were able to see and then analyze how the term "Lady Macbeth" was used to describe her in *multiple* articles published mere hours before class had started. We could have spent a unit defining what makes Lady Macbeth's actions monstrous, and what makes her "witch-like," but it was more interesting to see how different contexts again use the monstrous as shorthand to label other figures.

By the end of the course, we could have made the argument that if Doniger viewed myth as a neutral construct, monstrosity could be a similarly pliable term—one that exists more as a tool and less as definable set of qualities all types of monsters must share. Monsters are not identified by what they have done or what they look like; they are defined by the effect they have on the cultures that fear them (in other words, the monster hiding under a bed with a terrible and bloody history is no monster if it emerges to terrify a child but is viewed as cute and cuddly; the monster is a monster precisely because of the effect it has on the child).

It was this ability to see the monstrous repeatedly in various contexts that made the thematic strand essential to the course. I could have woven the mythological theory into a course that focused on various kinds of retold stories (monsters in one unit, cultural superheroes in another, tricksters in another, etc.), but by focusing on monsters throughout the year, we were able to build up a view of literature and supernatural storytelling that was unassailably connected to the outside world. To see how frequently we continue to use the monsters of myth and literature to describe the women of today (and to see how frequently we used the same monsters to describe the women of yesterday) is to have a far greater appreciation of the vitality of a category that seems to continue to exist only in the genre literature of "escapism." Secondary students of literature are inherently skeptical of forced connections—of "reading too much into" what is essentially entertainment—but when hours before class begins an article is published that links a 21st-century politician to a 17th-century literary monster, even skeptical teenagers have trouble arguing that our work is forced, or that we are reading too much into things. If we want students to see the humanities as more than just that discipline where we play games of getting way too specific about what students consider to be ultimately unimportant, we must work to make them see these connections to the outside world. And we must equip them with the skills to make these connections on their own rather than merely giving them the knowledge that comes with having read a few good books closely. It is no doubt true that courses centered on monsters attract students because they expect the topic to be easier to handle and less serious than courses centered on classic literature (likely because they assume that if the topic interests them outside of school it cannot be serious or challenging); that doesn't mean that we must meet those expectations. This is just another beneficial deception: make them think that a course on monsters will be fluff and then wow them with the level of thought it inspires—and the amount of work you get them to do with it.

This course is one example of how specific planning resulted in a different type of theory-informed analysis than most core courses offer beyond the New Critics' vision. Few of my students would have described themselves as interpreters of a series of macromyths that drew upon a careful evaluation and critique of various attempts to impose an ideological framework over different cultural moments using a mythological monster as reference. They accomplished this nonetheless.

We eventually discussed Lincoln's work openly in class, and students did not feel betrayed at some kind of theoretical deception played upon them; it was too insignificant for them to notice and too geeky for them to care. Nonetheless, I feel confident that, by taking a course that replaces both the typical Joseph Campbell approach to mythical figures and the typical New Criticism/Common Core restrictions on the text itself, these students are more capable of the complexity required of them later in their college careers and more likely to see literary study as something that exists beyond "close reading."

In the future, I plan to design courses that offer similar forms of deception with different theoretical foundations, but that I began with monsters should be indicative of the capability of the topic to produce profound thought and rigorous instruction. One thing that secondary education quickly taught me was that the content was never as important as the planning behind its presentation to students; the topic of monsters may seem as if it should be relegated to elective space, but when married with as serious a purpose as any course deserves, it can more than exceed the expectations we should have for a core course.

Appendix

This is a sample project from the course that asks students to take the fundamental concept that underscores the course and apply it through their own research. In essence, I'm asking students to do exactly what I did when planning the course in order to better understand the theory behind it. By breaking the project down into four separate phases the project becomes doable—though still challenging. This is the assignment sheet for the first phase of the project.

Yearlong Research: Monstrous Women in Myth, Literature and History

Throughout this year, you will conduct an extensive research project based on the central focus of this course: the connections between mythical monsters, literary women, and key moments in American history.

For instance, in October and November, we will study Medea, the monstrous figure of Greek myth who murdered her sons. We will see reflections of Medea in *Beloved*, the 20th-century novel about a slave who killed her daughter. We will then study how the issues of motherhood, violence, and oppression raised by these two texts appear in multiple moments and debates in American history.

Your job is to do something similar but with a different monster, a different literary work, and a different set of nonfiction pieces from key historical moments. The project will proceed in four phases: (1) researching topics and selecting your mythic monster and literary retelling; (2) reading your monster's mythical origins, reading the literary retelling, and writing an analysis of their connections; (3) researching the ways in which your monster has moved beyond the realm of myth and literature and into the real world, and (4) publicly presenting on this monster, its literary reinventions, and its historical relevance.

This is the assignment for phase one. At key moments throughout the year, you will receive the assignments for the remaining three phases.

The Process for Phase One:

1. Using the resources in our library and its extensive access to college research databases, locate a monstrous woman from a mythical text (it need not be Greek/Latin) that you find compelling and complex.
2. Research the various retellings of your monster's story over time. Ideally, you will locate a literary text that translates the mythic story into a new context.
    a. As an example, one successful project from a previous class researched the succubus, a female demon who uses her sexuality to imperil men. This project paired the monstrous succubus with the trope of the femme fatale in detective fiction and focused on *The Maltese Falcon* for its literary text.
3. Once you have sources on your monster and a literary text that reinvents the monster's story, read as much as you can of each. Become an expert on your monster and its history and then read the literary text carefully, focused on how that text's depiction of the monster differs from its origins (or retains them).
4. You will evidence your successful completion of phase one by writing a comparative essay explaining how key questions/narrative elements/problems raised by the monstrous myth are reinterpreted in the literary variant. How did the literary work reimagine and rework the myth?
    a. To successfully complete this task, you want to avoid merely demonstrating that there are similarities between the myth and the literary text. Instead, dwell on the differences that provoke varying analyses. Analyze key scenes that are representative

of the respective texts, focusing on how the language of each text reveals a difference in perspective on the issues raised by the monster.

1. For instance, myths of succubi seem to demonstrate a fear that women will use their sexuality to bring men to ruin. To what extent is the femme fatale in *The Maltese Falcon* a modern incarnation of that concept? Does the literary text view the femme fatale as an evil and affirm the fear of women (and their sexuality) that lies behind the original monster, or does it somehow use the trope to empower women, or even celebrate their power? Does it do a little bit of both, or a something else entirely? The essay would demonstrate that a careful reading of both sets of texts in comparison to one another can show a strong understanding of each, as well as an understanding of the larger issues that underscore them.

Notes

1. Rhonda Wilcox, "Buffy the Vampire Slayer: An Introduction," in *Reading Joss Whedon*, ed. Tanya Cochran, David Lavery, Cynthea Masson, and Rhonda Wilcox (Syracuse: Syracuse University Press, 2014), 17.

2. To provide two examples: (1) as it currently stands, New York State teachers are rated on student performance on exams that they do not necessarily prepare students to take. Spanish teachers can be rated on their students' performance on English exams; in fact, in the absence of a suitable Spanish standardized exam, Spanish teachers could be rated on their students' performance on a Physics exam if desired. Of the 185 students I taught in 2014–15, only 30 took the exam that I was rated on; the other 84 percent of students I worked with did not count towards my rating. Even if we were to agree in theory that it is a good idea to rate teachers on student performance, putting that theory to practice has been and will continue to be disastrous. (2) When I say "impossible levels of excellence" are demanded, consider the teachers who receive reduced ratings because their students were so good that they did not demonstrate adequate "yearly progress" on standardized exams (those who get near to perfect scores do not show growth).

3. This is not to suggest that the only way to provide "college ready" curricula is to use literary theory inspired by mythological scholarship and new historicism. Any literary theory beyond New Criticism could be employed, using the planning methods I will demonstrate, to shake the foundations of secondary English study.

4. "2009 English Language Arts Tests Standard And Performance Indicator Map with Answer Key Grade 8," *New York State Education Department*, www.nysedregents.org/Grade8/EnglishLanguageArts/20090120scoringkey.pdf (accessed June 15, 2015).

5. *The Simpsons*, "Much Apu About Nothing," directed by Susie Dietter, written by David S. Cohen (Fox Broadcasting, 1996).

6. National Governors Association Center for Best Practices, Council of Chief State School Officers, "Common Core State Standards for English language arts and literacy in history/social studies, science, and technical subjects," *Common Core State*

Standards Initiative, Washington, D. C., 2010, www.corestandards.org/ELA-Literacy/ (accessed June 15, 2015).

7. It turns out that one of my former professors from Hamilton College (Peter Rabinowitz) actually did take on this very standard in a co-written essay that deals with the Common Core (one section of the essay is titled "Searching for Big Themes Usually Leads to Banality"). That essay is also useful for anyone looking for more advice than is offered above about how to provide a more theoretically-sound education to secondary students; whereas my focus is on curricular structures that more carefully incorporate different theories of literature into unit plans, lesson plans, and assignments, Rabinowitz's work focuses on presenting an overall view of reading that will enable secondary students to engage with texts in a manner that will lead to success at the college level and beyond. See Corrine Bancroft and Peter Rabinowitz, "Euclid at the Core: Recentering Literary Education," *Style* 48.1 (2014): 19–21.

8. National Governors Association, "Common Core State Standards for English Language Arts and Literacy in History/Social Studies."

9. Alan Singer, "Reading Without Understanding—Common Core Versus Abraham Lincoln," *The Huffington Post*, 2014, www.huffingtonpost.com/alan-singer/reading-without-understan_b_4323239.html (accessed June 15, 2015). See this discussion for how David Coleman (key developer of the Common Core and current head of the College Board) proposes teaching "The Gettysburg Address" without historical context.

10. James Cercone, "Communities of Practice: Bridging the Gap Between Methods Courses and Secondary Schools," in *Reclaiming English Language Arts Methods Courses: Critical Issues and Challenges for Teacher Educators in Top-Down Times*, ed. Jory Brass and Allen Webb (New York: Routledge, 2014), 114.

11. P. L. Thomas, "'A Richer, Not a Narrower Aesthetic': The Rise of New Criticism in *English* Journal," *English Journal* 101.3 (2012): 52–57.

12. Bancroft and Rabinowitz, 7.

13. Thomas, 56.

14. I want to make it clear that in all of this I do not use the term deceit lightly. Though it has been years since I have been asked to define my "educational philosophy," deception would factor into it greatly. And if we are talking myth, then it is the myth of the "trickster" that has most guided my own methodologies. When I taught middle school and had the benefit of teaching in the same room throughout the day, one of the only times I would use the blackboard for anything beyond writing down the date and homework would be to jot messy notes that seemed to have been written in haste and for another class. When students walked in, the apparent lesson for the day would be queued up on the SmartBoard, but inevitably, one student would ask about the messy notes on the blackboard.

"It's not for you," I would tell them. "They got me off topic in another class, and we should try to stay focused on the lesson in this one."

The allure of "Off Topic Land" is too great for any student to resist, and I would quickly let them manipulate me into taking them to the same "off topic" that previous classes had allegedly taken me. Their engagement at near 100 percent, then we would begin discussing the content I had already prepared for that day's lesson, and pretend as if the spur of the moment conversation had inspired me to do something more engaging than the one planned on the SmartBoard.

Such a deception was often necessitated by a sense of dullness creeping into a unit and could be employed regardless of the content, but it exemplifies the depth of planning that goes into tricking people to learn. We can pretend that every student we teach is just so happy to be in school and soak up knowledge, but our experience tells us otherwise, and just as we must use the airplane trick to get our own very young children to eat their broccoli, we must go to greater lengths to get our students to do the educational equivalent.

I give the above example because it shows how much planning goes into one lesson built upon deception; if we are to structure a course around it, we must do far more than that.

15. Joseph Campbell, *The Hero with a Thousand Faces* (Novato, CA: New World Library, 2008), 17.

16. Wendy Doniger, *The Implied Spider: Politics & Theology in Myth* (New York: Columbia University Press, 1998), 80.

17. Bruce Lincoln, *Theorizing Myth: Narrative, Ideology, and Scholarship* (Chicago: University of Chicago Press, 1999), 147.

18. It should be noted that I had near complete freedom in developing this course from my administrators. As long as I maintained connections between the junior year curriculum and American history (and covered certain texts/authors), I was free to develop the rest of the course. Oddly enough, despite my disapproval of the Common Core's theoretical foundations, my interest in linking literary texts with nonfiction texts made this course decidedly "Common Core friendly" in one aspect, and I am certain that teachers who want to create courses with the freedom I had can always find creative ways to justify the validity of their planning within the political climate of the day.

19. David Skinner, "Andrea Yates—Not a Women's Issue: Explaining the Modern Medea Is Beyond the Powers of Feminism and Psychiatry," *The Weekly Standard,* March 13, 2002, www.weeklystandard.com/Content/Public/Articles/000/000/001/010agmve.asp (accessed June 15, 2015); Rebecca Hyman, "Medea of Suburbia: Andrea Yates, Maternal Infanticide, and the Insanity Defense," *Women's Study Quarterly* 32 (2004): 192–210.

20. Michael Moriarty, "Medea's Millennium and Nobel Prize Winning Barbarism," *Enter Stage Right,* September 24, 2007, www.enterstageright.com/archive/articles/0907/0907medea.htm (accessed June 15, 2015).

21. The influence of the New Historicists is clearly behind the theory this course teaches, with the non-fiction texts moving from being tools to add context to their being "co-texts" that demonstrate larger ideas about historical moments. The distinction is that whereas New Historicists would link a series fiction and nonfiction texts from one time and place without privileging one over the other, Doniger's method treats as co-texts those which share the same mythical tropes at their core (but are not necessarily focused on the same historical moments). In this way, students uses the mythical method to explore key elements of various historical moments in order to draw connections between myth, literature, and history, while also drawing connections between cultures and time periods.

22. Lincoln, 148–51.

The Monster Waiting Within
Unleashing Agon in the Community

HEATHER RICHARDSON HAYTON[1]

If the point of a small liberal arts college classroom is to create a welcoming or nurturing space to engage with big ideas and unanswerable questions, what happens when we bring the monstrous into that classroom? How does the classroom, as a "safe" place for transformational learning, get altered when we invite the lingering, abject, grotesque parts of ourselves into such intentional learning communities that encourage us to be our best selves? Is the very notion of "community" irrevocably polluted by contact with the undead or once-buried monsters that haunt our cultural imagination?

To answer these questions, I spent three years teaching courses on zombies at a Quaker-founded liberal arts college devoted to the core values of community, equality, diversity—and promising a transformational learning experience. As an interdisciplinary pre-modernist in a literature department, I had taught monsters for many years as part of my courses: from the demonic creatures in *Beowulf*, to the sexually-monstrous giants in Arthurian romances, from Dante's infernal hybrids, to *Paradise Lost*'s allegorical and bestial Sin, my students were used to examining the ways that "monsters show" (*monstrum monstrare*). Lisa Verner reminds us in *Epistemology of the Monstrous*, "the monster is always a sign of something else," and I had become comfortable teaching students to analyze the ways such monsters exposed the anxieties, fears, and fantasies of their pre-modern cultural moment.[2] Yet, none of us were prepared for what would happen when we invited a more recent, and relentless, kind of monster (the zombie) into our classroom. The transformations that occurred as a result, and the *agon* unleashed by the lingering zombie presence, challenged what we professed to believe as a campus community.

Across several courses, including a first-year seminar and a senior-capstone, students were tasked with testing many theoretical and pop culture assumptions about the monstrous undead and our own communities. I designed zombie courses to be intellectually rigorous, with heavy readings, multiple films, and plenty of opportunities to develop or refine analytical writing skills. The senior-level undergraduate English capstone had 18 students who read Georgio Agamben, Julia Kristeva, Slavoj Žižek, and Judith Butler to provide a theoretical structure, as well as several scholarly articles on the history and influence of zombies.[3] Students in both courses spent time analyzing popular zombie narratives such as Romero's Living Dead series, *Zombieland* (2009), *Shaun of the Dead* (2004), *Warm Bodies* (2012), *World War Z* (2007), and examining selections from *The Walking Dead* (2006-) television series and graphic novel.

Student learning was purposely designed to be experiential, student-centered, and *affectively* challenging. For example, I staged an all-night zombie simulation in the woods on the edge of our Southern gothic campus where 15 first-year students in the class "passed" the exam only if they survived until daybreak. I also used a RAFT, or audience-centered, writing prompt to require 20-year-old students to imagine they were trapped alone in our second-story classroom with zombies about to break through, and to write their "last thoughts" on the wall in case humanity eventually survived the outbreak and campus was reclaimed by the living.[4] (Afterward, we used that writing assignment as the basis for ongoing discussions about ethics, memorializing loss, and what is worth saving or remembering in the collapse of a civilization—all enduring questions explored by the humanities writ large.) Students in my senior capstone course had to investigate campus geography and infrastructure to develop, and publish, a campus zombie survival plan—including determining how to get supplies, move safely from building to building, and practice "sustainability" as resources dwindled (see appendix; www.quakerzombies.org).

Our campus had long embraced engaged learning models and transformative learning pedagogies promising to challenge students so that they critically assess deeply held assumptions and beliefs about the world and their place in it. Through hands-on learning practices, experiential activities, or "flipped classroom" scenarios—followed by critical reflection—students are encouraged to become change-agents who likewise empower others in their communities. Although the basic premise of an education that transforms students and communities alike dates back to John Dewey's work in the 1930s, and is revitalized by Paolo Freire's call for students to take ownership of their own educational process in the early 1970s, terms for this kind of pedagogy perpetually evolve: one only needs to glance at the latest version of the *Chronicle of Higher Education* to see the rise and fall of certain educational theory catch-phrases ("active learning," "experiential learning," "inquiry-based learning," "high impact pedagogies," are just a few of the most popular in the past few years).[5]

Remaining constant throughout the changing terminology, however, is an impulse to treat students as co-creators of their own learning process and the unyielding hope that education has the power to transform. Also essential to such pedagogies is a conceptual reframing of the educational experience that will transcend traditional classroom boundaries and empower students through an emphasis on critical inquiry. Robert Boyd, especially, argues that the change instigated by transformational learning activities occurs first on an emotive rather than rational plane, and that, as such, it is a psychosocial rather than purely cognitive practice. Likewise, J. Gordon Myers argues that it cannot occur unless a student is willing and *able* to process the experience in an authentic fashion.[6]

Transformational learning, then, has much in common with many of the claims for what occurs in the humanities, and at liberal arts colleges, around the country. Promising engaged learning opportunities in an intimate classroom environment, liberal arts colleges (like my own) actively recruit students who *seek* transformational learning—who want to be challenged by their learning experience, and imagine themselves then going on to "be the change" in their own communities. Guilford College even used that Gandhian phrase as its recruitment slogan from 2003 through 2007, as they tried to highlight the transformational education offered by progressive faculty on an intimate campus in North Carolina.

Ultimately, my experiment inviting the undead and abject into our classroom helped us interrogate the progressive ideals of our community and the promises touted by transformational learning pedagogies. My multi-year experiment exposed how the campus and classroom was a site of *agon* as frequently as it was a hub of collaboration. Teaching zombies also made visible the ways that certain members of our own communities reside perpetually in liminal states of being or in undead peripheries (e.g., the homeless, mentally ill, undocumented persons). Finally, our zombie pedagogy put to test recent research about leadership and group communication when under duress from Dan Wilson's CoLAB at Harvard University, and exposed how quickly a classroom can turn monstrous or embody a well-worn cliché of zombie movies as students in one particular class sacrificed each other to survive a night with monsters.

Exceptional Monsters

Over the span of three years, I offered courses that explicitly invited the monstrous into the classroom. While all monsters reflect pieces of ourselves and our culture that we fear and magnify into inescapably grotesque shapes and proportions, zombies are a particularly dangerous form of monster.[7] Because they are both human and inhumane, simultaneously alive and dead, all-consuming and empty, zombies blur the lines between "us" and "them." Zombies heighten "our awareness of ourselves as individuals because our individuality is endangered" by zombie hordes.[8] Unlike other monsters, zombies are, at least initially, indistinguishable from the humans they threaten (and once were). Their monstrosity, then, draws attention to the ambiguous peripheries and liminal states that challenge our very definitions of society. Theorist Georgio Agamben reminds us that the basis of human civilization—juridical sovereignty—contains the undoing of itself. Agamben notes, in *Homo Sacer*, that law itself is always predicated on the exception to law; boundaries are created with regard to their surplus or breach.[9] Zombies, then, read in tandem with Agambian theory, threaten to expose that untenable reality upon which our society is based, and force us to confront our complicity in maintaining the lie that order and justice are not *already* predicated upon exceptions waiting to be punished.

My students found the "quislings" (living humans who had become so zombie-like that they were virtually indistinguishable and often more dangerous) of Max Brooks' *World War Z* to be an especially resonant depiction of Agamben's theories, and Agamben's theories an apt way to understand why the quislings were even more disturbing monstrosities than the zombies. Classroom discussion came alive as we mapped on the whiteboard all the ways that *World War Z* exemplified the *homo sacer*, the state of exception that entitles yet constantly challenges the norm—ranging from the obvious zombies and quislings, to Brooks' depiction of Cuba, North Korea, California domestic workers, and so on, as states of exception that expose the inherent fragility of juridical order. Zombies became much more interesting to my advanced students once they were coupled with theoretically complex secondary readings about postcapitalism, resource management and sustainable communities, undocumented worker rights, and queer identities. Zombies forced us to consider the horrors unleashed when we try to build community by building walls, literally and metaphorically. We found time and again that, like other monsters, zombies fail to reside in any neat categories, or stay "outside" of the barricades we create to protect ourselves. They are hybrids, prodigious, and challenging to our very definitions of what it is to exist; in short, as Verner points out, "the monster, enigmatic, chaotic, awesome, resists."[10]

Resistance and Persistence

Even more than other monster narratives, zombie movies expose the lie behind our most cherished manifestations of order and justice. Watching

Romero's *Night of the Living Dead* initially felt "disturbingly banal" and "campy but realistic" to most of my 20-something year old students in North Carolina (the "new south," but still a slave state until 1865, and the site of the Woolworth counter sit-ins during the civil rights movement).[11] Indeed, students initially appeared bored by the film in our first classroom discussion. When pressed further in discussion, they claimed they were adamantly *not* shocked by Romero's ending, where a black man who has managed to survive the zombies is killed by a posse of white men approximating a lynch-mob the next morning. The famous shot of Ben's body, thrown onto a pile of zombies, perfectly encapsulates Agamben's *homo sacer*: Ben's black body is juxtaposed with the zombies and any distinction between monster and human is erased in the pile of corpses. Students in this 2011 course recognized Romero's horrific fantasy as their own living reality—a world where black and brown bodies, even heroic ones, are routinely sacrificed and discarded, inevitably becoming zombie-like corpses living on in narratives of oppression from yet another socioeconomically-depressed region.

After more critical reflection in a recursive teaching approach, and with excerpts from Judith Butler's *Precarious Life* and Agamben's *Homo Sacer* under their belt, students later began to articulate how "heavy" the film felt. In part this was due to despair over Romero's bleak vision of humanity—a place Dan Drezner, in the *Theory of International Politics and Zombies*, says all zombie narratives go: "where every man is enemy to every man."[12] Discussion of the film's relevance to current events continued in our final capstone presentation in front of the campus community, as well. One student described the film itself as a "zombie" that continued to live on beyond its cultural moment, and which persisted in his memory each time he read about another racially-motivated killing in America. For him, and I suspect other students, the monstrous persistence of the zombie became an iconic representation of American injustices from which we cannot escape. As W. Scott Poole reminds us, "the monster reifies very real incidents, true horrors, true monsters."[13]

Yet, in part the heaviness students felt was also due to our geographical and historical location exerting force over their understanding of Romero's narrative. Students were watching *Night of the Living Dead* on a 175-year old campus that once belonged to the family of Levi Coffin, the reputed leader of the underground railroad, and whose woods contained a southern-most stop on the journey toward freedom undertaken by enslaved people. Students had, from the first weeks of college, heard stories of how Coffin built carts with false bottoms and hid black bodies underneath stacks of vegetables, cotton, and grains going to market—claiming, when challenged, that he had nothing but "earthen vessels" in his cart.[14] First-year students had taken tours of the Guilford woods and had seen the 350 year old tree that most likely was a marker for escaping slaves, who would hide in our woods and await local Quaker families to bring food, give directions, and often personally escort them north through networks of other sympathetic community members. Much like geospatial mapping, to see Ben's body being stacked on top of the zombies by McLelland's posse was to resurrect a kind of racial narrative of the "living dead" that overlaid the movie with historical resonances and atemporal dissonance. Students affectively, not just rationally, comprehended Butler's claims that some lives are worth more than others simply because of geography or corporality. They grasped Romero's now famous reflection that "there is nothing scarier than the neighbors."[15]

This example suggests that teaching zombies to students in a progressive community devoted to transformational learning was successful in promoting changed attitudes as well as behaviors. Certainly, it worked better with seniors in a capstone course. The student cohort became a tighter learning community who actively practiced patient listening, developed bonds that have persisted several years past graduation (there was even a mini-reunion last year), and included one group of students who crowd-sourced funds to maintain their course website called "quakerzombies.org." Student evaluations for the course were unanimously high, and the students' final campus-wide presentation of their research was one of the best-attended and most interactive in the last decade of English department capstone presentations.

However, when applied the following year to first-year students, this pedagogical experiment proved more complicated and had some very real challenges to the kind of "deep, structural shift" hoped for by Edmund O'Sullivan.[16] When adapted to a first-year seminar in 2012, the same kinds of transformational learning did *not* occur in a consistent fashion and, more troubling, did not provide the kind of cohort cohesion that could promote persistence in college. Indeed, it seems the opposite occurred, where monstrosity infected the group and destabilized the community. Of the eighteen first-year students who enrolled in the zombie course, only eight have persisted to their senior year: five women and three men.[17]

This first-year seminar offered an experientially-based course thematized around zombies and the zombie apocalypse. With many of the same readings included, albeit in shorter selections and with several movie versions substituted, the course content was remarkably similar to the senior-capstone. What differed, however, was the scaffolding of the course and the expectations for student analysis. In short, this first-year course devoted less time to deep analysis of zombie material and offered more opportunities for experiential-learning and self-discovery, as appropriate to a first-year seminar. I hoped it would help students develop sustainable academic habits or modes of thinking and create lasting communities on campus. Institutional course outcomes for all first-year seminars focused on empowering students to perform quality work in teams, improving their oral (rather than written) communication and presentation skills, and exhibiting an ability for sustained deliberation on a range of ethical questions.

Thus, in my course design, I was influenced by Dan Wilson's Project Zero and Primal Quest Extreme Team research at Harvard University—a multiyear investigation into how adults learn and teams function optimally, through communication, especially in crisis or high-stress situations.[18] Some of Wilson's research, for example, followed high-achieving teams as well as those who failed in the dangerous international Primal Quest all-terrain race, and mapped how teams navigated tension through language and group roles. He found that successful teams managed their group dynamics through proactive linguistic sharing of vulnerability and acknowledging uncertainty. Failing teams did the opposite—team members asserted their views as absolute truths or with verbal certainty even when wrong, and projected strength through false certainty rather than admit vulnerability. Wilson's research team mapped participants' verbal patterns across several years and several teams' worth of audio recordings while in the multiple day-long race, and his research seemed to imply that once a team-member identified themselves as a leader, they felt more pressure to project certainty, even if detrimental to the group's success.[19]

Like Wilson, I was interested in seeing how my students would deal with the pressure and stress of a crisis—a monstrous threat of the zombie-sort, with all of its uncertainty, lack of trust, and challenge to social order. Indeed, this is the "meat" of any good zombie or monster narrative. As Shawn McIntosh reminds us, "The unique balancing act that zombies represent between control and enslavement, strength and weakness, us and them, and group versus individual identity offers a window into better understanding why we enjoy the horror genre in particular and how we perceive ourselves and certain aspects of popular culture in general."[20] Intentionally using decentered teaching techniques, experiential learning opportunities, and role-playing, I constructed a semester filled with unpredictability and simulated crisis. My students had to learn not just to react, but to discern ethical and sustainable paths forward. Post-activity reflective assignments provided us with plenty of opportunities to examine our own and the group's ethical behavior, oral communication skills, and community building. I hoped my zombie simulations would be the perfect assessment for all of the learning outcomes in a first-year seminar at Guilford College. But in the example I am about to describe, the result was nothing like what I imagined; indeed, what happened to this zombie experiment challenged everything I took for granted about learning communities, how they are sustained, and how easily their ideals can be challenged.

Becoming Monstrous

On the first Friday night of the semester, when my freshmen had only been on campus one week and barely knew each other, I recreated the narrative arc of a typical zombie text: a small group of near strangers comes under threat from a horde of monstrous zombies.[21] Like a scene out of *The Walking Dead*, *Shaun of the Dead*, or Romero's films, the group had to find temporary shelter, figure out how to work together as a team, reallocate resources, and process fear, in order to survive the night. For my simulation, I enlisted recently graduated seniors from the previous zombie and monster courses who dressed up as zombies and, at an appointed time, interrupted our 10:00 p.m. moonlight tour of the campus woods and graveyard. The first-year seminar students had *not* been warned in advance (although their parents and campus officials had), and as the "zombies" came slowly shuffling our way, students were quickly told they must get to the first "safe house" across campus and await my arrival for further instructions. They were also told of two important rules: they could not hurt or harm the zombies in any way, and would be graded on whether they survived the night without getting a (fake) bloody handprint on their clothes from the zombies. Over the next five hours, this group of students had to respond to three separate "attacks" on their safe-houses, navigate a 300-acre campus they barely knew geographically, and liberate *and allocate* up to six pizzas after the pizza delivery guy was attacked and carried off by the zombies (later to return as a zombie and harass them).[22] Student Life administrators and other campus personnel were involved in the night-long experiment, and campus public safety officers helped stage one of the attacks to exemplify the sacrifice of authority and safety personnel in a typical zombie narrative. Finally, I took all of their cell phones away after the first 20 minutes, to symbolize the loss of technology and isolation that occurs in most monster or zombie survival narratives. For the rest of the night, both groups of students (survivors and zombies) had to work together in their respective groups to coordinate individual actions, achieve their mission, communicate effectively while under threat—and to manage individual as well as collective fear alternated with bouts of boredom.

If done well according to our campus Quaker ethos, we should see each of the groups act with integrity in a manner that promotes inclusion and equality, being good stewards of resources and distributing things fairly, and communicating cohesively by listening and encouraging a diversity of voices. Yet, by turning campus into a monstrous geography (even a *simulated* version of monstrosity and horror), all of our college's progressive ideals were being challenged, and the actions of the two cohorts exposed the fragility of those core values.

This was especially clear in the first-year cohort, who had only been on campus for a short time and had not yet internalized our community values. Almost immediately they abandoned the campus principle of patient listening and consensus for decision-making, defaulting instead to the commands of a "hero" figure who happened to be the tallest and loudest man in the group (a 6'6" center for our basketball team). Time and again, I watched in disbelief as the group consistently ignored or rejected ideas from the petite, 5'2" tall, but astute, woman who almost always offered a better solution or strategy. When it came to resource allocation (of the four out of six pizzas freshmen managed to liberate from the zombies at midnight for their group of 18 students), they were not fair or equitable, nor did they exhibit any of the manners for which the South is so well-known. In painfully stereotypical fashion, several larger men pushed women out of the way to grab food—even only moments after some of those same women had played crucial roles in the pizza-liberation mission.[23] Finally, in the most horrific and monstrous moment of the night-long experiment, the group chose to sacrifice one of its own members to the zombies. Fully-knowing that any student who got "caught" by the zombies would earn an "F" in the graded, high-stakes simulation, students worked against one of their own to ensure he was caught and expelled from the group.

This particular student had challenged the authority of the two most vocal students vying for leadership roles within the group throughout much of the experiment. A first-generation football player with a booming voice and even bigger personality, he got more independent and difficult to include in planning sessions as the night wore on. At one point he mocked the survival plan developed by the rest of the group and insisted he would "go it alone" if they didn't adopt his version. Finally, and with only 90 minutes left in the experiment, most of the group seemed to turn on him. In fact, the incident played out almost precisely like the Shane-Rick struggle for power in *The Walking Dead* series—and replicated what Dan Wilson saw happening in the failing-teams he followed through the Primal Quest extreme team challenge. As Wilson points out with his linguistic research, once a group under extreme stress stops using interrogative, collaborative sentence structure and adopts short, declarative commands even when facing high uncertainty of being correct or knowing the outcome, group cohesion has been lost. According to Wilson's research, a well-functioning team handles danger and extreme stress best by maintaining a linguistic and socio-psychological commitment to sharing the burden of uncertainty.[24] But when group members begin to assert their own opinions and ideas as factual, this represents a shift in the dynamic whereby the group no longer exists as an entity that must be protected; instead, it has become a collection of individuals in struggle against once another.

That is precisely what I watched happen to the freshmen cohort in this zombie simulation, and observed in other experiential-learning activities throughout the semester. When under threat from external monsters, humans became monstrous—replicating what most zombie narratives (from *28 Days* to *The Walking Dead* to even *I, Zombie*) point out. Like the zombies who sought to mindlessly consume anything that got in their way, my freshmen became voracious individuals willing to jettison progressive practices, core values, and even other community members.[25] Once monsters entered the safety of our classroom, and Habermasian struggle replaced progressive Quaker ethos, our community was destabilized. McIntosh points out that part of the fear-inducing effect of zombies historically has been that they appear to be "horrific sanctions for anti-social behavior," and that modern zombies highlight a postmodern fear of losing individuality and "becoming one among 'many.'"[26] When put into simulated zombie crisis situations, my first-year students seemed to bear witness to that fear throughout the semester.

Whereas the seniors, in the English capstone course or working together as zombies during the simulated attack, could welcome the destabilizing effect of monstrous *agon* as another challenge to face together, the freshmen could not—they simply did not have the critical reflection skills yet developed to transform their thought and action. Nor had they developed as deep an ethical commitment to the core values of a progressive community, as had the seniors over three previous years. The first-year students were still in *individual* survival mode even at the end of the semester, while the seniors embraced the opportunity to bond as a community almost immediately.

Even in the guided reflection activities held after that all-night zombie raid, first-year students remained unable to process critically their own complicity within the group's actions. Over the residual weeks of the semester, these same students pointed out how *other* literary and film characters acted out of self-interest rather than protecting the community, and fell into stereotypical leadership roles, in zombie narratives. Yet they were not able to see their own actions as part of a similar trajectory and refused to be transformed by their experience of (staged) monstrous horror. That cognitive dissonance precluded them from acknowledging the veracity and psycho-social critique inherent in zombie stories, and rendered them more zombie-like in their mindless consumption of the genre than they could ever acknowledge.

"Slate-Wipers"

Max Brooks has famously said that zombies are the most dangerous or fear-inducing of all monsters because they are "slate-wipers" who can wipe out the "entire human race" rather than just a handful of individuals. He also points out that "most monsters, you have to go to the swamp or the forest or under the pyramid or whatever. Zombies come right to you."[27] I will confess that—along with the fact they are relentless and mindless in their pursuit—is what enticed me to teach courses on zombies. From their categorical challenge to our deepest held beliefs about what it means to be living, sentient beings, to the way they semiotically represent multiple categories of monstrosity, deprivation, and "otherness," to the horrific totality of their consumption, there is just something *extreme* about zombies. My students are attracted to such extremity, as well, and were eager to experience it firsthand. Like me, however, they were not fully prepared for what happens when such monsters are invited, unleashed, into a learning community.

Bringing zombies to campus infected the group of learners, exposing the fragility of our community and ethical values we professed. For example, one of the Quaker testimonies under which our campus continues to operate is integrity. Beyond an honor code, Guilford College encourages all members of its community to "walk our talk" and endeavor to put our beliefs to practice daily. This can mean having the courage to speak to injustice, as many of our students and faculty have done across the years as conscientious objectors, peace protestors, or practitioners of civil disobedience. The burden of that testimony was made abundantly clear, however, while teaching zombies: by putting students into simulated crisis situations where their professed ethics required self-less action, we had to face the uncomfortable evidence of our lack of integrity. Seniors, who had developed a stronger commitment to the community and its ideals, better used critical reflection opportunities to become a more cohesive group of survivors who understood their own limitations. They had used the semester-long opportunity to refine their own practice of how to belong in a group they may not have chosen, how to cultivate tolerance under pressure, and how to resist knee-jerk or reactive thinking. For them, the experience was transformative and the pedagogical promises of such teaching paid ongoing dividends. Indeed, it appears to have *remained* transformative—four years post graduation, they continue to be connected to and supportive of one another and the college via social media, group correspondence, return visits, and campus giving.

Ed Greenwood defends writing zombie fiction by invoking another way that *monstrum monstrare*: arguing that "if voiceless, as my zombies always are, they really let me 'show' rather than 'tell.' Zombies let me explore what it is to be human."[28] That was true for all of my zombie students, as well. Academically, the senior zombie cohort was better able to translate theoretical complexity to a broad audience in their capstone presentation, and their writing exhibited a clearer sense of audience and exigency than previous capstone research papers. Even the first-years figured out how to work collectively as a team by the last few weeks of the semester and staged a "zomBcon" (a six-hour festival of movies, games, and zombie activities) for campus. After 14 weeks together, they began to correct their early issues with teamwork in the zombie raid simulation: they exhibited better mastery of group project management, and problem solving skills, than other first-year seminar cohorts I had taught.

One foundation of zombie stories is that, in a time of crisis, civilization is fragile and that individuals cannot be counted upon to do what is best for the common good. Yet, the narrative arc of even the most pessimistic zombie text also simultaneously offers hope that a small pocket of survivors will be able to come together to create a new kind of post-apocalyptic community with more integrity. One need only think of how most recent zombie movies end to see this pattern: *Zombieland*'s "new" family structure adopted at the end of the movie (symbolized by a family road trip and by Tallahassee finally getting the much sought-after twinkie from Little Rock), *Shaun of the Dead*'s reconciliation of pub-life and family responsibility, or even *Warm Bodies*' happy zom-rom-com ending. Teaching zombies and introducing monstrous *agon* into the classroom powerfully replicated zombie narrative arcs by disrupting my pedagogy and our learning community in both transformative and monstrous ways. Using a simulated monster attack as part of the course structure forced me to reconsider my own teaching assumptions. It also affirmed the need for both analytical activities and reflection about how easy it is for us all to become monsters, especially when the monsters are unleashed from the books and films to take over our learning spaces. Zombies became, for me, a true "slate wiper" like no other monster I had taught.

The transformative pedagogies attempted by introducing zombies into the classroom were not uniformly successful; nor were they a failure. W. Scott Poole reminds us that monsters are a "messy subject," and their stories are "tales of excess" that contain contradictions and conflict and, most often, refuse happy endings.[29] Likewise, unleashing monstrous *agon* into my classroom and onto my campus became "messy" or overdetermined in its excess. Once freed, the zombies threatened to consume and infect us, truly flipping our classroom of students who had gleefully consumed such monsters so long as they were trapped on the pages of favorite books or within scenes of cult movies. What we learned from our struggle with these monsters was that we must cultivate resilience *and* patience, grit *and* compassion, if we had any hope of surviving together. The zombies were certainly disruptive—and there is a radical promise in embracing disruptive educational acts. As Flavia M. C. Bastos and Jeffrey Di Leo remind us in their call for a new kind of pedagogy to revitalize the humanities, disruptive pedagogies can generate "paradigm shifts, creating consciousness raising that alters the ways in which we see ourselves and society."[30] That, to me, is the worth the danger of unleashing monsters and monstrosity into the classroom.

Appendix A
RAFT Assignment Sheet (2012)
Surviving the Zombie Apocalypse

The zombie apocalypse has begun! Zombies have invaded Guilford College, and you and a handful of other students have survived thus far. You are holed-up in the King Hall, but you are running out of water and protein bars. You can hear shuffling and moaning outside, and you know the end is near....

At first you just thought it was a just a game of Humans vs. Zombies. Then you saw Professor Hayton chewing on Professor Jeske's leg. Still, you didn't get truly scared until you saw a zombified RA in the dorm, eating one of his residents.

Please write a "survivor's journal" documenting this last night at Guilford. Your final record of existence should be between 3–4 pages, and be written to a future historian who will uncover your words scrawled onto a wall 150 years into the future, when humanity has been reestablished and the zombies have been eradicated.

- What part of your story is important to tell?
- What lasting thoughts or observations about the apocalypse deserve to be remembered?

The Zombies are coming—

Appendix B
Zombie Seminar—Campus Presentation Discussion Questions (ENGL 400Z, 2011)

1. So I get it: Zombies are everywhere. Why should I care, when I can read Shakespeare or Melville or Bronte or Morrison?
2. What have you learned this semester, beyond the obvious fact that Zombies represent our cultural anxieties?
3. For a class on Zombies, it seems like you spent a lot of time talking about "post capitalism," sustainability, or resource management. Why is that?
4. For a class on Zombies, you seemed to spend a lot of time talking about *humans* and how they try to get along. Why? What's the connection?

5. What's the connection between apocalypse and Zombies?

6. I like Zombies; I think these stories are fun. But I don't get all the fuss. How is it fun to play video games shooting them, or watching gory movies about them eating brains, for a whole semester? Once you've seen one shambling "walker" haven't you pretty much seen 'em all

7. What have Zombies taught you about community?

8. What have Zombies taught you about the line between human vs. animal and living vs. dead?

9. Where did Zombies come from, and why are they so popular right now?

10. Can you problematize the concept of "survival" and what that means for Zombies (or in Zombie stories)?

11. Why does *Night of the Living Dead* remain so popular?

12. What is the "abject" I keep hearing you talk about?

13. What is "homo sacer" and what does it have to do with Zombies?

14. Who among you will be the first to get bitten?

15. Why do we feel okay killing Zombies, but not other "living humans" or animals?

16. What would a Quaker do when confronted with a Zombie?

Notes

1. An earlier, abbreviated, version of this essay was presented at the Inter-Disciplinary.Net 4th Global "Monstrous Geographies" conference in Lisbon, Portugal, on March 22, 2015. I am grateful for astute and helpful suggestions from colleagues in our session.

2. Lisa Verner, *Epistemology of the Monstrous* (New York: Routledge, 2005), 156.

3. Of particular use were selections from Georgio Agamben's *Homo Sacer: Sovereign Power and Bare Life* (Stanford: Stanford University Press, 1998), Julia Kristeva, *Powers of Horror: An Essay on Abjection* (New York: Columbia University Press, 1982), the movie *Zizek!* by Astra Taylor (2006), and Judith Butler's *Precarious Life* (New York: Verso, 2006).

4. RAFT assignments are designed to help students improve their writing by appealing to, and crafting a persuasive document for, a specific audience. Such assignments are set in an "authentic" or real-world context that requires students to pay particular attention to audience awareness, as well as develop their own voice in their argument—and promises to feel more meaningful than many standard academic assignments written "for the professor." (RAFT stands for reading, audience, format, theme.) See John C. Bean's *Engaging Ideas: The Professor's Guide to Integrating Writing, Critical Thinking, and Active Learning in the Classroom,* 3d ed. (San Francisco: Jossey-Bass, 2011) for specific examples of how to construct RAFT assignments across the curriculum, or Deborah Dean's *Strategic Writing: The Writing Process and Beyond in the Secondary English Classroom* (Urbana: NCTE, 2006).

5. See, especially, John Dewey, *Experience and Education* (New York: Macmillan, 1938) and Paolo Freire, *Pedagogy of the Oppressed* (New York: Herder and Herder, 1970). Transformational pedagogy theories have proliferated over the past 30 years, with important contributions by John Mezirow, J. Gordon Myers, Robert D. Boyd,

Edward Taylor, and David Kolb, among others. See Mezirow and Taylor's *Transformative Learning in Practice* (San Francisco: Wiley & Sons, 2011), the Kolb Learning Style Inventory (LSI), and George Slavich and Philip Zimbardo, "Transformational Teaching: The Theoretical Underpinnings, Basic Principles, and Core Methods," *Educational Psychology Review* 24 (2012): 569–608. Of particular use to me as I designed my zombie pedagogy was John C. Bean's *Engaging Ideas*.

6. Robert D. Boyd and J. Gordon Myers, "Transformative Education," *The International Journal of Lifelong Education* 7.4 (1988): 261–84. For a more recent review of transformative educational practices, see Shelley White and Mindell Nitkin's excellent article detailing their own experiential course at Simmons College ("Creating a Transformational Learning Experience: Immersing Students in an Intensive Interdisciplinary Learning Environment," *International Journal for the Scholarship of Teaching and Learning* 8.2 [2014]).

7. A fascinating article about how zombies highlight human failure to create just and sustainable communities is by June Pulliam, "Our Zombies, Ourselves: Exiting the Foucauldian Universe in George A. Romero's Land of the Dead," *Journal of the Fantastic in the Arts* 20.1 (2009): 42–56.

8. Sarah Juliet Lauro and Karen Embry, "A Zombie Manifesto: The Nonhuman Condition in the Era of Advanced Capitalism," *boundary 2* 35 (2008): 85–108; 89. They go on to say, "Whereas the vampire and even the intangible ghost retain their mental faculties, and the werewolf may become irrational, bestial only part of time, only the zombie has completely lost its mind, becoming a blank—animate, but wholly devoid of consciousness" (89).

9. Georgio Agamben, *State of Exception*, trans. Kevin Attell (Chicago: University of Chicago Press, 2005). Of use to my students was Agamben's discussion of how the very foundations of law and community are predicated on a need for "an exception" who, although indistinguishable from ourselves, must be seen as intrinsically challenging to the entire system. See especially chapters five and six in *State of Exception*.

10. Verner, 41.

11. In the three years that I was teaching these zombie courses, about half of our student body was from North Carolina, while the remaining students hailed predominantly from the northwest corridor (Virginia, Maryland, Pennsylvania, New Jersey, New York, Connecticut, Delaware, Massachusetts).

12. Daniel W. Drezner, *Theories of International Politics and Zombies* (Princeton: Princeton University Press, 2011) 9.

13. W. Scott Poole, *Monsters in America: Our Historical Obsession with the Hideous and the Haunting* (Waco: Baylor University Press, 2006) xvi.

14. According to Quaker historian Max Carter, Levi Coffin's family was active in the movement, but the first *recorded* instance of him using a fake-bottom cart to convey enslaved people came two years after he left Guilford County, in Indiana. Similar carts, however, have been found in Guilford County. The "New Garden Woods" (part of the Guilford College campus) was described as the southernmost land terminus of the underground railroad as early as 1819–20. (Private conversations and tours with Max Carter, 2007–15.) For more on Levi Coffin's work in Indiana, see Ryan Jordan, "Quakers, 'Comeouters,' and the Meaning of Abolitionism in the Antebellum Free States." *Journal of the Early Republic* 24.4 (2004): 587–608. Guilford College has an extensive collection of early Quaker documents pertaining to the Coffins and the campus woods—our students have opportunities to work with the Friends Archive at Hege Library throughout their undergraduate education.

15. Romero has repeated a version of this line several times since *Night of the Living Dead* was made in 1967. See, most recently, the transcript of his July 20, 2014, interview with NPR (Weekend Edition): www.npr.org/2014/07/20/i-made-them-the-neighbors (last accessed August 2015), or *Generation Zombie: Essays on the Living Dead in Modern Culture*, ed. Stephanie Boluk and Wylie Lenz (Jefferson, NC: McFarland Press, 2011) 19.

16. Edmund O'Sullivan, "Bringing a Perspective of Transformative Learning to Globalized Consumption," *International Journal of Consumer Studies* 27.4 (2003): 326–30; 326.

17. In 2014, Guilford College's first to second year retention rate was the same as the national average: 74 percent. On average, Guilford College has graduated 43 percent of students in four years and 58 percent in six years. See also U.S. Department of Education statistics: *The Condition of Education 2014* (NCES 2014–083), Institutional Retention and Graduation Rates for Undergraduate Students: http://nces.ed.gov/programs/coe/indicator_cva.asp (last accessed March 2015).

18. Information about Daniel Wilson's leadership and communication research in K–12 as well as workplace environments, can be found on his profile at Harvard's Graduate School of Education, where he is the Director of Project Zero: www.gse.harvard.edu/faculty/daniel-wilson (last accessed July 2015).

19. For an overview of Wilson's research with Primal Quest extreme racing, see Hannah Clark, "Leadership in the Wild," *Forbes Magazine*, www.forbes.com/2006/06/26/adventure-racing-leadership cx_hc_o626leadershipwild.html (last accessed June 2015).

20. Shawn McIntosh, "The Evolution of the Zombie: The Monster that Keeps Coming Back," *Zombie Culture: Autopsies of the Living Dead*, ed. Shawn McIntosh and Marc Leverette (Lanham, MD: Scarecrow Press, 2008) 1.

21. I should note that the first Friday night of the Fall semester, as on many campuses, is the biggest "party" night for our students. Thus, by staging the experiment on this particular night, I was directly challenging student expectations for what their night would be like. While their parents knew of the event in advance, students did not. Several students talked afterward about their initial anger and frustration at being unable to join the rest of their college peers, and how those initial feelings either made them feel closer to their zombie-survival cohort, or "left behind."

22. The scenario was an homage to Glenn from *The Walking Dead* and I am grateful for J.J. Crass, one of my former students, for insisting upon its inclusion—as well as agreeing to play the role of delivery guy. Unlike Glenn, who has survived (in 2015) through many seasons of *The Walking Dead* television show, we decided our delivery guy would be more effective if he came back as a zombie, to remind the group of what happens when someone is *not* saved from the zombie horde.

23. Simon Pegg, in the afterword of *Miles Behind Us*, *The Walking Dead* 2 (Image Comics, 2004) argues that zombies represent the fear "that deep down, we may be little more than animals, concerned only with appetite." As quoted by Kyle Bishop in "Raising the Dead," *Journal of Popular Film and Television* 33 (2006): 196–205; 204. My zombie pizza-liberation simulation exposed this claim to be especially true.

24. Daniel Gray Wilson, "Team Learning in Action," PhD dissertation, Harvard Graduate School of Education, 2007.

25. To be fair, these same students did develop good team-work skills by the end of the semester and have, over the remaining 3.5 years on campus, become adept at practicing many of the progressive values of our campus. But their inability to recognize in themselves and transcend the most antisocial and individualist elements

of apocalyptic monster narratives—even with opportunity for reflection and practice—undermined much of my own high hopes for the course.

26. McIntosh, 3.

27. This quotation is widely repeated in various articles, scholarly books, and internet sources. It appears to have originated in press-materials and interviews given during Brooks' very successful 2008 book tour. Cited here from "A Grave Situation: Max Brooks and Zombie Satire," *Washington Post* (November 5, 2008).

28. Ed Greenwood, "Humans in the Foreground: 11 Writers on Writing Zombie Fiction" by Christopher L. Dinkins and Jeremy L. C. Jones in *Booklife* (July 2010): www.booklifenow.com/2010/07/humans-in-the-foreground-11-writers-on-writing-zombie-fiction/ (last accessed August 2012).

29. Poole, xv.

30. Flavia M. C. Bastos and Jeffrey Di Leo, "The Sites of Pedagogy," *Symplokē* 10.1 (2002): 7–12; 11.

Afterword

Monster Classroom (Seven Theses)

JEFFREY JEROME COHEN

Thesis I: The Monster's Body Is a Pedagogical Body

Adam Golub and Heather Richardson Hayton invited me to compose an afterword to this rich, generous, and timely book because of something I wrote more than 20 years ago, at a time when monsters were seldom discussed in college and high school classrooms—except, perhaps, as a foil to heroism or an allegory for unthinkable vice. "Monster Culture (Seven Theses)" was first published in 1996. The essay introduced *Monster Theory*, a book that collects work by 13 authors from a variety of disciplines, exploring what monsters reveal about the times and cultures they haunt: as demonstrations, as admonitions, as bodies feared and desired. The first collaborative project with the imprimatur of a well-respected university press to argue that monsters matter to critical theory and cultural studies, *Monster Theory* insists that its subject is more than a guilty pleasure or pop culture trifle. Its contributors examine intimate aliens without reducing them to psychological parables, or disembodied cultural metaphors. Among the creatures that populate the book are reanimated dinosaurs, sexy vampires, the undead of the Icelandic sagas, marauding Grendel, alluring hermaphrodites, conjoined twins, and demonized Muslims.

I wrote "Monster Culture (Seven Theses)" to provide an overview of the trans-historical, shared endeavor of *Monster Theory*. Yet the essay is also the product of a lively classroom. The Experimental College at Tufts University offers a welcoming home to weird courses that fit nowhere else. The program's director was intrigued when I proposed a class on "Reading Monsters," but wondered what students would gain from examining texts not for their resplendent prose or participation in a canon of masterpieces but for the ability to trigger anxiety, to bestow an archive of fear. At the interview I explained that western literature has been monstrous from the start (as a medievalist it comes easily to me to explain in boring detail why things that seem contemporary are actually quite ancient).[1] *Gilgamesh*, the Torah, Homer's *Odyssey*, Vergil's *Aeneid*, *Beowulf*, Shakespeare's *The Tempest*, Shelley's *Frankenstein*: these works offer a long chronicle of ghosts, dragons, cannibals, the misbegotten, and the undead. I was hired—and allowed to design and teach my first monstrous course. Students enrolled simply because they were drawn to the topic. The class fulfilled no requirements, and was led by an unknown instructor (I had never taught at Tufts before). Thinking through with these young women and men the work of the monster across time was essential to composing "Monster Culture." Born of pedagogical collaboration, the essay ruminates over the books and films we enjoyed together, from Arthurian myths and *Interview with the Vampire* to the *Odyssey* and *The Werewolf of Paris*. I owe the genesis of the essay to a program that had faith in nontraditional teaching at a time when academia was not all that hospitable to freaks, deviants, aliens, queers, and other unnatural things. "Monster Culture" is the record of a collective of learners eager to discover together where the errant tracks of the monster lead.

Now a familiar prod to high school and college writing assignments, the native domain of "Monster Culture (Seven Theses)" remains, 20 years on, the classroom.[2]

Thesis II: The Monster Finds Strange Welcome

Just before I taught that class at Tufts, I completed a doctoral thesis on the ubiquitous giants of medieval literature. I was astonished that no scholar had yet written about these fascinating stories, with their cannibalism, decapitations, licentiousness, violence, surprising comedy, and (sometimes) amity and affection. These narratives insist that monsters are not limit cases, but separated from the familiar only by weak and traversable boundaries. What is the ghastly giant after all but the human body writ large? Completing my dissertation had been an exercise in solitude, though: it turns out that little had yet been published on giants because most academics found monsters unworthy of serious attention. I assembled *Monster Theory* in an attempt to convene a community of scholars willing to accept the monster's invitation to knowledge. While the manuscript was under consideration at the University of Minnesota Press, I used "Monster Culture (Seven Theses)" as my job talk at the George Washington University (GW). I framed monster theory as a way to teach cultural studies without the temporal segregations that structure most literature departments. The monster crosses history promiscuously, and makes a ruin of neat periodizations. Had I not been offered the GW job (and I was not at all certain I would be: it was my third and last year on the market, and a faculty member stormed out during the Q&A), then I likely would not have published the essay, nor made a career out of welcoming monsters into the classroom. My monstrous obsessions continue to guide the critical conversations that unfold when I teach—no matter if the text in question has been composed by Geoffrey Chaucer, Marie de France, Octavia Butler, or China Miéville.

Reading through the wonderful essays collected in *Monsters in the Classroom* has reminded me of how forceful a presence the monster asserts. These thoughtful pieces suggest numerous new ways of harnessing that power to provoke student engagement. Writing on what the grotesque enables in the classroom, Nancy Hightower describes the monster as "a moment rather than an object, as an action rather than thing," a description that well conveys the figure's activity. Monsters are also an invitation to consider the previously unthought (even if, as Bernice M. Murphy points out in her essay, the invitation to the unfamiliar is often concealed within a "Trojan Horse" of familiarity). The uncanny, the abnormal, the impossible, and the queer are especially intriguing to young people at that pivotal point in their intellectual development when they are critically evaluating their past and all things seem possible. As Jessica Elbert Decker emphasizes, students are trying to figure out what *normal* consists of, what belongings and what differences they may desire. Pamela Bedore describes how her capstone seminar addresses feminism, gender equality, and queer sexuality through vampires. Kyle William Bishop vividly demonstrates what unfolds when we literally transport our students outside of comfortable and accustomed space, into a shared and experiential pedagogy. Phil Smith has his students zombie-walk. Heather Richardson Hayton goes farther, asking her students to participate in a zombie apocalypse, a "transformational learning exercise" that spurs some to realize they are the very creature they fear. Through Japanese monsters Charlotte Eubanks encourages her students to realize the limits of their American imagination, while through demons and ghosts Joshua Paddison invites his classroom to grapple with their own religious beliefs. Our students are often deciding how much family inheritance to carry forward, how much uncertainty and risk to embrace, how much affect (an essential component of learning to which these essays repeatedly return) to share. Brian Sweeney movingly details how the monster might be creatively deployed within the classroom to fight against the dreary forces of educational standardization, "fighting monsters with monsters." To welcome the monster means treading strange byways rather than roads of predetermined destination.

Thesis III: The Monster Arrives in Crisis

Students depart our classrooms to difficult, attenuated futures. College graduates are frequently saddled with a decade of debt from loans that assisted in covering exorbitant tuition charges. They compete against friends for jobs that do not pay a sufficient wage. They discover that to the machinery propelling the U.S. economy, young people are a resource for the extraction of labor at minimized cost. Though it might reward entrepreneurial drive and some forms of creativity, this system mandates compliance and cares little for the psychological and intellectual well being of those who sustain it—and even less for the animals it reduces to products. Natural resources and what had been wilderness become territory and consumable commodities (Adam Golub gets at this process well in this book, writing about the classroom use of literature and film to think about monsters and the space of the natural). People who have benefited from this economy seem to feel little impulse to ensure the thriving of those who follow, rendering the road behind them narrow, steep, and lonely. The Earth meanwhile is rapidly losing species diversity, green space, and drinkable water while gaining an overheated climate and catastrophe-limned future. Economic disparity and environmental injustice flourish together.

Prospects are especially bleak for those who have studied to earn an advanced humanities degree. The number of permanent teaching positions is small and continues to dwindle. The life of the mind has always been an unreliable way to make a living, but in the course of the last decade a constricted market has only worsened. Precarious employment is the new academic norm. When I wrote "Monster Culture (Seven Theses)" I was working as an adjunct instructor seeking a more stable job—preferably one that included health insurance and maybe sufficient salary to start repaying my student loans. Looking to supplement my income and attempt something new in the process, I applied to teach a night course on monsters at the Tufts Experimental College. I would like to think that experience assisted in my hiring by GW the following year, and acknowledge I was very fortunate to secure that position. Two of the early career contributors to *Monster Theory* never found permanent academic jobs, and eventually left the field. Two others lost positions that they had held for a while, the result of complicated tenure struggles. One suffered a breakdown. Those contributors already in established positions when *Monster Theory* was published have continued to have good careers, but, like all of us within the university system, have repeatedly had to fight against cost cutting measures that disproportionately impact the humanities as well as administrators and trustee boards who imagine that postsecondary education ought to be run like a profit-oriented business (where *profit* is numerical and easily assessable quantity rather than an intellectual and long term gain).

Each year I write a great many letters of recommendation for would-be teachers seeking positions at colleges, universities, high schools. Not enough are offered the stable, well supported positions they deserve. Many at the front of the classroom do not have the resources, remuneration or security they merit. Academic life is precarious, limned by the monsters we dream as well as the monsters we dread. Pamela Bedore observes in her essay that the classroom monster can make the teacher "sometimes feel vulnerable." We *are* vulnerable. So are our students. And not just emotionally or rhetorically.

Thesis IV: The Monster Stands at the Door

I am composing this afterword a few days before Halloween 2015. This year has so far seen 52 shootings on school grounds and 23 on college campuses. Since the Sandy Hook Elementary School massacre of 2012, at least 149 shootings have occurred at schools. Campus security is among the "one button dial contacts" on my cell phone, just in case an incident should unfold at GW. We have been told that we should be able to make such a call while sheltering behind a desk or table. My daughter's middle school practices the protocols for an active shooter (Code Blue) once per quarter, just in case. While I was writing this essay, I received email, text and voicemail alerts from her school that her classes had spent the morning in lockdown due to two unspecified threats. Emergency procedures for most schools and universities mostly entail remaining quietly in a locked or barricaded room with the lights off, and hoping.

It is easy to think that the monster is an entity external to us rather than a creature of our own fashioning, the product of a contemporary love of destruction, explosion, violence, guns. All the firepower in the world will not stop the monster, but fewer guns might at least mean more people act less monstrously. And more students remain alive.

Thesis V: The Monster Breaches the Borders of the Possible

Relieved to have *Monster Theory* placed under contract with a press, I did not think much about the future of the book. Two decades later, the volume sells well enough never to have gone out of print. "Monster Culture (Seven Theses)" has inspired conferences, museum exhibits, television shows (John Logan mentions the queer worlds the piece opened to him in his pitch to sell *Penny Dreadful* to Showtime in 2013). When Disney and Pixar were sued for copyright infringement after the release of *Monsters, Inc.* (2001), their legal counsel retained me as an expert witness on the history of monstrosity—mainly because a paralegal working for the firm had read the essay in a college writing class. *Monster Culture* and "Monster Theory" did not arrive out of nowhere. Many other scholars were working on monsters and abnormality at the same time (most visibly, Rosemarie Garland-Thomson, J. Jack Halberstam, and Jeffrey Weinstock). *Monster Theory* is only one participant within a collective scholarly endeavor that continues. W. Scott Poole makes this point eloquently in his excellent foreword to this book, tracing the long lineage of contemporary teratology.

Because "Monster Culture" is so historically promiscuous—placing Dracula in the good company of revenants from Norse sagas, the creature from *Alien* (1979), and the dinosaurs of Jurassic Park alongside Polyphemus and the biblical Nephilim, the American West with the Delta Quadrant—the essay has been repeatedly cited, contemplated, and taught, especially in first year writing programs. The downside to its popularity is that the piece really is 20 years old and more accessible, more vibrant, and more nuanced work is now widely available. When one text is too often returned to as source, the vitality of what came alongside and afterwards is easy to obscure. Much of this more recent work has refined, rethought, and at times rejected what is contained in "Monster Culture," often through conversations scholars have staged in their own classrooms. Rick Godden gets at this collaborative nexus well in the rubric he composed for a composition course he teaches at Tulane that focuses on the monster: "Because of their inherent ambiguity, monsters encourage open-mindedness, productive questioning, careful scrutiny, and flexible research, all of which are the hallmarks of good scholarship."[3] Because the field is lively—because the classroom is a dynamic habitat—the monster endures.

Thesis VI: Desire for the Monster Is Desire for a Different World

Monsters in the Classroom demonstrates how these figures engage students and hone critical faculties. The pedagogical models this book offers are inspirational. Most invite students to think with the monster and thereby queer what passes itself off as natural, or to discover in the supernatural a realm that exists not at some impossible distance but intimately, alongside everything that appears ordinary. To romanticize monsters is dangerous, since these creatures frequently incarnate misogyny, homophobia, xenophobia, anti–Semitism, racism. But the monster also offers alternatives to the everyday world, realms in which solid reality dissolves into possibility. As I composed this afterword I asked fellow teachers on social media to contemplate what the monster offers their classroom. Most stressed the esprit de corps that monstrous study engenders, so that students make lasting friendships through difficult but shared pedagogical endeavor. Though the monster is often inimical to collectives, a reminder of who has been left outside at the closing of the door, imagining the future through the monster paradoxically builds community.

Thesis VII: The Monster Stands at the Threshold of Belonging

"Monster Culture (Seven Theses)" has been used to teach composition, cultural studies, American studies, religion, literature, philosophy, and critical theory. Sometimes the essay has been a shared text in required Freshman writing classes (Columbia, Rutgers, Indiana University). Often the piece has found its way into a course on monsters. I have received as a result a thank you card signed by an entire class; the Seven Theses inscribed on cardboard tablets as if they were the Ten Commandments; and photographs of Halloween costumes inspired by the essay. Although I worry that the writing style is not a good example to emulate (when I read the essay now it seems to me rather stilted and precious), I am always pleased when a student who has been thinking with the essay writes to me on Twitter or Facebook or email to tell me what worlds they have opened for themselves through their classroom experience. *Monsters in the Classroom* is a record of how such lively and creative communities continue to be engendered through a variety of catalysts—and this book will no doubt be a trigger to many more such collectives.

Twenty years after its publication, the essays collected in *Monster Theory* have been joined by so many monstrous books, essays, and websites that call out for classroom conversation that it is difficult not to agree with Adam Golub and Heather Richardson Hayton that we live in "a peak moment of monster pedagogy." The Fellowship of Monsters is always looking for new members. Sometimes (as Asa Simon Mittman so well describes in his essay) that invitation is a trap, a call to swim dangerous waters. Yet if thinking through what a monster means and does (as character in a narrative and partner in the process of learning) invites a student to frame critically their own cultural moment, as well as perhaps the long histories behind that moment's formation, then the monster classroom is in the end a good place in which to dwell.

Notes

1. Not that this super power is reserved to medievalists: W. Scott Poole makes this point about the Western canon well in his foreword to this book.

2. I want to thank Hope D. Swearingen for sending me a thorough description of how she uses "Monster Culture (Seven Theses)" in her AP English class at Bastrop High School. I am also deeply grateful to the following scholars, who shared reflections on using the essay in the classroom with me, providing valuable material for what I have written in this afterword: Bonnie Jett Adams, Tracy Adams, Shaun Bryan, Brantley Bryant, Sakina Bryant, Kristi Janelle Castleberry, Melissa Ridley Elmes, Fen Farceau, Ted Geier, Rick Godden, Ana Grinberg, Simon Grüning, Brian Hardison, Jenny Howe, Beth Belgau Human, Dan Kline, Sally Livingston, Kathleen Long, Roberta Magnani, Lauryn Mayer, Asa Simon Mittman, Adam Roberts, Emily Schmidt, Corey Sparks, James K. Stanescu, Liza Strakhov, Hope D. Swearingen, Arngrímur Vídalín, Amy Vines, David Wallace, Jeffrey Weinstock, and Helen Young.

3. I am thankful to Rick Godden for sending me a detailed description of the three monsters courses he teaches, and for conversations about monsters in the classroom.

***Jeffrey Jerome Cohen** is a professor of English at George Washington University and director of the Institute for Medieval and Early Modern Studies. The author of* Medieval Identity Machines *(2003),* Hybridity, Identity, and Monstrosity in Medieval Britain *(2006), and* Stone: An Ecology of the Inhuman *(2015), he is also the editor of several works including* Prismatic Ecology *(2014).*

Bibliography

"ACTFL Proficiency Guidelines 2012." *American Council on the Teaching of Foreign Languages.* Accessed January 15, 2015. www.actfl.org/publications/guidelines-and-manuals/actfl-proficiency-guidelines-2012.

Adams, Colin. *Zombies and Calculus.* Princeton: Princeton University Press, 2014.

Aeschylus. *Oresteia: Agamemnon, Libation Bearers, Eumenides.* Loeb Classical Library. Cambridge: Harvard University Press, 2009.

Agamben, Georgio. *Homo Sacer: Sovereign Power and Bare Life.* Stanford: Stanford University Press, 1998.

_____. *State of Exception.* Translated by Kevin Attell. Chicago: University of Chicago Press, 2005.

Ahmad, Aalya, and Sean Moreland, eds. *Fear and Learning: Essays on the Pedagogy of Horror.* Jefferson, NC: McFarland, 2013.

Amador, Victoria. "The LGBTQ Message in *True Blood* and Charlaine Harris' Sookie Stackhouse Novels." In *The Scourges of the South? Essays on 'The Sickly South' in History, Literature, and Popular Culture*, edited by Thomas Aervold Bjerre and Beata Zawadka, 165–179. Newcastle upon Tyne: Cambridge Scholars, 2014.

American Psychiatric Association Major Depressive Disorder and the "Bereavement Exclusion." Accessed July 9, 2015. www.dsm5.org/Documents/Bereavement%20Exclusion%20Fact%20Sheet.pdf.

Anderson, Benedict. *Imagined Communities: Reflections on the Origin and Spread of Nationalism.* New York: Verso, 1983.

Aristotle. Vol. I of *The Complete Works of Aristotle*, edited by Jonathan Barnes. Princeton: Princeton University Press, 1984.

Armstrong, Susan J., and Richard Botzler, eds. *Environmental Ethics: Convergence and Divergence.* New York: McGraw-Hill Humanities, 2003.

Asma, Stephen T. *On Monsters: An Unnatural History of Our Worst Fears.* Oxford: Oxford University Press, 2009.

Atwood, Margaret. *Oryx and Crake.* New York: McClelland and Stewart, 2003.

Avila, Erica. *Popular Culture in the Age of White Flight: Fear and Fantasy in Suburban Los Angeles.* Berkeley: University of California Press, 2004.

Bain, Ken. *What the Best College Teachers Do.* Cambridge: Harvard University Press, 2004.

Ball, Eric L., and Alice Lai. "Place-Based Pedagogy for the Arts and Humanities." *Pedagogy: Critical Approaches to Teaching Literature, Language, Composition, and Culture* 6.2 (2006): 261–287.

Bancroft, Corrine, and Peter Rabinowitz, "Euclid at the Core: Recentering Literary Education," *Style* 48.1 (2014): 19–21.
Barber, Stephen. *Projected Cities: Cinema and Urban Space*. London: Reaktion Books, 2002.
Bastos, Flavia M. C., and Jeffrey Di Leo, "The Sites of Pedagogy." *Symplokē* 10.1 (2002): 7–12.
Baudelaire, Charles. *The Mirror of Art*. New York: Doubleday, 1956.
Beal, Timothy K. *Religion and Its Monsters*. London: Routledge, 2002.
Bean, John C. *Engaging Ideas: The Professor's Guide to Integrating Writing, Critical Thinking, and Active Learning in the Classroom*. 3rd edition: San Francisco: Jossey-Bass, 2011.
Benshoff, Harry M. *Monsters in the Closet: Homosexuality and the Horror Film*. New York: Manchester University Press, 1997.
Betterton, Rosemarie. "Promising Monsters: Pregnant Bodies, Artistic Subjectivity, and Maternal Imagination." *Hypatia* 21:1 (2006): 80–100.
Bishop, William Kyle. *American Zombie Gothic: The Rise and Fall (and Rise) of the Walking Dead in Popular Culture*. Jefferson, NC: McFarland, 2010.
_____. "Raising the Dead." *Journal of Popular Film and Television* 33 (2006): 196–205.
Bissonette, Melissa Bloom. "Teaching the Monster: Frankenstein and Critical Thinking." *College Literature* 37:3 (Summer 2010): 106–120.
Boluk, Stephanie, and Wylie Lenz, eds. *Generation Zombie: Essays on the Living Dead in Modern Culture*. Jefferson, NC: McFarland, 2011.
Bowman, Matthew. "A Mormon Bigfoot: David Patten's Cain and the Conception of Evil in LDS Folklore." *Journal of Mormon History* 33 (2007): 62–82.
Boyd, Robert D., and J. Gordon Myers. "Transformative Education." *The International Journal of Lifelong Education* 7.4 (1988): 261–284.
Braidotti, Rosi. *Metamorphoses: Towards a Materialist Theory of Becoming*. Cambridge: Blackwell, 2002.
Braxton, Greg. "Chris Hardwick's 'Talking Dead' Walks Off with Zombie Fans." *Los Angeles Times*. Last modified March 30, 2013. http://articles.latimes.com/2013/mar/30/entertainment/la-et-st-talking-dead-walking-dead-amc-20130330.
Brightman, Robert A. "The Windigo in the Material World." *Ethnohistory* 35.4 (1988): 338–379.
Brooks, Max. *World War Z: An Oral History of the Zombie War*. New York: Three Rivers Press, 2006.
_____. *The Zombie Survival Guide: Complete Protection from the Living Dead*. New York: Basic Books, 2002.
Browning, John Edgar. "Towards a Monster Pedagogy: Reclaiming the Classroom for the Other." In *Fear and Learning: Essays on the Pedagogy of Horror*, edited by Aayla Ahmad and Sean Moreland, 40–55. Jefferson, NC: McFarland, 2013.
Buhs, Joshua Blu. *Bigfoot: The Life and Times of a Legend*. Chicago: University of Chicago Press, 2009.
Bullard, Thomas E. "UFO Abduction Reports: The Supernatural Kidnap Narrative Returns in Technological Guise." *Journal of American Folklore* 102 (1989): 147–70.
Bundtzen, Lynda K. "Monstrous Mothers: Medusa, Grendel, and Now Alien." In *The Gendered Cyborg*, edited by Hirhup, Janes, Woodward, and Hovenden, 101–109. New York: Routledge, 2000.
Burgess, Chris. "Multicultural Japan? Discourse and the 'Myth' of Homogeneity." *Japan Focus* 5.3 (2007). Accessed June 23, 2015. www.japanfocus.org/-Chris-Burgess/2389/article.html.

Butler, Judith. *Gender Trouble: Feminism and the Subversion of Identity.* New York: Routledge, 2006.

_____. "Performative Acts and Gender Constitution: An Essay in Phenomenology and Feminist Theory." *Theatre Journal* 40.4 (1988): 519–31.

_____. *Precarious Life.* New York: Verso, 2006.

Butler, Octavia. *Lilith's Brood.* 1987, 1988, 1989; reprint New York: Warner Books, 2000.

Campany, Robert. *Strange Writings: Anomaly Accounts in Early Medieval China.* Albany: SUNY Press, 1996.

Campbell, Joseph. *The Hero with a Thousand Faces.* California: New World Library, 2008.

Capuit, Jane. *Goddesses and Monsters: Women, Myth, Power, and Popular Culture.* Madison: University of Wisconsin Press, 2004.

Carroll, Noël. *The Philosophy of Horror: Or, Paradoxes of the Heart.* New York: Routledge, 2010.

Cercone, James. "Communities of Practice: Bridging the Gap Between Methods Courses and Secondary Schools." In *Reclaiming English Language Arts Methods Courses: Critical Issues and Challenges for Teacher Educators in Top-Down Times,* edited by Jory Brass and Allen Webb. New York: Routledge, 2014.

Cherry, Bridget. *Horror.* New York: Routledge, 2009.

Chickering, Arthur W., and Zelda F. Gamson. "Seven Principles for Good Practice in Undergraduate Education." *AAHE Bulletin,* March 1987.

Christie, Deborah. "A Dead New World: Richard Matheson and the Modern Zombie." In *Better Off Dead: The Evolution of the Zombie as Post-Human,* edited by Deborah Christie and Sarah Juliet Lauro, 67–80. New York: Fordham University Press, 2011.

Clark, Hannah. "Leadership in the Wild." *Forbes Magazine.* June 26, 2006. Accessed June2015. www.forbes.com/2006/06/26/adventure-racing-leadershipcx_hc_0626leadershipwild.html.

Clark, Simon. "The Undead Martyr: Sex, Death and Revolution in George Romero's Zombie Films." In *The Undead and Philosophy: Chicken Soup for the Soulless,* edited by Richard Greene and K. Silem Mohammad, 197–209. Chicago: Open Court, 2006.

Clery, E.J. "The Genesis of 'Gothic' Fiction." In *The Cambridge Companion to Gothic Fiction,* edited by Jerrold E. Hogle. Cambridge: Cambridge University Press, 2002.

Clover, Carol J. *Men, Women, and Chain Saws: Gender in the Modern Horror Film.* Princeton: Princeton University Press, 1992.

Coats, Lauren, et al. "Those We Don't Speak Of: Indians in The Village." *PMLA* 123 (2008): 358–74.

Cohen, Jeffrey Jerome, ed. *Monster Theory: Reading Culture.* Minneapolis: University of Minnesota Press, 1996.

"College Courses Study Monsters?" Accessed July 2015. http://chssundergrad.gmu.edu/articles/6193.

Collings, Beth, and Anna Jamerson, *Connections: Solving Our Alien Abduction Mystery.* Newberg, OR: Wild Flower Press, 1996.

Colombo, Robert John. *Windigo: An Anthology of Fact and Fantastic Fiction.* Saskatoon, Saskatchewan: Western Producer Prairie Books, 1982.

Connelly, Frances. Introduction to *Modern Art and the Grotesque,* edited by Frances Connelly. Cambridge: Cambridge University Press, 2009.

Craft, Christopher. "'Kiss Me with Those Red Lips': Gender and Inversion in Bram Stoker's *Dracula*." *Representations* 8 (1984): 107–33.

Creed, Barbara. *The Monstrous Feminine*. New York: Routledge, 1993.

Cronon, William. "The Trouble with Wilderness; or, Getting Back to the Wrong Nature." *Uncommon Ground: Rethinking the Human Place in Nature*, edited by William Cronon. New York: W. W. Norton, 1995.

Daston, Lorraine, and Katharine Park. "Unnatural Conceptions: The Study of Monsters in Sixteenth and Seventeenth-Century France and England." *Past & Present* 92 (August 1981): 20–54.

Davidson, Amy. "Darren Wilson's Demon." *The New Yorker*. November 26, 2014. Accessed March 12, 2015. www.newyorker.com/news/amy-davidson/demon-ferguson-darren-wilson-fear-black-man.

Davies, Gill. "London in *Dracula*; Dracula in London." *The Literary London Journal* 2.1 (2004). Last modified August 21, 2014. www.literarylondon.org/london-journal/march2004/davies.html.

Dean, Deborah. *Strategic Writing: The Writing Process and Beyond in the Secondary English Classroom*. Urbana: NCTE, 2006.

Denzler, Brenda. *The Lure of the Edge: Scientific Passions, Religious Beliefs, and the Pursuit of UFOs*. Berkeley: University of California Press, 2001.

Dewey, John. *Experience and Education*. New York: Macmillan, 1938.

Dick, Philip K. *Do Androids Dream of Electric Sheep?* New York: Del Rey, 1996.

Dinkins, Christopher, and Jeremy L.C. Jones. "Humans in the Foreground: 11 Writers on Writing Zombie Fiction." *Booklife* (July 2010). Accessed August 2012. www.booklifenow.com/2010/07/humans-in-the-foreground-11-writers-on-writing-zombie-fiction/.

Dixon, Glenn. "A Grave Situation: Max Brooks and Zombie Satire." *Washington Post*. November 5, 2008. Accessed March 2015. www.washingtonpost.com/express/wp/2008/11/06/a_grave_situation_max_brooks_and_zombie/

Doniger, Wendy. *The Implied Spider: Politics and Theology in Myth*. New York: Columbia University Press, 1998.

"The Double Dead Walking Tour." *City of the Dead*. Accessed June 13, 2015. http://www.cityofthedeadtours.com/the-double-dead-walk/.

Drezner, Daniel W. *Theories of International Politics and Zombies*. Princeton: Princeton University Press, 2011.

Dunn, George A., and Rebecca Housel, eds. *True Blood and Philosophy: We Wanna Think Bad Things with You*. New York: Wiley, 2010.

Edelman, Lee. *No Future: Queer Theory and the Death Drive*. Durham: Duke University Press, 2004.

Elliot-Smith, Darren. "The Homosexual Vampire Is a Metaphor for ... the Homosexual Vampire? *True Blood*, Homonormativity and Assimilation." In *True Blood: Investigating Vampires and Southern Gothic*, edited by Brigid Cherry, 139–154. London: I.B. Tauris, 2012.

Emmerich, Michael. *Read Real Japanese Fiction: Short Stories by Contemporary Authors*. Tokyo: Kodansha, 2008.

Erb, Cynthia. *Tracking King Kong: A Hollywood Icon in World Culture*. Detroit: Wayne State University Press, 2009.

Eubanks, Charlotte. *Miracles of Book and Body: Buddhist Textual Culture and Medieval Japan*. Berkeley: University of California, 2010.

Fabris, Casey. "A MOOC Hopes to Sink Its Teeth into a New Audience: TV Fans." *The Chronicle of Higher Education*. Last modified May 13, 2015. Accessed August

2015. http://chronicle.com/blogs/wiredcampus/a-mooc-hopes-to-sink-its-teethinto-a-new-audience-tv-fans/56577.
Fardi, Sara. "Knock Knock, Go Away!" Student work, 2014. Used with permission.
Fessenden, Tracy. *Culture and Redemption: Religion, the Secular, and American Literature.* Princeton: Princeton University Press, 2006.
Figal, Gerald. *Civilization and Monsters: Spirits of Modernity in Meiji Japan.* Durham: Duke University Press, 2000.
Filene, Peter. *The Joy of Teaching: A Practical Guide for New College Instructors.* Chapel Hill: University of North Carolina Press, 2005.
Fontaine, Claire. *Human Strike Has Already Begun & Other Writings.* Lüneburg: PML Books, 2013.
Foote, Kenneth E. *Shadowed Ground: America's Landscapes of Violence and Tragedy.* Austin: University of Texas Press, 2003.
Foresman, Galen A., ed. *Supernatural and Philosophy: Metaphysics and Monsters ... for Idjits.* Oxford: Wiley-Blackwell, 2013.
Foster, Michael Dylan. *Pandemonium and Parade: Japanese Monsters and the Culture of Yokai.* Berkeley: University of California Press, 2008.
Franklin, Wayne, and Michael Steiner. "Taking Place: Toward the Regrounding of American Studies." In *Mapping American Culture*, edited by Franklin and Steiner, 3–26. Iowa City: University of Iowa Press, 1992.
Freire, Paolo. *Pedagogy of the Oppressed.* New York: Herder and Herder, 1970.
Freud, Sigmund. "The Uncanny." In Vol. XVII of *The Standard Edition of the Complete Psychological Works of Sigmund Freud*, edited by James Strachey, 219–52. London: Hogarth, 1953.
Friedan, Betty. *The Feminine Mystique.* New York: W. W. Norton, 1963.
Fuller, Robert C. *Spiritual, but Not Religious: Understanding Unchurched America.* New York: Oxford University Press, 2001.
Gibson, Cascene. "REI Hosting 'Zombie Preparedness' Classes." *Q13 Fox.* November 15, 2013. Accessed August 1, 2016. http://q13fox.com/2013/11/15/rei-prepares-you-for-zombie-apocalypse/.
Giertson, Donald E. *Miraculous Retribution: A Study and Translation of Tang Lin's Ming Pao Chi.* Berkeley: University of California Press, 1989.
Gilmore, David. *Monsters: Evil Beings, Mythical Beasts and All Manner of Imaginary Terrors.* Philadelphia: University of Pennsylvania Press, 2003.
Goddu, Theresa. *Gothic America: Narrative, History and Nation.* New York: Columbia University Press, 1997.
Grant, Barry Keith, ed. *The Dread of Difference: Gender and the Horror Film.* Austin: University of Texas Press, 1996.
Halberstam, J. Jack. *Skin Shows: Gothic Horror and the Technology of Monsters.* Durham: Duke University Press, 1995.
Hales, Peter Bacon. "Topographies of Power: The Forced Spaces of the Manhattan Project." In *Mapping American Culture*, edited by Wayne Franklin and Michael Steiner, 251–290. Iowa City: University of Iowa Press, 1992.
"Hanzai jōhō mappu." Accessed 15 April 2015. http://www.keishicho.metro.tokyo.jp/toukei/annai/map_annai.htm.
Haraway, Donna J. "A Cyborg Manifesto." In *Philosophy of Technology: The Technological Condition*, edited by Robert C. Scharff and Val Dusek, 429–50. London: Wiley Blackwell, 2003.
_____. *Simians, Cyborgs, and Women: The Reinvention of Nature.* New York: Routledge, 1991.

Harpham, Geoffrey Galt. *On the Grotesque: Strategies of Contradiction in Art and Literature*. Princeton: Princeton University Press, 1982.

Hawthorne, Nathaniel. "Young Goodman Brown." In *Young Goodman Brown and Other Tales*, edited by Brian Harding, 111–24. Oxford: Oxford University Press, 2009.

Hay, Thomas. "The Windigo Psychosis: Psychodynamic, Cultural and Social Factors in Aberrant Behavior." *American Anthropologist* 73 (1971): 1–19.

Henderson, Jan-Anderson. "The Mackenzie Poltergeist." *City of the Dead*. Accessed June 13, 2015. http://www.cityofthedeadtours.com/the-mackenzie-poltergeist.

Hervey, Ben. *Night of the Living Dead*. Basingstoke: Palgrave Macmillan/BFI, 2008.

Hill, Susan. *The Woman in Black*. 1983. New York: Vintage Books, 2011.

Holden, Rebecca J. "The High Cost of Cyborg Survival: Octavia Butler's *Xenogenesis* Trilogy." *Foundation: The International Review of Science Fiction* 72 (1998): 49–56.

Hsia, Linda, and Roger Yeu. *Strange Stories from a Chinese Studio*. New Haven: Yale University Press, 1977.

Huet, Marie-Helene. *Monstrous Imagination*. Cambridge: Harvard University Press, 1993.

Hunt, Leon, Sharon Lockyer, and Milly Williamson. "Introduction: Sometimes They Come Back—The Vampire and Zombie on Screen." In *Screening the Undead: Vampires and Zombies in Film and Television*, edited by Hunt, Lockyer, and Williamson, 1–16. London: I. B. Tauris, 2008.

Huss, John, ed. *Planet of the Apes and Philosophy: Great Apes Think Alike*. Chicago: Open Court, 2013.

Hutchison, William R. *Errand to the World: American Protestant Thought and Foreign Missions*. Chicago: University of Chicago Press, 1987.

Hyman, Rebecca. "Medea of Suburbia: Andrea Yates, Maternal Infanticide, and the Insanity Defense." *Women's Study Quarterly* 32 (2004): 192–210.

Igarashi, Yoshikuni. *Bodies of Memory: Narratives of War in Postwar Japanese Culture, 1945–1970*. Princeton: Princeton University Press, 2000.

"Infrastructure, UC Irvine Reveal Results of 'The Walking Dead' MOOC." Accessed July 2015. http://ps.uci.edu/news/8289.

Irigaray, Luce. *This Sex Which Is Not One*. Ithaca: Cornell University Press, 1985.

Ivy, Marilyn. *Discourses of the Vanishing: Modernity, Phantasm, Japan*. Chicago: University of Chicago Press, 1995.

"Jack the Ripper Tour: A Walk Worth Investigating." *Discovery Tours & Events*. Accessed June 13, 2015. http://www.jack-the-ripper-tour.com.

Jacobs, Naomi. "Posthuman Bodies and Agency in Octavia Butler's *Xenogenesis*." In *Dark Horizons: Science Fiction and the Dystopian Imagination*, edited by Raffaella Baccolini and Tom Moylan, 91–111. New York: Routledge, 2003.

James, E.L. *Fifty Shades of Grey*. New York: Vintage Books, 2012.

James, William. *The Varieties of Religious Experience: A Study in Human Nature*. New York: Longmans, Green, and Co., 1903.

Jing, Wang. *China's Avantgarde Fiction*. Durham: Duke University Press, 1998.

"Jogguingu kōsu no aru kōen." Accessed April 14, 2015. http://www.tokyopark.net/park_jogging.html.

Johnson, Sylvester. "Monstrosity, Colonialism, and the Racial State." *J19: The Journal of Nineteenth-Century Americanists* 3 (2015): 173–81.

Jones, Sumie. *An Edo Anthology: Literature from Japan's Mega-City, 1750–1850*. Honolulu: University of Hawai'i Press, 2013.

Jordan, Ryan. "Quakers, 'Comeouters,' and the Meaning of Abolitionism in the Antebellum Free States." *Journal of the Early Republic* 24.4 (2004): 587–608.

Jung, C.G. *Flying Saucers: A Modern Myth of Things Seen in the Skies.* Princeton: Princeton University Press, 1978.

Kaprow, Allan. *Essays on the Blurring of Art and Life.* Berkeley: University of California Press, 2003.

Kern, Adam L. *Manga from the Floating World: Comicbook Culture and the Kibyoshi of Edo Japan.* Cambridge: Harvard University Press, 2006.

Kerner, Aaron. "*Gojira* vs. *Godzilla*: Catastrophic Allegories." In *Ritual and Event: Interdisciplinary Perspectives,* edited by Mark Franko, 109–124. New York: Routledge, 2007.

King, Stephen. *Pet Sematary.* London: Hodder and Stoughton, 1989.

Kirby, Michael. *A Formalist Theatre.* Philadelphia: University of Pennsylvania Press, 1987.

_____. Introduction to *Happenings and Other Acts,* edited by Mariellen R. Sandford, 1–24. New York: Routledge, 1995.

Kolb, David A. *Experiential Learning: Experience as the Source of Learning and Development.* Englewood Cliffs, NJ: Prentice-Hall, 1984.

Kowalski, Dean, ed. *The Philosophy of The X-Files.* Lexington: University Press of Kentucky, 2009.

Kristeva, Julia. *Powers of Horror.* New York: Columbia University Press, 1982.

Larkin, William S. "*Res Corporealis*: Persons, Bodies, and Zombies." In *The Undead and Philosophy: Chicken Soup for the Soulless,* edited by Richard Greene and K. Silem Mohammad, 15–26. Chicago: Open Court, 2006.

Lauro, Sarah Juliet. *The Transatlantic Zombie: Slavery, Rebellion, and Living Death.* New Brunswick: Rutgers University Press, 2015.

Lauro, Sarah Juliet, and Karen Embry. "A Zombie Manifesto: The Nonhuman Condition in the Era of Advanced Capitalism." *boundary 2* 35.1 (2008): 85–108.

Le Fanu, Sheridan. *Carmilla.* Doylestown, PA: Wildside Press, 1872.

Lincoln, Bruce. *Theorizing Myth: Narrative, Ideology, and Scholarship.* Chicago: University of Chicago Press, 1999.

Loughran, John. "Pedagogy: Making Sense of the Complex Relationship Between Teaching and Learning." *Curriculum Inquiry* 43.1 (2013): 121.

Loza, Susana. "Vampires, Queers, and Other Monsters: Against the Homonormativity of *True Blood.*" In *Fanpires: Audience Consumption of the Modern Vampire,* edited by Gareth Schott and Kirstine Moffat, 91–117. Washington, D.C.: New Academia Press, 2011.

Lykke, Nina. "Between Monsters, Goddesses, and Cyborgs: Feminist Confrontations with Science." In *The Gendered Cyborg,* edited by Hirhup, Janes, Woodward, and Hovenden, 74–88. London: Routledge, 2000.

Mann, Jake. "How Chris Hardwick's Talking Dead Is Changing TV." *The Motley Fool.* Last modified December 3, 2013. www.fool.com/investing/general/2013/12/03/how-chris-hardwicks- talking-dead-is-changing-tv.aspx.

Marano, Lou. "Windigo Psychosis: The Anatomy of an Emic-Etic Confusion." *Current Anthropology* 23:4 (August 1982): 385–412.

Marder, Elissa. *The Mother in the Age of Mechanical Reproduction: Psychoanalysis, Photography, Deconstruction.* New York: Fordham University Press, 2012.

Matheson, Richard. *I Am Legend.* 1954; reprint New York: Tom Doherty, 1995.

May, Elaine Tyler. *Homeward Bound: American Families in the Cold War Era.* New York: Basic Books, 1988.

McAlister, Melani. *Epic Encounters: Culture, Media, and U.S. Interests in the Middle East Since 1945*. Berkeley: University of California Press, 2005.

McCloud, Sean. *American Possessions: Fighting Demons in the Contemporary United States*. New York: Oxford University Press, 2015.

McGray, Douglas. "Japan's Gross National Cool." *Foreign Policy*. Accessed June 24, 2015. http://foreignpolicy.com/2009/11/11/japans-gross-national-cool/

McIntosh, Shawn. "The Evolution of the Zombie: The Monster That Keeps Coming Back." In *Zombie Culture: Autopsies of the Living Dead*, edited by Shawn McIntosh and Marc Leverette, 1–18. Lanham, MD: Scarecrow Press, 2008.

Meyer, Stephenie. *Twilight*. New York: Little, Brown, 2005.

Mezirow, John, and Edward Taylor. *Transformative Learning in Practice*. San Francisco: Wiley & Sons, 2011.

Mies, Maria, and Vandana Shiva. "Introduction to *Ecofeminism*." In *Environmental Ethics: Convergence and Divergence*, edited by Susan J. Armstrong and Richard Botzler, 429–437. New York: McGraw-Hill Humanities, 2003.

Miller, Lee. "Playing Undead." *Studies in Theatre and Performance*. 34.3 (2014): 191–200.

Modern, John Lardas. "Introduction: Duty Now for the Future," *J19: The Journal of Nineteenth-Century Americanists* 3.1 (2015): 165–173.

______. *Secularism in Antebellum America*. Chicago: University of Chicago Press, 2011.

Mohammad, K. Silem. "Zombies, Rest and Motion, Spinoza and the Speed of Undeath." In *The Undead and Philosophy: Chicken Soup for the Soulless*, edited by Richard Greene and K. Silem Mohammad, 91–102. Chicago: Open Court, 2006.

Morgan, Jack. *The Biology of Horror: Gothic Literature and Film*. Carbondale: Southern Illinois University Press, 2002.

Moriarty, Michael. "Medea's Millennium and Nobel Prize Winning Barbarism." *Enter Stage Right*. September 24, 2007. Accessed June 15, 2015. www.enterstageright.com/archive/articles/0907/0907medea.htm

Murphy, Bernice. "Going Windigo: Civilization and Savagery on the New Frontier." In *The Rural Gothic in American Popular Culture*, edited by Bernice Murphy, 108–32. Basingstoke: Palgrave Macmillan, 2013.

Murphy, Bryn. "Dual Process." Student work. 2014. Used with permission.

Myers Hall Ghost. Twitter Post. August 6, 2012, 5:35 a.m. https://twitter.com/myershallghost.

National Governors Association Center for Best Practices. Council of Chief State School Officers. "Common Core State Standards for English Language Arts and Literacy in History/Social Studies, Science, and Technical Subjects." *Common Core State Standards Initiative*. Washington D. C., 2010. Accessed June 15, 2015. www.corestandards.org/ELA-Literacy/.

Nevarez, Lisa A., ed. *The Vampire Goes to College: Essays on Teaching with the Undead*. Jefferson, NC: McFarland, 2014.

Noriega, Chon A. "Godzilla and the Japanese Nightmare: When *Them!* Is Us." *Cinema Journal* 27.1 (1987): 63–77.

O'Connor, Flannery. *Mystery and Manners*. New York: Farrar, Straus and Giroux, 1969.

O'Hare, Erin. "Monster Mash: Modern-Day Dr. Frankensteins Bring Creatures to Life." *Virginia: The UVA Magazine*. Last modified October 16, 2012. Accessed August 2015. www.uvamagazine.org/articles/monster_mash/.

Osamu, Dazai. *No Longer Human*. New York: New Directions, 1958.
O'Sullivan, Edmund. "Bringing a Perspective of Transformative Learning to Globalized Consumption." *International Journal of Consumer Studies* 27.4 (2003): 326–30.
Paddison, Joshua. "Disorderly Doctrines: Religion, Race, and the Fountaingrove Sex Scandal of 1891–1892." *Journal of the Gilded Age and Progressive Era* 14 (2015): 475–502.
Partridge, Christopher. "Alien Demonology: The Christian Roots of the Malevolent Extraterrestrial in UFO Religions and Abduction Spiritualities." *Religion* 34 (2004): 164–89.
Pegg, Simon. "Afterword." *Miles Behind Us, The Walking Dead 2*. Image Comics, 2004.
Perrault, Melanie. "American Wilderness and First Contact." In *American Wilderness: A New History*, edited by Michael Lewis, 15–35. Oxford: Oxford University Press, 2007.
Poole, W. Scott. *Monsters in America: Our Historical Obsession with the Hideous and the Haunting*. Waco: Baylor University Press, 2011.
Powell, Anna. *Deleuze and Horror Film*. Edinburgh: Edinburgh University Press, 2005.
Phillips, Erica. "Zombie Studies Gain Ground on College Campuses." *The Wall Street Journal*. Last modified March 3, 2014. Accessed July 2015. www.wsj.com/articles/SB10001424052702304851104579361451951384512.
Phillips, Kendall R. *Projected Fears: Horror Films and American Culture*. Westport, CT: Praeger, 2005.
Piccinini, Patricia. "The Naturally Artificial World." *Tender Creatures Exhibition Catalogue*. Atrium: ARTIUM of Alva, 2007. Accessed June 2015. www.patriciapiccinini.net/printessay.php?id=29.
Podruchny, Carolyn. "Werewolves and Windigos: Narratives of Cannibal Monsters in French-Canadian Voyageur Oral Tradition." *Ethnohistory* 51 (2004): 677–700.
Pulliam, June. "Our Zombies, Ourselves: Exiting the Foucauldian Universe in George A. Romero's Land of the Dead." *Journal of the Fantastic in the Arts* 20.1 (2009): 42–56.
Redfern, Catherine, and Kristin Aune, *Reclaiming the F Word: Feminisms Today*. London: Zed Books, 2013.
Regal, Brian. *Searching for Sasquatch: Crackpots, Eggheads, and Cryptozoology*. New York: Palgrave Macmillan, 2011.
Renda, Mary A. *Taking Haiti: Military Occupation and the Culture of U.S. Imperialism, 1915–1940*. Chapel Hill: University of North Carolina Press, 2001.
Rich, Adrienne. "Compulsory Heterosexuality and Lesbian Existence." *Journal of Women's History* 15.3 (2003): 11–48.
Romero, George. *The Secret Behind Romero's Scary Zombies: 'I Made Them the Neighbors.'* By NPR Staff. Weekend Edition, Sunday, July 20, 2014. www.npr.org/2014/07/20/332644099/the-secret-behind-romeros-scary-zombies-i-made-them-the-neighbors.
Rothstein, Mikael. "'His Name Was Xenu. He Used Renegades…': Aspects of Scientology's Founding Myth." In *Scientology*, edited by J. R. Lewis. New York: Oxford University Press, 2009.
Rowlandson, Mary. "The Sovereignty and Goodness of God." In *The Mayflower Papers: Selected Writings of Colonial New England*, edited by Nathaniel Philbrick and Thomas Philbrick, 166–212. Oxford: Oxford University Press, 2007.
Rudnick, Lois P., Judith E. Smith, and Rachel Lee Rubin, eds. *American Identities: An Introductory Textbook*. Malden, MA: Blackwell, 2006.

Saraiya, Sonia. "Review of *Talking Dead*." *The A.V. Club*. Last modified April 1, 2013. Accessed July 2015. www.avclub.com/tvclub/emtalking-dead-em-95849.

Schuller, Dorothea. "'Something Black and of the Night': Vampirism, Monstrosity, and Negotiations of Race in Richard Matheson's *I Am Legend*." *Inklings-Jahrbuch für Literatur und Ästhetik* 27 (2009): 78–94.

Sconce, Jeffrey. "Dead Metaphors/Undead Allegories." In *Screening the Undead: Vampires and Zombies in Film and Television*, edited by Leon Hunt, Sharon Lockyer and Milly Williamson, 95–111. London: I. B. Tauris, 2014.

Sedgwick, Eve Kosofsky. *Between Men: English Literature and Male Homosocial Desire*. New York: Columbia University Press, 1985.

Shildrick, Margrit. *Embodying the Monster: Encounters with the Vulnerable Self*. London: SAGE, 2002.

Singer, Alan. "Reading Without Understanding—Common Core Versus Abraham Lincoln." *The Huffington Post*. 2014. Accessed June 15, 2015. www.huffingtonpost.com/alan-singer/reading-without-understan_b_4323239.html.

Singer, Peter. "Equality for Animals?" In *Environmental Ethics: Convergence and Divergence*, edited by Susan J. Armstrong and Richard Botzler, 323–330. New York: McGraw-Hill Humanities, 2003.

Skinner, David. "Andrea Yates—Not a Women's Issue: Explaining the Modern Medea Is Beyond the Powers of Feminism and Psychiatry." *The Weekly Standard*. March 13, 2002. Accessed June 15, 2015. www.weeklystandard.com/Content/Public/Articles/000/000/001/010agmve.asp.

Slavich, George, and Philip Zimbardo. "Transformational Teaching: The Theoretical Underpinnings, Basic Principles, and Core Methods." *Educational Psychology Review* 24 (2012): 569–608.

Smith, Don G. "Teenage Monsters and Their Meaning." In *Images of Youth: Popular Culture as Educational Ideology*, edited by Michael A. Oliker and Walter P. Krolikowski, 96–111. New York: Peter Lang, 2001.

Smith, Phil. "History, Terrain and Tread: The Walk of Demons, Zombie Flesh Eaters and the Blind Dead." In *European Nightmares: Horror Cinema in Europe Since 1945*, edited by Patricia Allmer, Emily Brick and David Huxley, 131–40. New York: Wallflower Press, 2012.

_____. *On Walking*. Axminster: Triarchy Press, 2014.

_____. "Pedagogy and the Zombie Mythos: Lessons from Apocalyptic Enactments." In *Schooling Zombies*, edited by Esther Priyadharshini. New York: Springer, 2015.

_____. "Performative Walking in Zombie Towns." *Studies in Theatre and Performance* 34, no. 3 (2014): 219–29. London: Routledge.

_____. "A Taxonomy of 'Zombie Space' for Walking in Monstrous Cties." (under consideration).

_____. *Walking's New Movement*. Axminster: Triarchy Press, 2015.

Soja, Edward. "Inside Exopolis: Scenes from Orange County." In *Variations on a Theme Park: The New American City and the End of Public Space*, edited by Michael Sorkin, 94–122. New York: Hill and Wang, 1992.

Speilmann, Guy, and Mary L. Radnofsky, "Language Learning Under Tension: New Directions from a Qualitative Study." *The Modern Language Journal* 85:2 (Summer 201): 259–78.

Steiner, Michael C. "Introduction: Varieties of Western American Regionalism." In *Regionalists on the Left: Radical Voices From the American West*, edited by Steiner. Norman: University of Oklahoma Press, 2013.

Stoker, Bram. *Dracula*. 1897. Reprint New York: Signet, 1992.

Stoker, Bram. *Dracula*. Edited by Nina Auerbach and David J. Skal. New York: W.W. Norton, 1996.

Sullivan, Winnifred. *The Impossibility of Religious Freedom*. Princeton: Princeton University Press, 2007.

Summers, David. "The Archaeology of the Modern Grotesque." In *Modern Art and the Grotesque*, edited by Francis Connelly, 22–24. Cambridge: Cambridge University Press, 2009.

Taylor, Charles. *A Secular Age*. Cambridge: Harvard University Press, 2007.

Thomas, P.L. "'A Richer, Not a Narrower Aesthetic': The Rise of New Criticism in *English Journal*." *English Journal* 101.3 (2012): 52–57.

Tsutsui, William. *Godzilla on My Mind: Fifty Years of the King of Monsters*. New York: Palgrave, 2004.

Tuan, Yi-Fu. *Landscapes of Fear*. New York: Pantheon Books, 1979.

_____. *Space and Place: The Perspective of Experience*. Minneapolis: University of Minnesota Press, 2001.

Tucker, Veta Smith. "Purloined Identity: The Racial Metamorphosis of Tituba of Salem Village." *Journal of Black Studies* 30 (2000): 624–34.

Turner, Cathy. "Porous Dramaturgy and the Pedestrian." In *New Dramaturgy: International Perspectives on Theory and Practice*, edited by Katalin Trencsenyi and Bernadette Cochrane, 199–213. London: Bloomsbury, 2014.

Turner, Frederick. "The Invented Landscape." In *Environmental Ethics: Convergence and Divergence*, edited by Susan J. Armstrong and Richard Botzler, 294–306. New York: McGraw-Hill Humanities, 2003.

Twitchell, James B. *Dreadful Pleasures: An Anatomy of Modern Horror*. New York: Oxford University Press, 1985.

"2009 English Language Arts Tests Standard and Performance Indicator Map with Answer Key Grade 8." *New York State Education Department*. Accessed June 15, 2015. www.nysedregents.org/Grade8/EnglishLanguageArts/20090120scoringkey.pdf

Urbanski, Heather. *Plagues, Apocalypses, and Bug-Eyed Monsters: How Speculative Fiction Shows Us Our Nightmares*. Jefferson, NC: McFarland, 2007.

Ury, Marian. *Tales of Times Now Past: Sixty-Two Stories from a Medieval Japanese Collection*. Ann Arbor: University of Michigan, 1993.

U.S. Department of Education. *The Condition of Education 2014*. NCES 2014–083. Institutional Retention and Graduation Rates for Undergraduate Students. Accessed March 2015. http://nces.ed.gov/programs/coe/indicator_cva.asp.

U.S. House of Representatives Oversight and Government Reform Committee. February 24, 2010. https://www.toyota.co.jp/announcement/100209address.html.

_____. February 24, 2010. Accessed June 23, 2015. https://www.toyota.co.jp/announcement/100217address.html.

_____. February 24, 2010. Accessed June 23, 2015. https://www.toyota.co.jp/announcement/0224_2.pdf.

Ussher, Jane M. *Managing the Monstrous Feminine: Regulating the Reproductive Body*. New York: Routledge, 2006.

Verner, Lisa. *Epistemology of the Monstrous*. New York: Routledge, 2005.

Weber, Max. *From Max Weber: Essays in Sociology*, edited by H. H. Gerth and C. Wright Mills. New York: Routledge, 2009.

White, Eric. "The Erotics of Becoming: *Xenogenesis* and *The Thing*." *Science Fiction Studies* 20 (1993): 394–408.

White, Shelley, and Mindell Nitkin. "Creating a Transformational Learning Experience:

Immersing Students in an Intensive Interdisciplinary Learning Environment." *International Journal for the Scholarship of Teaching and Learning* 8.2 (2014).

Whitman, Glen, and James Dow, eds. *Economics of the Undead: Zombies, Vampires, and the Dismal Science.* Lanham, MD: Rowman & Littlefield, 2014.

Whitmore, John. "Religious Dimensions of the UFO Abductee Experience." In *The Gods Have Landed: New Religions from Other Worlds,* edited by James R. Lewis, 65–84. New York: SUNY Press, 1995.

Whyte, William. *The Organization Man.* New York: Simon & Schuster, 1956.

Wilcox, Rhonda. "Buffy the Vampire Slayer: An Introduction." In *Reading Joss Whedon,* edited by Tanya Cochran, David Lavery, Cynthea Masson, and Rhonda Wilcox. Syracuse: Syracuse University Press, 2014.

_____. *Why Buffy Matters: The Art of Buffy the Vampire Slayer.* New York: I.B. Tauris, 2005.

Wilcox, Rhonda V., and David Lavery. "Introduction." *Fighting the Forces: What's at Stake in Buffy the Vampire Slayer,* edited by Wilcox and Lavery. Lanham, MD: Rowman & Littlefield, 2002.

Williams, Evan Calder. *Combined and Uneven Apocalypse.* Ropley, UK: Zero Books, 2011.

Wilson, Daniel Gray. "Team Learning in Action." Ph.D. dissertation, Harvard Graduate School of Education, 2007.

Wittig, Monique. "One Is Not Born a Woman." In *The Straight Mind and Other Essays.* New York: Beacon Press, 1992.

Wood, Robin. *Hollywood from Vietnam to Reagan.* New York: Columbia University Press, 1986.

Wrights & Sites. About. Company website. 2012. Accessed May 5, 2015. www.misguide.com/ws/about.html.

Young, Elizabeth. *Black Frankenstein: The Making of an American Metaphor.* New York: New York University Press, 2008.

Young, Mark R. "The Art and Science of Fostering Engaged Learning," *Academy of Educational Leadership Journal* 14, Special Issue (2010): 5.

Yuen, Wayne. *The Walking Dead and Philosophy: Zombie Apocalypse Now.* Chicago: Open Court, 2012.

Zeitlin, Froma. *Playing the Other: Gender and Society in Classical Greek Literature.* Chicago: University of Chicago Press, 1996.

"Zombie Preparedness." Center for Disease Control. Accessed August 1, 2016. www.cdc.gov/phpr/zombies.htm.

About the Contributors

Pamela **Bedore** is an associate professor of English at the University of Connecticut, teaching courses in American literature and popular culture, including "The Monster in Literature and Culture," "Tracking the Vampire," and "American Detective Fiction." She wrote *Dime Novels and the Roots of American Detective Fiction* (2013) and several articles on detective fiction, science fiction, and writing program administration.

Kyle William **Bishop** is a third-generation professor at Southern Utah University, where he directs the Honors Program and teaches courses in American literature, film studies, and horror. He has written on a variety of popular culture texts and cinematic adaptations, including his 2010 book *American Zombie Gothic: The Rise and Fall (and Rise) of the Walking Dead in Popular Culture* (McFarland).

Jessica Elbert **Decker** is an assistant professor of philosophy at California State University, San Marcos, and also teaches courses in women's studies. Her research explores images of women in Greek myth through a feminist psychoanalytic lens. Her work has been published in *Epoche: A Journal for the History of Philosophy*; *Philosophia: A Journal of Continental Feminism*, and *Women's Studies: An Interdisciplinary Journal*.

Charlotte **Eubanks** is an associate professor of comparative literature, Japanese, and Asian studies at Penn State. She studies the material culture of books and word/image relations, with a focus on Japanese literature from the medieval period to the present. She is the author of numerous articles and the monograph *Miracles of Book and Body: Buddhist Textual Culture and Medieval Japan* (2011).

Adam **Golub** is an associate professor and director of the M.A. program in American studies at California State University, Fullerton, where he teaches courses on literature, popular culture, childhood, and monsters. His academic writing has appeared in various journals, including *Film and History*, *American Quarterly*, *Hybrid Pedagogy*, and *Anthropology Now*.

Heather Richardson **Hayton** is a professor in the English Department and director of the Honors Program at Guilford College. She co-edited *Translating Desire in Medieval and Early Modern Literature* (2005), is co-editing *Siena in the Middle Ages* *and Early Modern Period* (forthcoming, 2017), and is the president of the Society for Comparative Literature and the Arts.

Nancy **Hightower** for a number of years taught the grotesque in art and literature through the Program for Writing and Rhetoric at the University of Colorado, Boulder. Along with Carrie Ann Baade, she authored the *Cute and Creepy Exhibition Catalogue* in 2011, and from 2012 to 2013 was the art columnist for *Weird Fiction Review*.

Asa Simon **Mittman** is a professor and chair of art and art history at California State University, Chico. He is the author of *Maps and Monsters in Medieval England* (2006) and *Inconceivable Beasts: The Wonders of the East in the Beowulf Manuscript* (with Susan Kim, 2013) and editor of *Research Companion to Monsters and the Monstrous* (2012). He serves as president of MEARCSTAPA and is a founding member of the Material Collective.

Bernice M. **Murphy** is a lecturer at the School of English, Trinity College, Dublin, and director of the school's M. Phil in popular literature. She is the author of *The Suburban Gothic in American Popular Culture* (2009), *The Rural Gothic: Backwoods Horror and Terror in the Wilderness* (2013) and *The Highway Horror Film* (2014) and editor of *Shirley Jackson: Essays ...* (McFarland, 2005) and co-editor of *It Came from the 1950s! Popular Culture, Popular Anxieties* (2011).

Joshua **Paddison** teaches classes on religion, race, and the American West at Texas State University in San Marcos. He received his Ph.D. from UCLA. He is the author of *American Heathens: Religion, Race, and Reconstruction in California* (2012).

Phil **Smith** is an associate professor (reader) in the School of Humanities and Performing Arts at Plymouth University, UK, a member of arts collective Wrights & Sites, and company dramaturg for TNT Theatre (Munich). His publications include "Walking's New Movement" (2015), "On Walking" (2014), "Counter-Tourism: The Handbook" (2012), and "Mythogeography" (2010).

Brian **Sweeney** has been teaching in New York City since 2008. He studied at Hamilton College and the University of Chicago, where he pursued a course of study that brought together topics in classical civilization, mythology, literature and religion. He also consults on designing and implementing secondary literacy curricula.

Index